TREASURE SCHOOLS

AMERICA'S COLLEGE GEMS

School profiles written by Jessica Allen.

Illustrations by Frank Webster.

SparkCollege is an imprint of SparkNotes LLC

Spark Publishing
A Division of Barnes & Noble
120 Fifth Avenue
New York, NY 10011
www.sparknotes.com

ISBN-13: 978-1-4114-9988-1
ISBN-10: 1-4114-9988-3

Library of Congress Cataloging-in-Publication Data is available upon request.

Please submit changes or report errors to www.sparknotes.com/errors.

Printed and bound in Canada.

1 3 5 7 9 10 8 6 4 2

TREASURE SCHOOLS

AMERICA'S COLLEGE GEMS

SPARKCOLLEGE

AN IMPRINT OF SPARK PUBLISHING

WWW.SPARKCOLLEGE.COM

Contents

Introduction

There's something to be said for popular, well-known bands. They put on expensive concerts with a lot of lights in huge, crowded arenas. And if you remember to bring binoculars, you might even catch a glimpse of the lead singer.

On the other hand, have you ever felt that indescribable joy of discovering the next great band? You watch in wonder as your friends catch on, and you politely say, "Oh, they're not new. I've been listening to them for years." But secretly, you think to yourself, "Well, that's what happens when you only listen to music from the Billboard Top 100."

The colleges and universities in this guide are like those indie bands. They inspire and surprise, and they cause you to ask out loud, "Why hasn't anyone ever told me about these schools?"

Here at SparkCollege, we read about an awful lot of schools. We've noticed a few disappointing, all-too-common realities in today's college experience. There's so much degree-mill drudgery and schools that treat students like commodities.

But we also noticed a handful of schools that are truly special, that offer truly exceptional educational opportunities. We noticed 95 of these schools, in fact—95 colleges that put learning and community above a national football championship; 95 colleges that offer you more than cookie-cutter majors; 95 schools that think more of you than to entrust your education to a teaching assistant and a 300-student lecture hall.

We got so excited about these schools that we had to write a book about them. We call these schools *Treasure Schools*, because that's exactly what they are—hidden treasures. Gems. And you *need* to know about them.

What Makes a Treasure School?

A Sense of Community: While Treasure Schools come in all shapes and sizes, they all value and actively try to build academic community. Teachers discourage cutthroat competition, and they demonstrate a commitment to learning, not grading. In fact, at some schools in this guide, like The Evergreen State College in Washington, Hampshire College in Massachusetts, and Prescott College in Arizona, students receive narrative evaluations instead of letter or number grades.

Teachers Teach: Imagine buying $100 tickets to see U2 and being treated to two hours with a U2 cover band instead. Wouldn't you demand a full refund? Surprisingly, each year thousands of students accept a similar practice as part and parcel to earning a degree—more and more, teaching duties are passed on to graduate students, and professors are barely seen. Treasure Schools reject this practice. When you go to class, you'll get an actual professor who will take an active interest in your educational progress. Moreover, Treasure Schools hire *teachers*, first and foremost—not just people with long research résumés and publication records.

It Doesn't Stop in the Classroom: The schools in this book are among the nation's leaders in study abroad, service-learning, and residential life programs that don't involve weekday keggers. Students at Treasure Schools also give back to their communities in the form of countless volunteer hours and public service. In addition, students get hands-on experience in their chosen fields.

Bright Ideas: Treasure Schools often do things their own way. Take St. John's College, for example, which uses readings from the great books of history to teach lessons that can be applied in virtually any field. Or Marlboro College in Vermont, which lets students develop individualized plans of concentrations based on their unique skills and interests. Or Goucher College in Maryland, which *requires* students to study abroad. Or the College of the Ozarks, nicknamed "Hard Work U," at which tuition is waived in exchange for 15 hours of work per week.

Affordability: Several schools in this guide are public, including Purchase College and Binghamton University in New York, Sonoma State University in California, and the University of Montevallo in Alabama. For state residents, these schools are true treasures, offering an elite education with a very affordable price tag. Most of the private schools in this guide offer tremendous scholarship packages for students with demonstrated financial need. And in addition to the College of the Ozarks, two other schools—Berea College in Kentucky and Cooper Union in New York—are tuition-free.

Yes. Free. As in *no charge*.

Proven Success Records: Treasure Schools work. Their student success rates rival those of Ivy League colleges in terms of prestigious fellowships, graduate and professional school appointments, and job placement.

An Attainable Goal: We think you'll be able to get into most of these schools. Although a handful may have some challenging entry requirements, most Treasure Schools are selective in their own unique way—meaning that you don't have to be the valedictorian of your high school class to get in.

At this point, if you haven't already realized it, you should probably hide this guide from anyone who graduated from a college not listed in the following pages. Buyer's remorse is a terrible sight to behold.

Remember: You're not just choosing a college—you're choosing the next four years of your life. You owe it to yourself to at least visit a Treasure School. If we were choosing schools for ourselves right now, we certainly would.

Happy hunting and good luck!

TREASURE SCHOOLS

AMERICA'S COLLEGE GEMS

Agnes Scott College

141 East College Avenue	**(404) 471-6000**
Decatur, GA 30030	**http://www.agnesscott.edu/**

Why It's Cool

Every night is ladies' night at Agnes Scott, though students are more likely to be up late studying rather than partying. But don't worry: Schoolwork isn't dull and dry at this women's liberal arts college. Through the Global Connections program, profs don't just lecture about a city or country—they take you there! Don't want your hand held? The Global Awareness program lets you do your own thing in the non-Western country of your choice. This school truly lives up to its slogan, "The World for Women."

THE BLACK CAT CELEBRATION ENDS ORIENTATION WITH A DANCE, A BONFIRE, AND GAMES.

The Details

Campus setting:	suburban
Degrees:	bachelor's, master's
Calendar:	semesters
Public/Private:	private religious
Number of full-time faculty:	74
Student-to-teacher ratio:	11:1

Admissions requirements:

- **Options:** common application, deferred entrance, early admission, early decision, electronic application
- **Application fee:** $35
- **Required:** essay or personal statement, high school transcript, 2 letters of recommendation, SAT or ACT
- **Application deadlines:** 3/1 (freshmen), 3/1 (transfer)
- **Early decision:** 11/15
- **Notification:** 5/1 (freshmen), continuous (transfer), 12/15 (early decision)

Average high school GPA:	3.62
Average freshman SAT verbal/math score:	615 / 570
Average freshman ACT score:	24
Number of applicants:	1,252
Number of applicants accepted:	741
Percentage of students from out of state:	46%
Total freshman enrollment:	256
Total enrollment:	1,002
Percentage of students who live in campus housing:	87%
Total tuition fee:	$22,050
Total cost with fees and expenses:	$31,110
Average financial aid package:	$23,111

Where It's At

Agnes Scott is located in the historic district of Decatur, a community of about 18,000 people in Georgia. Each October, Decatur hosts the Oakhurst Art and Music Festival. Skateboarders head to McKoy Park, while picnickers stop at Adair Park and hikers climb Stone Mountain. A trip to Atlanta via the rapid transit system takes only 11 minutes. Once there, students can enjoy professional basketball, baseball, and hockey teams, as well as Zoo Atlanta, a memorial dedicated to Martin Luther King Jr., and a museum devoted entirely to Coca-Cola.

What It's Like

"Motivated to make a difference" is one way the school describe its students, who are very active in campus life. Mostly made up of southern women, the student body is definitely driven to excel. Scotties, as students are known, run nearly 70 organizations, from the Joyful Noise gospel group to the Faust Club (devoted to everything German). There are also seven Division III athletic teams.

To offer the world to its students, Agnes Scott encourages everyone to study abroad, and more than 40 percent accept the challenge. The student body prides itself on diversity, and more than 30 percent of students have minority backgrounds.

Live like a princess . . . then see the world

Everyone is required to live on campus in standard dorms or theme housing like C.H.O.I.C.E, designed for students who want to live in a healthy community. All Scotties must adhere to the Honor System, a series of academic and social regulations designed to foster a community of trust and personal responsibility.

Students choose from among approximately 30 majors, 25 minors, and three preprofessional programs. Every spring, the Atlanta Semester allows students to explore women's issues, develop leadership skills, and learn about social change by completing an internship and research project.

Dual-degree programs allow students to get the best of two academic worlds: a BA from Agnes Scott and a BS from Emory University in nursing or from Georgia Tech in engineering. Future architects can also take a combined BA–MA course of study through Agnes Scott and Washington University in St. Louis, Missouri.

In the twenty-first century, Agnes Scott has actively sought to increase its reputation and size: The faculty has increased by 25 percent and the student body by 50 percent. But some things remain the same. According to tradition, when seniors receive a job offer or a letter of admission to graduate or professional school, they ring the campus bell—a sonic symbol of another Scotty's official entrance into the world.

Albertson College of Idaho

2112 Cleveland Boulevard
Caldwell, ID 83605
(208) 459-5011
http://www.albertson.edu/

Why It's Cool

Albertson will hook you up—and not just with potatoes. The 50-acre campus is totally wireless, which means you can IM your roommate from the 75,000-square-foot, newly refinished athletic center or the huge Centennial Amphitheater, an outdoor auditorium styled to look like something out of the ancient world. If you prefer face-to-face interaction, Albertson's got you covered: All first-year students get upperclass mentors. Most important, Albertson connects its graduates to careers: Close to 80 percent of Albertson preprofessional students go on to law and medical schools. And that's no small potatoes.

TIME CHECK? IN THE MORRISON QUADRANGLE, ALBERTSON'S CLOCK TOWER GETS MANY LAST-SECOND GLANCES AS STUDENTS BOLT OFF TO CLASS.

The Details

Campus setting:	suburban
Degrees:	bachelor's, master's
Calendar:	semesters, plus 6-week winter term
Public/Private:	private nonprofit
Number of full-time faculty:	57
Student-to-teacher ratio:	13:1

Admissions requirements:

- **Options:** common application, deferred entrance, early admission, early action, electronic application
- **Application fee:** $50
- **Required:** essay or personal statement, high school transcript, letter of recommendation, SAT or ACT
- **Application deadlines:** 5/1 (freshmen), continuous (transfer)
- **Early action:** 11/15
- **Notification:** continuous (freshmen), continuous (transfer), — (early action)

Average high school GPA:	3.58
Average freshman SAT verbal/math score:	589 / 579
Average freshman ACT score:	23
Number of applicants:	634
Number of applicants accepted:	521
Percentage of students from out of state:	26%
Total freshman enrollment:	190
Total enrollment:	807
Percentage of students who live in campus housing:	52%
Total tuition fee:	$15,200
Total cost with fees & expenses:	$23,065
Average financial aid package:	$14,534

Where It's At

Just 30 minutes from Boise, Idaho, Albertson is located in rural Caldwell, a community of about 25,000 people along the Boise River. Every summer, the Caldwell Night Rodeo arrives for five nights of cattle roping and bronco and bull riding. The Bogus Basin Ski Resort hosts skiers and snowboarders every winter. As the state capital, Boise has several museums, an orchestra, and a science center. While there, you can visit a memorial to Anne Frank, as well as the only museum devoted to Basque culture in North America. Sebree and Luby Parks are two of the ten city parks, all of which have picnic spots and playing fields.

What It's Like

Residential life and academics at Albertson embody the school's slogan: "Small School, Huge Possibilities." First-years and sophomores are required to live on campus in four traditional dorms: one is co-ed by neighbor, and three are co-ed by floor. Two apartment-style clusters, designed for upperclass students, are equipped with kitchens, washers and dryers, cable TV, and internet access.

Athletics play a big part in student life. About a third of the students play on one of the college's intercollegiate teams, all known as the "Coyotes." Nonvarsity Coyotes break a sweat in the Intramural Program, which schedules noncompetitive play and friendly tournaments, most of which are co-ed. Just about everybody plays some sport.

Fraternities and sororities have an on-campus presence, but there's plenty of non-Greek stuff to do too, including such campus groups as the philanthropic Intercollegiate Knights and the theater troupe Scarlet Masque. The student-run Outdoor Program sponsors activities like inner tubing and snowshoeing and even lends out equipment for free.

Small school, huge possibilities

Students choose from more than 25 majors, 35 minors, and 10 preprofessional programs. Should students not find what they're looking for in the specializations ranging from leadership studies to exercise science, the Gipson Scholar program lets motivated self-starters create their own interdisciplinary concentrations. Albertson uses an innovative academic calendar that features two 12-week terms in the fall and spring and one intense six-week term in the winter.

Many students study abroad during the short winter quarter, taking such courses as the Cuba Experience and Costa Rican Biology. Albertson works the minds—and bodies—of its 800 students through the Liberal Arts Core, a set of required classes in math, writing, history, natural science, fine arts, and physical education. In 2002, Albertson enacted a tuition decrease of 30 percent to help keep this school affordable for all families.

Allegheny College

520 North Main Street
Meadville, PA 16335

(814) 332-3100
http://www.allegheny.edu/

Why It's Cool

Three's company at Allegheny. You have to take three classes in Communications and three in Academic Planning. During the three-week Experiential Learning term, you can study the environment in Alaska, culture in Canada, or political systems in Ukraine. You're even required to live on campus for three years. Plus, you'll choose from more than 30 majors. But what really makes Allegheny special is its emphasis on mixing eclectic skills, talents, and interests. You'll be encouraged to maybe major in computer science, minor in dance, and do an independent study in German or to double-major in economics and English, with an internship in neuroscience. Here, three's always cool—and never a crowd.

TRENT REZNOR STUDIED COMPUTER SCIENCE AT ALLEGHENY. TODAY, HE MAKES MUSIC WITH NINE INCH NAILS AND PLAYS VIDEO GAMES AS POOPER SNIFFER.

The Details

Campus setting:	small town
Degrees:	bachelor's
Calendar:	semesters
Public/Private:	private nonprofit
Number of full-time faculty:	136
Student-to-teacher ratio:	13:1

Admissions requirements:

- **Options:** common application, deferred entrance, early admission, early decision, electronic application
- **Application fee:** $35
- **Required:** essay or personal statement, high school transcript, 2 letters of recommendation, SAT or ACT
- **Application deadlines:** 2/15 (freshmen), 7/1 (transfer)
- **Early decision:** 11/15
- **Notification:** 4/1 (freshmen), 8/1 (transfer), 11/30 (early decision)

Average high school GPA:	3.74
Average freshman SAT verbal/math score:	611 / 613
Average freshman ACT score:	24
Number of applicants:	3,279
Number of applicants accepted:	2,438
Percentage of students from out of state:	34%
Total freshman enrollment:	649
Total enrollment:	1,955
Percentage of students who live in campus housing:	75%
Total tuition fee:	$26,650
Total cost with fees & expenses:	$34,300
Average financial aid package:	$20,370

Where It's At

Allegheny's 540-acre campus includes a 72-acre main campus, a 182-acre recreational complex, and a 283-acre nature preserve. Everything's located in Meadville, a town in the Lake Erie region of northwestern Pennsylvania. In addition to museums, wineries, and galleries, Meadville has many parks and an almost 9,000-acre wildlife refuge, with trails, fishing holes, picnic spots, and hunting areas. Nearby are several preserved historical sites, including the John Brown Farm and the David Mead Log Cabin. Each February, the local barbershop quartet provides singing Valentines, and the town celebrates Memorial Day and Labor Day with Doo-Wop weekends and 1950s-themed festivals. Pittsburgh is 90 minutes away, and Cleveland is about two hours away.

What It's Like

Allegheny attracts bright students looking for an affordable education in a supportive atmosphere. Close to 95 percent receive financial aid, and Allegheny's small size means that everyone will know your name. Volunteering is big, and community projects range from tutoring through Creek Connections to exploring resources through the Meadville Community Energy Project.

To help students combine diverse passions, Allegheny requires courses in the humanities, social sciences, and natural sciences. Everybody must also complete three advising courses, known collectively as "Academic Planning," in which they discuss extracurricular activities and career plans with faculty mentors. Experiential Learning courses are optional, but lots of students do travel to seminars in such places as Mexico or internship programs in Boston and New York City.

Academic life is structured around three core components: the first-year/sophomore program (FS), the junior seminar, and the senior project. As part of FS, students take three courses designed to strengthen reading, writing, and speaking skills: Descriptive Communication and Inquiry, Persuasive Communication, and Communication in a Discipline (taken in the department in which students think they might want to major). All students take a seminar in their major as juniors and later complete a big project, such as doing research or performing a creative work, as seniors. Just about every department also requires students to defend their projects during an oral examination.

Everybody will know your name.

Most students—about 75 percent—live on campus in town houses, traditional dorms, and theme houses. First-years might live in the co-ed Ravine, Schultz, or Walker Hall. And everybody can participate in the more than 100 student organizations, including Dobro Slovo (a Slavic language honor society), the Student Experimental Theatre, and Golem (a creative writing group). About a quarter of all students belong to one of nine Greek houses. There are 18 Division II athletic teams. Club sports include kung fu and skiing/boarding. The Allegheny Outing Club has been around since 1928 and leads adventures in the outdoors.

Alma College

614 West Superior Street **(989) 463-7111**
Alma, MI 48801 **http://www.alma.edu/**

Why It's Cool

Alma will make your soul sweat—but in a good way. An education here emphasizes the liberal arts, the sciences, *and* community service, which means your mind and your character will get a workout. Many courses have a volunteering component, so you serve while you study. Premed students might volunteer at clinics in Mexico, while English majors can teach in India. Want more? Move into the Service Learning House and live with other civic-minded students. In return, Alma boasts a 92 percent job- and school-placement rate for all students within six months of graduation.

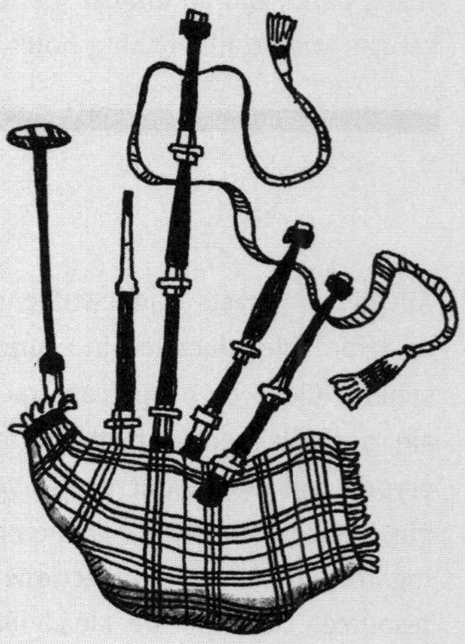

SCOTTISH HERITAGE IS BIG AT ALMA. THE SCHOOL'S MARCHING BAND PERFORMS IN KILTS, AND ALMA HAS ITS VERY OWN TARTAN PLAID.

The Details

Campus setting:	small town
Degrees:	bachelor's
Calendar:	4-4-1
Public/Private:	private religious
Number of full-time faculty:	82
Student-to-teacher ratio:	13:1

Admissions requirements:

- **Options:** common application, deferred entrance, early admission, early action, electronic application
- **Application fee:** $25
- **Required:** high school transcript, letter of recommendation, SAT or ACT
- **Application deadlines:** continuous (freshmen), continuous (transfer)
- **Early action:** 11/1
- **Notification:** continuous (freshmen), continuous (transfer), 11/15 (early action)

Average high school GPA:	3.42
Average freshman SAT verbal/math score:	568 / 560
Average freshman ACT score:	24
Number of applicants:	1,305
Number of applicants accepted:	1,092
Percentage of students from out of state:	4%
Total freshman enrollment:	323
Total enrollment:	1,268
Percentage of students who live in campus housing:	84%
Total tuition fee:	$19,786
Total cost with fees & expenses:	$27,718
Average financial aid package:	$17,188

Where It's At

Alma's 100-acre campus is located in Alma, Michigan, a small town about an hour north of Lansing, the state capital. Both the college and the town take pride in their Scottish heritage. Each May, the Highland Festival arrives, complete with clan reunions and bagpipes, and the school calls its athletic teams the "Scots." Students shop and eat along Superior Street. White-water rafters and sunbathers head to the area's many parks, including Lake Alma State Park, while skiers and snowboarders can tackle Apple Mountain. Home to Michigan State University, Lansing also has the All Around the African World Museum and the Impression 5 Science Center.

What It's Like

Alma offers several study abroad programs, and many students use the monthlong spring term to take advantage of them. Some programs, such as those in Europe and South America, allow students to visit multiple cities during the course of their international education. Domestic opportunities range from the New York City Arts Program to the Urban Life Center in Chicago. Since 1990, Alma has maintained an exchange program with Stillman College, a historically African American school in Alabama.

Prepare to expand your mind, body, *and* soul.

All students must fulfill general education requirements, which include courses in a foreign language, writing, fine arts, history, and a laboratory science. Before graduating, seniors sit for comprehensive evaluations, usually an oral or written exam or a final project in their major.

There are more than 40 academic departments, with lots of interdisciplinary majors currently offered, including new media studies and gerontology, and four preprofessional programs, including predentistry and prelaw. Alma's strength in the sciences is due, in part, to its 185-acre ecological station, an outdoor laboratory for biology students.

Alma's multidisciplinary programs attract a variety of people, but most come from the Great Lakes states. Although Alma's science programs are great, 25 percent of students also participate in the top-notch music program. In total, 20 percent of students receive scholarships in recognition of dance, theater, music, and other performing arts. The many student performance groups, including the Kiltie Marching Band and the Highland Dancers, hold shows at the Heritage Center for Performing Arts, which has state-of-the-art sound systems and a 500-seat auditorium.

Other student organizations include ten fraternities and sororities, the Adventure Club, and the Association for Intercultural Understanding. More than 35 percent of students play on the 18 Division III varsity athletic teams, including a football team.

Antioch College

795 Livermore Street **(937) 769-1000**
Yellow Springs, OH 45387 **http://www.antioch-college.edu/**

Why It's Cool

You got a problem? Antioch's got a solution. In fact, the Antioch Solution offers students some of the most innovative programs in the country. You'll design your own major, which can range from traditional subjects like economics to interdisciplinary specializations like African American studies. Plus, you'll get narrative feedback from your profs, not letter grades. And the Co-Op Program lets you alternate between on- or off-campus study and work during three or four "cooperative" semesters. Hey, the Antioch Solution worked for these notable alumni: activist Coretta Scott King and scientist Stephen Jay Gould. It can work for you too.

GENDERF*CK, ONE OF ANTIOCH'S MOST POPULAR PARTIES, ENCOURAGES STUDENTS TO COME DRESSED IN DRAG—OR WEARING JUST THEIR BIRTHDAY SUITS.

The Details

Campus setting:	small town
Degrees:	bachelor's
Calendar:	trimesters
Public/Private:	private nonprofit
Number of full-time faculty:	54
Student-to-teacher ratio:	12:1

Admissions requirements:

- **Options:** common application, deferred entrance, early action, electronic application
- **Application fee:** $35
- **Required:** essay or personal statement, high school transcript, 2 letters of recommendation
- **Application deadlines:** 2/1 (freshmen), continuous (transfer)
- **Early action:** 11/15
- **Notification:** 4/1 (freshmen), continuous (transfer), 12/15 (early action)

Average high school GPA:	3.1
Average freshman SAT verbal/math score:	620 / 569
Average freshman ACT score:	23
Number of applicants:	458
Number of applicants accepted:	270
Percentage of students from out of state:	71%
Total freshman enrollment:	93
Total enrollment:	599
Percentage of students who live in campus housing:	97%
Total tuition fee:	$24,260
Total cost with fees & expenses:	$33,315
Average financial aid package:	$27,424

Where It's At

A very small but progressive town, Yellow Springs, Ohio, is home to Antioch, as well as a community of independently owned businesses, shops, restaurants, and movie theaters. Twice yearly, the Yellow Springs Street Fair features 160 booths of artists, crafters, entertainers, and food vendors. The town also hosts farmers' markets, book fairs, and concerts. At the Glen Helen Ecology Institute, visitors can roam 1,000 undeveloped acres, all the while looking for raptors and learning about sustainability. Bikers and walkers alike enjoy the 60-mile Little Miami Scenic Trail through southwestern Ohio. Columbus, the state capital, is less than an hour away and features an aquarium, the historic German Village, and the Motorcycle Hall of Fame.

What It's Like

Antioch takes seriously its motto, "Be ashamed to die until you have won some victory for humanity." Students really live this ideal and make a point of rallying behind their political views. As part of the Co-Op Program, students work locally, domestically, or internationally at a wide range of positions in the nonprofit, corporate, educational, or research fields. Planning a major involves combining classroom study with community service and co-op work. Everything at Antioch is geared toward integrating academics with the real world.

Antioch = academics + the real world

Rather than take plain old English or biology, students participate in learning communities. In these themed interdisciplinary courses, students are team-taught by professors from different departments. For example, professors from the departments of dance, environmental and biological studies, and psychology all teach Embodied Mind/Thinking Body. The Core Program Learning Community requires first-years to take a foreign language and seniors to participate in a specialized seminar in the humanities, natural sciences, or the social sciences. Sophomores and juniors join learning communities that relate to their majors. Antioch calls this educational model the "Connected Curriculum."

Students may also study abroad as part of the Co-Op Program, and everybody is encouraged to spend at least one summer abroad learning a new language. Other Antioch programs include Buddhist Studies in Japan or India and African Art and Culture in Mali. Close to 80 percent of students take advantage of these opportunities.

On campus, students choose from an array of activities, from organizing a debate at the Coretta Scott King Center for Cultural and Intellectual Freedom to swimming in the Poole Pool. Students can also be found singing in the annual fall opera and writing for the *Antioch Review,* one of the oldest literary magazines in the United States. Antioch awards financial aid to approximately 90 percent of students, so the Antioch Solution is affordable for everybody.

Portraits of Artists: Schools with the Most Creative Students

Hey, you artists, musicians, actors, designers, photographers, and artsy types of all stripes. Getting your imaginative freak on isn't just OK at these colleges—it's downright encouraged.

College for Creative Studies (P. 52)

College of Santa Fe (P. 58)

Elmira College (P. 82)

Emerson College (P. 88)

Hampshire College (P. 106)

Purchase College (P. 162)

Savannah College of Art and Design (P. 182)

Stephens College (P. 194)

Appalachian State University

PO Box 32004
Boone, NC 28608

(828) 262-2000
http://www.appstate.edu/

Why It's Cool

Appalachian State isn't your ordinary behemoth university. Its size (roughly 14,653 students, 91 majors, a 250-acre main campus, 1,500 courses offered each year) guarantees you'll have plenty of opportunities for livin' and learnin'. But its emphasis on individual education means you won't be just another face in the crowd. A low student-to-faculty ratio lets you get to know your profs as people—not lecture hall ghosts—and first-year seminars and learning communities will help you make friends fast. At ASU, every student is a big fish in a big pond.

HEAD FOR THE MOUNTAINS. ASU'S OUTDOOR PROGRAMS TAKE STUDENTS ROCK CLIMBING, BACKPACKING, HIKING, AND CAVING.

The Details

Campus setting:	small town
Degrees:	bachelor's, master's, doctoral
Calendar:	semesters
Public/Private:	public state
Number of full-time faculty:	674
Student-to-teacher ratio:	19:1

Admissions requirements:

- **Options:** deferred entrance, early admission, electronic application
- **Application fee:** $45
- **Required:** high school transcript, SAT or ACT
- **Application deadlines:** continuous (freshmen), continuous (transfer)
- **Early decision:** —
- **Notification:** continuous (freshmen), continuous (transfer)

Average high school GPA:	3.67
Average freshman SAT verbal/math score:	565 / 569
Average freshman ACT score:	22
Number of applicants:	9,683
Number of applicants accepted:	6,553
Percentage of students from out of state:	10%
Total freshman enrollment:	2,516
Total enrollment:	14,653
Percentage of students who live in campus housing:	42%
Total in-state tuition, fees & expenses:	$9,121
Total out-of-state tuition, fees & expenses:	$18,488
Average financial aid package:	$6,091

Where It's At

ASU is located in Boone, North Carolina, a rural town in the Blue Ridge Mountains named for Daniel Boone. There are outdoor activities aplenty in the High Country, as the area is known, including skiing, hiking along the Appalachian Trail, hunting, rafting, and fishing. Each spring, visitors and residents alike enjoy the High Country's wildflower blooming season. Local restaurants, such as the Southern Sideboard Cafeteria, serve all types of cuisines, from soul food to fusion. Several annual festivals feature bluegrass and Americana musicians, including the Grandfather Mountain's Singing on the Mountain. Raleigh, the state capital, is about four hours away.

What It's Like

ASU is the sixth-largest school in the University of North Carolina system. A university this big offers its students lots of great resources, including the annual Appalachian Summer Festival, which brings 30,000 people to campus for music, dancing, fireworks, and talks. The Forum Series hosts such luminaries as Elie Wiesel and Spike Lee as they give free lectures on contemporary issues.

Students are called "Happy Appys."

Nicknamed "Happy Appys," students at ASU have a meaningful mix of social and political perspectives. The more than 300 extracurricular activities include 26 fraternities and sororities, the Appalachian State Knitters, and Hip-Hop Oasis. There are also 19 Division I-A varsity sports, and the football team is Division I-AA. Athletes and amateurs have access to weight rooms, a dance studio, and a cross-country course.

Required first-year seminars help newbies transition from high school to college by teaching study skills. Students also take a personality test designed to help them choose a major and career path. Some first-years participate in learning communities, in which small groups take the same two or three classes. For example, the Forensic Science community takes three courses together: Chemistry, Chemistry Lab, and Introduction to Criminal Justice.

All students fulfill core curriculum requirements by taking courses in the humanities, social sciences, and natural sciences, as well as a physical education class. Other required courses teach students about diversity, technology, and cross-disciplinary scholarship.

ASU has five undergraduate colleges: the Hayes School of Music, the College of Arts and Sciences, the Reich College of Education, the Walker College of Business, and the College of Fine and Applied Arts. Majors range from anthropology with a specialization in sustainable development to health-care management to safety studies. If you want a big university that acts like a small college, ASU is your kind of place.

Arcadia University

450 South Easton Road **(215) 572-2900**
Glenside, PA 19038 **http://www.arcadia.edu/**

Why It's Cool

In a hurry to see the world? Consumed by wanderlust? If you've ever dreamed of packing your bags and taking off, Arcadia might be the place for you. The First-Year Study Abroad Experience (FYSAE) lets you spend your first semester in the United Kingdom. How's that for a start to college? Or you can head there for just $245, all expenses paid, during your spring break on the London/Scotland Preview. And get this: If you're accepted into the honors program, you can go for free. Arcadia is committed to making the world a smaller place, one first-year at a time.

THIS GORGEOUS 71-ACRE CAMPUS FEATURES A NATIONAL HISTORIC LANDMARK, THE GREY TOWERS CASTLE, NOW HOME TO STUDENT DORMS.

The Details

Campus setting:	suburban
Degrees:	bachelor's, master's, doctoral
Calendar:	semesters
Public/Private:	private religious
Number of full-time faculty:	105
Student-to-teacher ratio:	12:1

Admissions requirements:

- **Options:** common application, deferred entrance, early admission, early decision, electronic application
- **Application fee:** $30
- **Required:** essay or personal statement, high school transcript, 2 letters of recommendation, SAT or ACT
- **Application deadlines:** continuous (freshmen), continuous (transfer)
- **Early decision:** 11/1
- **Notification:** 9/1 (freshmen), 9/1 (transfer), 12/1 (early decision)

Average high school GPA:	—
Average freshman SAT verbal/math score:	561 / 541
Average freshman ACT score:	—
Number of applicants:	2,567
Number of applicants accepted:	1,843
Percentage of students from out of state:	27%
Total freshman enrollment:	476
Total enrollment:	3,391
Percentage of students who live in campus housing:	68%
Total tuition fee:	$23,990
Total cost with fees & expenses:	$34,370
Average financial aid package:	$16,465

Where It's At

Arcadia is located in Glenside, a suburb of Philadelphia, Pennsylvania. Public transportation carries students back and forth to such sites as the Philadelphia Museum of Art, the National Constitution Center, the galleries and bars in the Old City, and the shops at the Reading Terminal Market (each trip takes about 30 minutes). Glenside is home to the Keswick Theatre, a small performing arts space that brings theater troupes and other performers to the area. Each year, the town hosts one of the longest-running July 4th parades in the United States. New York City is two hours away by car, and Washington, D.C., is three hours away.

What It's Like

Arcadia helps its students go global. Its Center for Education Abroad (CEA) sponsors 70 programs in 11 countries. FYSAE lets first-years spend the fall semester in either England or Scotland. Through the Spring-Break Preview, first-years travel to London or Edinburgh for $245, including airfare and hostel accommodations. CEA helps students pick courses abroad so that going global doesn't disrupt graduation plans. Nearly two-thirds of first-years take advantage of FYSAE or the preview programs.

Go global for practically peanuts.

All students must satisfy general education requirements—foreign language, math, social sciences, and laboratory science—designed to develop communication skills. An additional requirement is the International Experience, which can be fulfilled by either studying abroad or taking such on-campus courses as Cross-Cultural Psychology and Modern Africa.

The more than 30 majors at Arcadia lead to a bachelor of fine arts, a bachelor of science, or a bachelor of arts. Popular majors include biology, education, and business administration. Qualified undergraduates are automatically accepted into Arcadia's graduate programs in physical therapy and physician assistant studies. Recently, Landman Library got a $12 million update, so it's now home to a huge reading room, state-of-the-art multimedia classrooms, and 140,000 volumes.

Each year, the Arcadia Theatre puts on several productions, including plays and musicals. Student organizations include the Abstract Club, Phi Alpha Theta (a history honorary society), the International Club, and Rocapella (a singing group). Intramural and club sports include cheerleading, the Tai Chi Club, and the Roller Hockey Club, and there are 15 Division III athletic teams.

Although on-campus housing is not required, most students live in one of Arcadia's seven residence halls, composed of traditional dorms, apartments, and converted suites in the Grey Towers Castle. Built in 1881, the castle now houses fancy meeting rooms, the president's offices, and laundry facilities, in addition to some student rooms. But at Arcadia, regardless of where you live, you'll definitely be treated like royalty.

Augsburg College

2211 Riverside Avenue
Minneapolis, MN 55454
(612) 330-1000
http://www.augsburg.edu/

Why It's Cool

Minnesota might be chilly, but the awesome academics at Augsburg are guaranteed to keep you warm and toasty. The required Augsburg Experience combines school with real-world work. You might spend the semester learning math in Budapest or completing an internship with the Minnesota Center for Book Arts. No matter what, you'll get hot just thinking about all the cool courses. On campus, the more than 50 majors range from American Indian studies to teaching physical education and coaching. OK, so you'll still have to bring heavy sweaters and a parka, but your brain will be positively balmy.

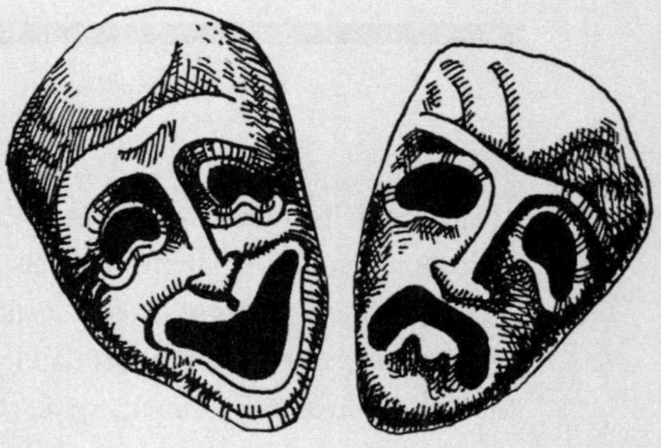

THE ARTS ARE HAPPENING AT AUGSBURG. THERE'S AN ON-CAMPUS PERFORMANCE, FREE LECTURE, DISCUSSION, OR EXHIBITION HELD JUST ABOUT EVERY DAY.

The Details

Campus setting: urban

Degrees: bachelor's, master's

Calendar: semesters for undergraduate programs; trimesters for graduate programs and weekend college

Public/Private: private religious

Number of full-time faculty: 157

Student-to-teacher ratio: 15:1

Admissions requirements:

- **Options:** deferred entrance, electronic application
- **Application fee:** $25
- **Required:** essay or personal statement, high school transcript, letter of recommendation, SAT or ACT
- **Application deadlines:** 8/15 (freshmen), 8/10 (transfer)
- **Early decision:** —
- **Notification:** continuous (freshmen), continuous (transfer)

Average high school GPA: 3.26

Average freshman SAT verbal/math score: 560 / 558

Average freshman ACT score: 21

Number of applicants: 954

Number of applicants accepted: 753

Percentage of students from out of state: 11%

Total freshman enrollment: 354

Total enrollment: 3,375

Percentage of students who live in campus housing: 54%

Total tuition fee: $20,260

Total cost with fees & expenses: $27,838

Average financial aid package: $12,467

Where It's At

Located in Minneapolis, Minnesota, Augsburg calls itself an "Urban Village": a metropolitan campus with a small-town feel. The funky neighborhoods of Seward, Cedar-Riverside, and Phillips are within walking distance of campus. St. Paul, the state capital, and Minneapolis make up the Twin Cities, whose numerous attractions include the Minnesota Twins (MLB), Vikings (NFL), Timberwolves (NBA), and Swarm (PLPA); the Walker Art Center; the Guthrie Theater; and the Science Museum of Minnesota. Serious shoppers head to the Mall of America, the nation's largest shopping complex, while hikers visit the Baker Park Reserve and Theodore Wirth Park. And then there are the area's many lakes, which host boaters and anglers.

What It's Like

In a word, *diverse*. Augsburg students come from 24 American Indian tribal nations/reservations, 36 foreign countries, and 45 states. The Weekend College program lets adults earn degrees by attending classes on Saturdays and Sundays, and the StepUP program gives disabled students or students in recovery from drug or alcohol abuse access to a liberal arts education—two more reasons for Augsburg's incredible diversity. Expect to meet people vastly different from you at Augsburg, no matter who you are or what you've done.

First-Year Feuds pit floormates against one another . . . in a friendly way.

The Augsburg Experience requires that students complete at least one off-campus experience chosen from among five categories: study abroad, internships, faculty/student research, community service, or weeklong immersion programs. Study abroad programs range from examining social and environmental justice in Latin America to thinking about globalization in Namibia. Other Experience options include student teaching in local schools or being "immersed" in the culture of Mexico through lectures and activities.

As part of Augsburg's academic program, students must complete the core curriculum, including courses in math, the humanities, and a foreign language. All students must also take the two-part Christian Vocation and the Search for Meaning.

Most first-years live in Urness Hall. First-Year Feuds pit teams of Urness floormates against one another in such activities as the Twisted Twister Tournament and Human Water Balloon Battleship. Upperclass students generally live in Anderson, New, or Mortensen Halls.

At the Center for Service, Work, and Learning, students can get information about all kinds of volunteering opportunities, as well as advice on finding a job. One popular community service activity is the Campus Kitchen. Participants use Augsburg kitchens to prepare meals for needy families and to help underemployed adults gain valuable work experience.

The Auggies compete on 18 Division III athletic teams, including wrestling and diving. Among the myriad student organizations are the *Augsburgian* (yearbook), the Unbounded Math Club, and the Pan-Afrikan Student Union.

Augustana College

639 38th Street
Rock Island, IL 61201
(309) 794-7000
http://www.augustana.edu/

Why It's Cool

Grab your dancing shoes and head to Augustana. One in three students here acts, draws, plays an instrument, or does something else related to the arts. So feel free to break out your inner diva and sing in one of the music department's two operas, or grab a paintbrush to teach kids through Kaleidoscope, a children's art program. Not the artsy type? Don't worry. Augustana's also super-strong in the sciences. Examine more than 1,500 rock specimens at the Fryxell Geology Museum, or go to the John Deere Planetarium and Carl Gamble Observatory to stare at stars. What more could you wish for?

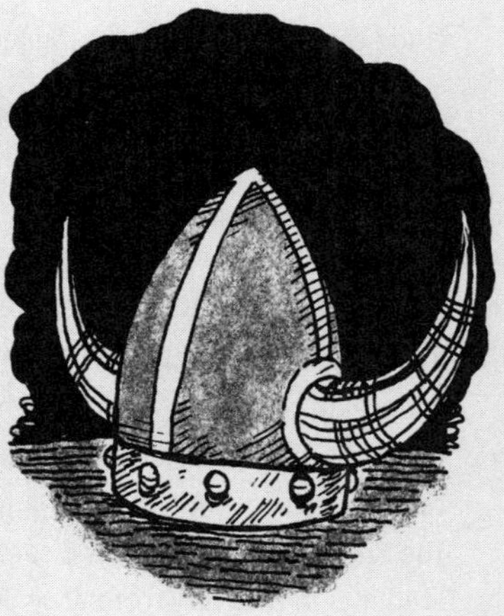

THE AUGUSTANA VIKINGS ARE BRAINY AND BRAWNY: THE SCHOOL RANKS FIFTH IN THE UNITED STATES FOR STUDENT ATHLETES NAMED ACADEMIC ALL-AMERICANS.

The Details

Campus setting:	suburban
Degrees:	bachelor's
Calendar:	quarters
Public/Private:	private religious
Number of full-time faculty:	145
Student-to-teacher ratio:	12:1

Admissions requirements:

- **Options:** common application, deferred entrance
- **Application fee:** $25
- **Required:** high school transcript, SAT or ACT
- **Application deadlines:** continuous (freshmen), continuous (transfer)
- **Early decision:** —
- **Notification:** continuous (freshmen), continuous (transfer)

Average high school GPA:	3.53
Average freshman SAT verbal/math score:	—/—
Average freshman ACT score:	24
Number of applicants:	3,021
Number of applicants accepted:	2,060
Percentage of students from out of state:	13%
Total freshman enrollment:	614
Total enrollment:	2,309
Percentage of students who live in campus housing:	72%
Total tuition fee:	$21,672
Total cost with fees & expenses:	$28,848
Average financial aid package:	$15,207

Where It's At

Augustana's 115-acre campus is located in Rock Island, near the Iowa border and Mississippi River in Illinois. The artsy downtown area, known as "the District," features the independent Brew and View movie house, the Circa 21 Dinner Theatre, and a renovated waterfront. As part of the metropolitan Quad City area, Rock Island has an international airport, the Quad City Botanical Center, and the Quad City Symphony Orchestra. Each summer, the Backwater Gamblers Water Ski Show Club performs; each fall, Rock Island hosts the largest go-kart street race in the United States. Chicago is about three hours away by car.

What It's Like

We love a college with massive resources in the arts *and* the sciences. The Augustana College Art Museum has a permanent collection of about 1,400 artworks, while the Bergendoff Hall of Fine Arts has two separate auditoriums, plus practice space for musicians and singers.

Augustana is one of just three schools in the United States with an independent research foundation, which means that students and professors don't have to go off campus to get funding for their projects. Students also have access to the 420-acre Green Wing Environmental Laboratory, as well as the Beling Ecological Preserve, which comes complete with its own island.

Massive resources in the arts *and* sciences

The top 10 percent of each entering class is automatically enrolled in the interdisciplinary Honors Program. Participants choose from two tracks: Foundations, which emphasizes the humanities, and Logos, which emphasizes the sciences. Each year, Augustana offers more than 900 classes.

All students must fulfill general education requirements, including courses in Christian traditions, writing, and the modern world. Students might elect to fulfill such requirements by taking classes in philosophy, Swedish, theater arts, or music.

Because Augustana requires first-years, sophomores, and juniors to live on campus, students have a lot of housing options. The co-ed, air-conditioned Erickson Residence Center contains mostly doubles and boasts a large-screen TV and pool tables. First-years usually live in the triples of Seminary Hall, as well as the singles and doubles of the Westerlin Residence Center, which has its own dining room. Some lucky women will find themselves living in the single-sex House on the Hill, a renovated mansion.

About 33 percent of students go abroad through the Freistat Center for Studies in World Peace. Students can spend the fall term in East Asia, Latin America, or Europe, among other places. And students here love to get sweaty: about 90 percent play some type of sport, whether intramural, club, or varsity (there are 21 Division III teams). Go Vikings!

Austin College

900 North Grand Avenue
Sherman, TX 75090
(903) 813-2000
http://www.austincollege.edu/

Why It's Cool

Start your new year off right. During Austin's monthlong January Term, you can study film or architecture in New York City, theater in London, Japanese in Japan, and Afro culture in Brazil and Uruguay. But you could just as easily hang out at the Ghost Ranch (an obstacle course and research center in New Mexico) or go scuba diving in Mexico. If you'd rather stick closer to home, you can take classes like Hollywood's Images of Capitalism; People in Tights: Carnivals, Freaks, and Superheroes; and Why Do Drugs . . . on campus. Jan Term lets you go somewhere cool or learn something new without making a major commitment. Out with the old, in with the new, indeed.

AUSTIN OFFERS SOME OF THE COOLEST CLASSES AROUND, INCLUDING AMERICAN ROAD STORIES (WHERE YOU'LL GET CREDIT FOR READING *ON THE ROAD* AND *THE ELECTRIC KOOL-AID ACID TEST*) AND THE MOST EXTREME PLACES IN THE SOLAR SYSTEM.

The Details

Campus setting:	suburban
Degrees:	bachelor's, master's
Calendar:	4-1-4
Public/Private:	private religious
Number of full-time faculty:	93
Student-to-teacher ratio:	12:1

Admissions requirements:

- **Options:** common application, deferred entrance, early admission, early decision, early action, electronic application
- **Application fee:** $35
- **Required:** essay or personal statement, high school transcript, 2 letters of recommendation, SAT or ACT
- **Application deadlines:** 5/1 (freshmen), 5/1 (transfer), 1/15 (early action)
- **Early decision:** 12/1
- **Notification:** — (freshmen), — (transfer), 1/10 (early decision), 3/1 (early action)

Average high school GPA:	3.51
Average freshman SAT verbal/math score:	632 / 629
Average freshman ACT score:	24
Number of applicants:	1,475
Number of applicants accepted:	1,016
Percentage of students from out of state:	8%
Total freshman enrollment:	370
Total enrollment:	1,323
Percentage of students who live in campus housing:	72%
Total tuition fee:	$20,310
Total cost with fees & expenses:	$28,671
Average financial aid package:	$20,391

Where It's At

Austin's 70-acre main campus is located in Sherman, Texas, which has been named one of the "most livable small cities" in the United States by *Money* magazine. A second campus, known as the Lake Campus, is about 20 minutes away on the shores of Lake Texoma. Here, various groups meet, host retreats, go swimming, and just hang out on the 30 undeveloped, recreational acres. Sherman is home to the Red River Historical Museum, dedicated to the history of North Texas. Bird-watchers and hunters alike head to the 11,320-acre Hagerman National Wildlife Refuge. The gigantic Dallas–Fort Worth Metroplex is about an hour away.

What It's Like

Austin's a tight community filled with young scholars raring to go. And go they do: Most students take advantage of Austin's strong study abroad programs, particularly the short travel courses offered during the Jan Term. On campus, students love to lead: More than 70 student organizations offer close to 400 leadership opportunities, includingrunning the Saturday Morning Program, which pairs Austin students with at-risk youth in Sherman.

A tight community of young scholars raring to go . . .

All students take Communication/Inquiry, a seminar designed to introduce students to communication and thinking skills required by college, as first-years. Past seminar offerings have included Food to Live For, Food to Die For (which examines the politics behind what we eat). In addition to taking the three-semester Heritage of Western Culture, students must also take one laboratory science, three humanities, and two social science courses.

Students choose majors from 30 departments, including international economics and finance. Biology, environmental studies, and other science majors do on-site research at one of Austin's five natural laboratories, including Garnett Prairie and McCarley Woods Nature Preserve. Austin also has several centers devoted to academics subjects like Southwestern and Mexican studies. Each year, 15 first-years and five sophomores are chosen to participate in the Posey Leadership Institute, a four-year program that teaches students to be good leaders.

On campus, about 70 percent of students live in one of five residence halls and two apartment complexes. Another housing option is the Jordan Family Language House, in which residents speak German, Japanese, French, or Spanish and have four native-speaker resident advisers. First-years generally live in the carpeted doubles and singles of co-ed Dean Hall.

Student groups range in diversity from 16 fraternities and sororities to 12 Division III athletic teams to Black Expressions and the Activators, which leads ministry youth groups throughout the Southwest. Other popular student activities include shopping at the Midway Mall and hanging out at the on-campus coffee shop, the Pouch Club.

Green Thumb, Green Tongue: Schools with Organic Farms

Some schools believe in cultivating more than just young minds. Go to one of these colleges and you could be tending alfalfa plants, selling fresh produce from a stand, picking apples, or raising cows and pigs. Better pack those overalls.

Berea College (P. 32)

College of the Atlantic (P. 62)

College of the Ozarks (P. 64)

Earlham College (P. 78)

Fairhaven College (P. 94)

Green Mountain College (P. 102)

Hampshire College (P. 106)

Hendrix College (P. 112)

Prescott College (P. 160)

Unity College (P. 200)

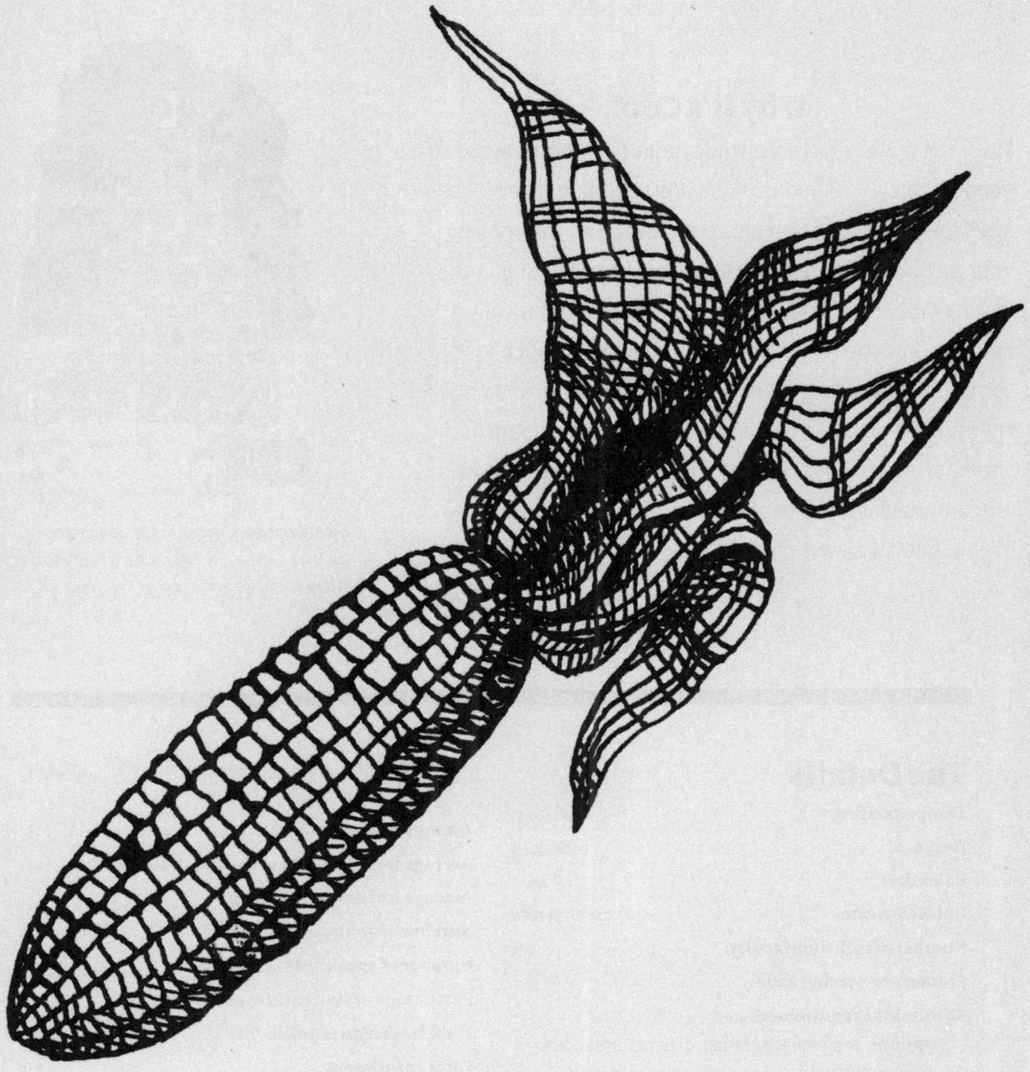

Bates College

Andrews Road | **(207) 786-6255**
Lewiston, ME 04240 | **http://www.bates.edu/**

Why It's Cool

Since 1855, Bates has admitted students without regard to gender, race, or religion. That's pretty cool, but cooler still are Bates's twenty-first-century innovations. Submitting your ACT or SAT scores is *optional*. So is participating in the Outing Club, to which everyone at Bates automatically belongs. But you might not want to opt out of such community-bonding events as the mega-popular clambakes at Popham Park. And you'll twice have to participate in the Short Term, a five-week-long semester in May that features on-campus classes or trips abroad. Sure, it gets cold in Maine, but it's always chill at Bates.

ON NEWMAN DAY, BATES STUDENTS TRY TO DRINK 24 BEERS IN 24 HOURS WHILE ALSO DOING THEIR NORMAL EVERYDAY ACTIVITIES.

The Details

Campus setting:	small town
Degrees:	bachelor's
Calendar:	4-4-1
Public/Private:	private nonprofit
Number of full-time faculty:	163
Student-to-teacher ratio:	10:1

Admissions requirements:

- **Options:** common application, deferred entrance, early admission, early decision, electronic application
- **Application fee:** $60
- **Required:** essay or personal statement, high school transcript, 3 letters of recommendation
- **Application deadlines:** 1/15 (freshmen), 3/1 (transfer)
- **Early decision:** 11/15
- **Notification:** 4/1 (freshmen), 4/1 (transfer), 12/20 (early decision)

Average high school GPA:	—
Average freshman SAT verbal/math score:	673 / 673
Average freshman ACT score:	—
Number of applicants:	4,098
Number of applicants accepted:	1,215
Percentage of students from out of state:	88%
Total freshman enrollment:	467
Total enrollment:	1,743
Percentage of students who live in campus housing:	90%
Total tuition fee:	—
Total cost with fees & expenses:	$41,650
Average financial aid package:	$25,836

Where It's At

Bates's 109-acre campus is located in Lewiston, Maine's second-largest city. Lewiston's attractions include the Creative Photographic Arts Center; the Maineiacs hockey club; L/A Arts, which sponsors lectures and arts events; and the Franco-American Heritage Center, which regularly hosts performances. In all, there are six museums and galleries. Skiers head to the nearby Sunday River resort, while anglers fish the Androscoggin River and hikers hang out in the Western Mountains. Each summer, Lewiston hosts the State of Maine Parade, the Liberty Festival, and the Great Falls Balloon Festival. Both Portland and the Atlantic Ocean are about 40 minutes away, and Boston is about three hours away.

What It's Like

Outdoorsy and *enthusiastic* best describe the typical Bates student. Each spring, students eagerly display their academic work at the Mount David Summit, while just about everybody spends the weekends at Popham Beach State Park or the Bates-Morse Mountain Conservation Area. But no tradition or activity better embodies Bates life than the annual Puddle Jump. On St. Patrick's Day, two brawny men, usually members of the men's rugby team, lower willing, naked souls into the frozen Lake Andrews for a brief dip.

The activities might be chilly, but academics at Bates are hot. Each new student is required to take a first-year seminar, ranging from Contemporary American Poetry to the Changing Climate of Planet Earth. Most departments require seniors to complete a thesis, a two-semester-long independent research project or paper.

Skinny-dipping on St. Patrick's Day

All students must do at least two Short Terms, five weeks of intense classes either on or off campus, during the month of May. Options range from The Development and Legacies of Slavery in Cuba to Molecular and Cellular Biology (nicknamed Cell Hell). About 66 percent of students study abroad in programs worldwide.

Bates offers more than 30 majors, from neuroscience to rhetoric. Popular majors include economics; English; and environmental studies, which combines courses from the sciences (such as Soils) and the social sciences (such as Nature in Human Culture).

Among the more than 80 clubs and organizations are the Investors Club, the Ballroom Society, the Strange Bedfellows comedy troupe, and the Outing Club, the largest group on campus. The Bobcats compete in 20 Division III athletic teams, which include alpine skiing, Nordic skiing, and squash.

About 90 percent of students live on campus in one of nine residence halls and 25 large Victorian houses, including Chase House (cooking), the first-year-only Milliken House, Howard House (cultural awareness), and the co-ed David House. There have never been fraternities or sororities at Bates, but students here find plenty of other ways to bond.

Belhaven College

1500 Peachtree Street **(601) 968-5928**
Jackson, MS 39202 **http://www.belhaven.edu/**

Why It's Cool

Move over, ABC, Belhaven has its own view—and it doesn't star Barbara Walters. Here, you'll spend your first two years doing the Worldview Curriculum. Each semester, you'll take the same four classes: Western Civilization, Form and Meaning, Literature, and Christian Perspective. Because each class moves at the same rate chronologically, you'll study the same time period in four different ways, which gives you an interdisciplinary outlook on history from biblical times to the present. You'll see how great art comes from big ideas and how human cultures have changed through the ages. Prepare to be amazed.

EACH YEAR IN DECEMBER, MEMBERS OF THE BELHAVEN CONCERT CHOIR STAND ON A SPECIAL TIERED PLATFORM AND PERFORM AS AN OUTDOOR SINGING CHRISTMAS TREE.

The Details

Campus setting:	urban
Degrees:	bachelor's, master's
Calendar:	semesters
Public/Private:	private religious
Number of full-time faculty:	65
Student-to-teacher ratio:	19:1

Admissions requirements:

- **Options:** deferred entrance, early admission
- **Application fee:** $25
- **Required:** essay or personal statement, high school transcript, letter of recommendation, SAT or ACT
- **Application deadlines:** continuous (freshmen), continuous (transfer)
- **Early decision:** —
- **Notification:** continuous (freshmen), continuous (transfer)

Average high school GPA:	3.34
Average freshman SAT verbal/math score:	593 / 558
Average freshman ACT score:	23
Number of applicants:	689
Number of applicants accepted:	399
Percentage of students from out of state:	37%
Total freshman enrollment:	180
Total enrollment:	2,505
Percentage of students who live in campus housing:	32%
Total tuition fee:	$13,400
Total cost with fees & expenses:	$20,880
Average financial aid package:	$9,376

Where It's At

Belhaven's 42-acre campus is located in Jackson, the capital of Mississippi. Jackson's museums include the Mississippi State Historical Museum, the Mississippi Museum of Natural Science, and the Mississippi Museum of Art. Other area attractions range from the Jackson Zoo to the antebellum Governor's Mansion to the Russell C. Davis Planetarium. The 305-acre LeFleur's Bluff offers many annual events, such as the Chimneyville Crafts Fair. The acclaimed International Ballet Competition comes to Jackson every fourth year, but Ballet Mississippi and Ballet Magnificat perform regularly. New Orleans and Memphis are each about three hours away by car.

What It's Like

A Christian perspective touches every aspect of life at Belhaven, from a specialized major in church music to a minor in ministries to the school's unofficial symbol of a sailboat and motto, "Catching the Wind of God." Not surprisingly, students here are mostly Christian and conservative.

But the devotion to Christ doesn't preclude Belhaven's devotion to the fine arts: In fact, Belhaven is the only evangelical school in the United States to offer bachelor's of fine arts degrees in theater, creative writing, dance, visual arts, and music. The highly regarded Joshua Squad uses such performing arts as mime and song to minister around the world.

Become a Master Learner.

Belhaven's Worldview Curriculum combines traditional study of great books with a Christian outlook. First-years also take the Master Learner Seminar, which helps students adjust to demanding college courses through discussions of time management and an emphasis on study skills. After completing the core curriculum, students choose from among over 20 majors, including pastoral studies and sports administration.

Through the Omega College program, students design their own courses of study or interdisciplinary major. The eight preprofessional programs at Belhaven include prephysical therapy and predental.

There are five residence halls on campus: Wells and Robertson Halls for men, and Caldwell, Helen White, and Gillespie Hall for women. First-years generally live in one of the doubles of Caldwell and Wells.

Thirteen teams, including dance and volleyball, compete as the Blazers. Each year, the entire campus stops studying and does something good as part of the Community Work Day.

Everybody hangs out at the Shoe Bird Café and Belhaven Lake. Located in the McCravey-Triplett Student Center, the café sells freshly baked goodies and Starbucks coffee. Plus, family and friends can send their Belhaven students care packages through the café's Gifts from Home program. The two-acre lake is considered the center of campus, and it's a favorite destination for sunbathers and anglers.

Beloit College

700 College Street **(608) 363-2000**
Beloit, WI 53511 **http://www.beloit.edu/**

Why It's Cool

Put the *earning* back in *learning*. Forget about a part-time job flipping burgers or babysitting kids. Beloit helps you think big through its CELEB program. Really big. At the Center for Entrepreneurship and Liberal Education at Beloit, you'll learn how to start your own business or not-for-profit group. But you'll get more than just advice. CELEB provides a cable-access television station, a computerized recording and editing studio, a suite designed for computer animation, and an art gallery, all in a recently renovated building downtown. After four years, you just might have a BA *and* be a CEO.

"INVENT YOURSELF" IS BELOIT'S UNOFFICIAL MOTTO.

The Details

Campus setting:	small town
Degrees:	bachelor's
Calendar:	semesters
Public/Private:	private nonprofit
Number of full-time faculty:	103
Student-to-teacher ratio:	11:1

Admissions requirements:

- **Options:** common application, deferred entrance, early admission, early action, electronic application
- **Application fee:** $30
- **Required:** essay or personal statement, high school transcript, letter of recommendation, SAT or ACT
- **Application deadlines:** 1/15 (freshmen), continuous (transfer)
- **Early action:** 12/15
- **Notification:** 4/1 (freshmen), continuous (transfer), 1/15 (early action)

Average high school GPA:	3.46
Average freshman SAT verbal/math score:	653 / 609
Average freshman ACT score:	25
Number of applicants:	1,875
Number of applicants accepted:	1,319
Percentage of students from out of state:	80%
Total freshman enrollment:	325
Total enrollment:	1,389
Percentage of students who live in campus housing:	93%
Total tuition fee:	$25,516
Total cost with fees & expenses:	$31,832
Average financial aid package:	$18,737

Where It's At

The small city of Beloit is located on the border between Illinois and Wisconsin on the Rock River. Anthropologist Margaret Mead once termed Beloit "a microcosm of America." A recent renovation revamped the city's waterfront area, which now features a park, a 3.5-mile walking trail, and a marooned eighteenth-century galleon. Each year, Beloit hosts 11 festivals, including Winterfest, a two-day celebration that features toboggan races and an indoor winter carnival. The Travel Series, which operates through the office of Student Activities, arranges free trips to the mall or movie theaters and gives students a lift into nearby Madison and Chicago.

What It's Like

Students crisscross Beloit's 40-acre campus on tree-lined paths, surrounded by 23 American Indian effigy mounds dating from AD 700. Recent campus improvements include making some streets pedestrian-only and building a state-of-the-art science center, complete with 100,000 square feet of office, laboratory, and classroom space. The campus also features an art museum and the Logan Museum of Anthropology, which holds what are thought to be the world's oldest pieces of jewelry.

WANTED: Young, able entrepreneurs

Most Beloit students live on campus in traditional dorms, Greek houses (three fraternities and two sororities), and special-interest houses. Theme houses include the Women's Center, the Voces Latinos House, and the Outdoor Environment House. Students participate in any of more than 100 organizations, from the Fencing Club to the Beloit Fair Action Labor Network. There are 18 Division III varsity athletic teams.

Some of the more than 50 majors and 30 minors offered at Beloit include directing for the theater, prelaw, and teaching English as a second language. The First-Year Initiative Program acclimates students to academic life through a small, seminar-style class during the first semester. During the second semester, the same groups of students meet outside of class for discussion and socializing, and they continue to meet with their advisers. Beloit also holds Sophomore-Year Initiatives, which include career, study abroad, and internship fairs. More than 50 percent of Beloit students end up studying abroad.

Through CELEB, students start entrepreneurial ventures, particularly in the arts and in communications. Another cool program, the Comprehensive Academic Plan, helps students thoughtfully map out their education. Under the CAP, sophomores decide on a major and possibly a minor. They then write up a short rationale for their remaining two years of study at Beloit. CAP helps students get the most out of this treasure school by making undergrads thoughtfully consider their academic and extracurricular choices.

Berea College

Edwards Building, CPO 2220
Berea, KY 40404
(800) 326-5948
http://www.berea.edu/

Why It's Cool

No moola? No problem. Berea gives every single student a tuition scholarship, plus financial aid for any other expenses. Talk about generosity. In return, you'll work at an on-campus job for about ten to 15 hours each week. You might make decorative objects through Broomcraft or sell them at the Log House Craft Gallery, teach nursery school at the Berea Children's Center, do computer mapping for the geology department, or process invoices for the utilities department. All told, there are 140 labor departments and hundreds of jobs from which to choose. At Berea, you'll work it . . . work it *real* good.

CRAFTS ARE COOL. BEREA'S ANNUAL HOLIDAY SALE OF STUDENT-MADE QUILTS, BROOMS, AND OTHER TRADITIONAL APPALACHIAN CRAFTS HAS GENERATED $20,000 IN JUST EIGHT HOURS.

The Details

Campus setting:	small town
Degrees:	bachelor's
Calendar:	4-1-4
Public/Private:	private nonprofit
Number of full-time faculty:	131
Student-to-teacher ratio:	11:1

Admissions requirements:

- **Options:** electronic application
- **Application fee:** —
- **Required:** essay or personal statement, high school transcript, letter of recommendation, SAT or ACT
- **Application deadlines:** continuous (freshmen), continuous (transfer)
- **Early decision:** —
- **Notification:** 4/30 (freshmen), continuous (transfer)

Average high school GPA:	3.4
Average freshman SAT verbal/math score:	564 / 569
Average freshman ACT score:	23
Number of applicants:	2,108
Number of applicants accepted:	562
Percentage of students from out of state:	64%
Total freshman enrollment:	400
Total enrollment:	1,556
Percentage of students who live in campus housing:	84%
Total tuition fee:	—
Total cost with fees & expenses:	$5,964
Average financial aid package:	$26,373

Where It's At

Berea's 140-acre campus is located in the town of Berea. As the "Folk Arts and Crafts" capital of Kentucky, Berea has the Old Town Artisan's Village, a group of artists' studios; the Kentucky Artisan Center, devoted to retailing Kentucky-made goods; and the Berea Arts Councils, which sponsors classes in quilting and other craftmaking. During the monthly Gallery Hop, artists open their studios to the public for browsing and socializing. The Renfro Valley Entertainment Center offers shopping, country music performances, and barn dances. Each February, the center hosts a bluegrass festival. Lexington and Knoxville are about two hours away by car.

What It's Like

Students from more than 70 countries are attracted to Berea and its motto, "Learning, Labor, Service"—and why not? In exchange for 140 hours of work per semester, students get a free education. Minorities and international students make up about a third of Berea's student body.

The Center for Excellence in Learning Through Service helps students find volunteering opportunities, such as with People Who Care, which pairs Berea students with nursing-home residents. Although community service is not required, the principle of "giving back" is built into Berea's atmosphere. For instance, through the Entrepreneurship for the Public Good Program, students can get an internship with a not-for-profit agency.

Pay nothing but get a lot.

Berea runs on a 4-1-4 schedule, with two 14-week terms in the fall and spring and a monthlong term in January. During the short term, students can do an internship; take an in-depth class on campus, such as African American Cinema, Foundations of Leadership, or Chemical Magic; or go abroad to study dancing in Argentina and Brazil or the culture of Ghana, among other international opportunities.

To fulfill the general studies requirements, designed to provide a strong background in the humanities and the sciences, students take such interdisciplinary courses as Appalachian Problems and Institutions; Western Traditions; and Service, Citizenship, and Injustice. Before graduating, all Berea students must attend several Convocation Series programs, including musical performances and lectures.

Among the more than 25 majors are child and family studies, technology and industrial arts, and agriculture. Self-designed majors range from ecological design to graphic communication, and students are urged to create their own interdisciplinary major.

About 88 percent of students live on campus in one of 14 residential halls and nine theme houses, including Talcott, Dana, and Blue Ridge for first-years. Another option is the sustainable Ecovillage, with totally "green" apartments for married and single-parent students.

Binghamton University
State University of New York

PO Box 6000
Binghamton, NY 13902
(607) 777-2000
http://www.binghamton.edu/

Why It's Cool

Sure, BU's got excellent programs in political science and chemistry. It's also got a rad way of teaching languages, which emphasizes practical knowledge, and National Book Award– and Pulitzer Prize–winning professors. Plus, BU's been super-successful at getting graduates into law and medical schools. And BU offers you all this—and more—for a low, low price. But what's really fabulous about this school is life on campus. You'll live in one of seven residential complexes, modeled on the living/learning colleges of England's Oxford. Each complex holds fun classes like How to Make Sushi and academic classes like Writing about Popular Music. Think Ivy League for less.

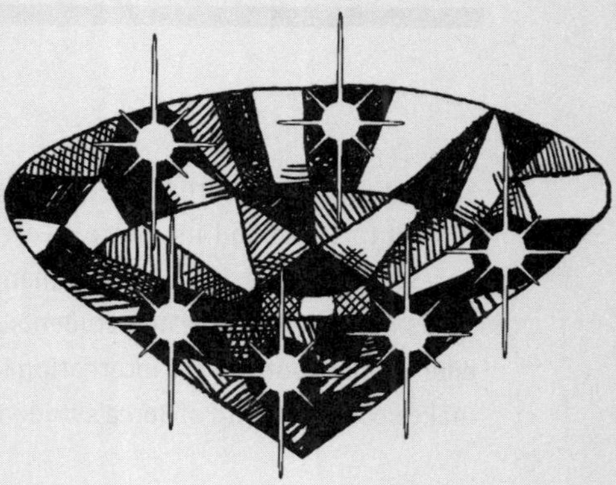

BINGHAMTON IS KNOWN AS THE "CROWN JEWEL" OF THE STATE UNIVERSITY OF NEW YORK'S 64 CAMPUSES BECAUSE OF ITS STRONG ACADEMICS AND GREAT PROGRAMS.

The Details

Campus setting:	urban
Degrees:	bachelor's, master's, doctoral
Calendar:	semesters
Public/Private:	public state
Number of full-time faculty:	512
Student-to-teacher ratio:	22:1

Admissions requirements:

- **Options:** common application, deferred entrance, early admission, early action
- **Application fee:** $40
- **Required:** essay or personal statement, high school transcript, letter of recommendation, SAT or ACT
- **Application deadlines:** continuous (freshmen), continuous (transfer)
- **Early action:** 11/15
- **Notification:** continuous (freshmen), continuous (transfer), 12/22 (early action)

Average high school GPA:	3.60
Average freshman SAT verbal/math score:	615 / 650
Average freshman ACT score:	25
Number of applicants:	20,116
Number of applicants accepted:	8,900
Percentage of students from out of state:	6%
Total freshman enrollment:	2,158
Total enrollment:	13,860
Percentage of students who live in campus housing:	58%
Total in-state tuition, fees & expenses:	$14,266
Total out-of-state tuition, fees & expenses:	$20,526
Average financial aid package:	$11,089

Where It's At

BU is located in the town of Vestal, a suburb of the greater Binghamton metro area in upstate New York. Sometimes called the "Carousel Capital of the World," the Binghamton area has six antique carousels. Ross Park boasts a carousel exhibit and the fifth-oldest zoo in the United States. Other attractions include the Cutler Botanic Gardens, the Binghamton Philharmonic, the Broadway Theater League, the Kopernik Observatory, and Chenango Valley State Park. Sports fans cheer on minor league baseball's Binghamton Mets and the Binghamton Senators (AHL), a hockey team affiliated with the Ottawa Senators. New York City is about four hours away by car.

What It's Like

A school this large draws all kinds of students, all of whom are attracted to the first-rate academics at bargain-basement prices. So don't worry about not fitting in at the Brain, as the campus is affectionately known. And with 41 Greek chapters on campus, fraternities and sororities are really popular.

The seven residential complexes at BU give students a sense of place within the large university. Each complex features several unique dorms, its own dining hall, and a Discovery Center, which has space for hanging out and resources for academic help. Students not only live together and take classes with one another but also participate in friendly competitions: Mutant Mania is nine days of games, including Ultimate Frisbee and Jeopardy.

Top-notch academics at bargain-basement prices

Academic life at BU is centered around five colleges: the Harpur College of Arts and Sciences, the School of Management, the Decker School of Nursing, the School of Education and Human Development, and the Watson School of Engineering and Applied Science. Specific requirements differ from school to school, but BU requires everyone to take classes in such subjects as composition and math. There's also a health and wellness requirement, fulfilled by classes like Wellness Through Power Yoga.

BU runs on the semester system but also offers an optional Winter Session. For three weeks in January, students take an in-depth class, including the popular Professional Writing. Majors range from cinema to Judaic studies. Roughly 28 percent of BU graduates go on to law or medical school.

In addition to traditional language classes, BU offers specialized ones, such as Business Spanish, to help students become bilingual professionals. Through the Office of International Programs, students can head to Grenada and Morocco, among other countries.

There are 21 Division I athletic teams at BU, including men's and women's lacrosse. Late Nite Binghamton offers all kinds of on-campus activities after 10 P.M., ranging from movies to pool tournaments.

Haunted Hallways: Schools with Ghosts

OK, we'll admit it: We're scared of ghosts. So what? Some of you might be scared too, so we've thoughtfully prepared a list of schools rumored to have skeletons in their closets—*literally*.

Arcadia University (P. 16)

A male ghost is said to roam the halls of Grey Towers Castle, a swanky dorm on campus.

Binghamton University (P. 34)

We hear there's a monster living in BU's Lake Lieberman. According to legend, a virgin must be sacrificed on the lake's shores each fall to keep the monster satisfied.

Coe College (P. 50)

The ghost of a young co-ed named Helen, who died in the influenza epidemic of 1918, supposedly lives in a clock inside Stuart Hall. Late at night, Helen leaves the clock to play piano or to pull the covers off sleeping co-eds.

University of Montevallo (P. 208)

Today, the ghost of Colonel Reynolds roams around Reynolds Hall, where Confederate soldiers were massacred during the Civil War.

The University of the South (P. 214)

Not one, not two, but *four* ghosts are said to haunt Sewanee's lovely campus. There's the Headless Gownsman, the ghost of a young man who was decapitated in a car accident while driving on the mountain; plus, the ghosts of three students rumored to have committed suicide in the same room haunt the third floor of Tuckaway Hall.

Birmingham-Southern College

900 Arkadelphia Road **(205) 226-4600**
Birmingham, AL 35254 **http://www.bsc.edu/**

Why It's Cool

Forget about the 411. BSC's all about the 4-1-4. You'll take roughly four classes during the two full-length semesters and one class during the short Interim Term in January. But you won't take just any old class. Instead, you'll stretch your mind with Sherlock Holmes Meets *CSI* or Mental Illness and the Media. Maybe you'll take up a new hobby like ballet or guitar. You don't even have to stay in Birmingham: You can volunteer in Mozambique or explore the ecology of Australia. Best of all, Interim Term is required, so you'll have lots of opportunities to try new stuff and see new places.

BIRMINGHAM'S "MR. & MISS APOLLO PAGEANT" IS THE SECOND-OLDEST CONTINUOUSLY RUNNING DRAG QUEEN FESTIVAL IN THE UNITED STATES.

The Details

Campus setting:	urban
Degrees:	bachelor's, master's
Calendar:	4-1-4
Public/Private:	private religious
Number of full-time faculty:	96
Student-to-teacher ratio:	12:1

Admissions requirements:

- **Options:** common application, deferred entrance, early admission, early action, electronic application
- **Application fee:** $25
- **Required:** essay or personal statement, high school transcript, letter of recommendation, SAT or ACT
- **Application deadlines:** continuous (freshmen), continuous (transfer)
- **Early action:** 12/1
- **Notification:** continuous (freshmen), continuous (transfer), 12/15 (early action)

Average high school GPA:	3.38
Average freshman SAT verbal/math score:	610 / 589
Average freshman ACT score:	25
Number of applicants:	1,157
Number of applicants accepted:	956
Percentage of students from out of state:	25%
Total freshman enrollment:	367
Total enrollment:	1,453
Percentage of students who live in campus housing:	79%
Total tuition fee:	$20,425
Total cost with fees & expenses:	$29,135
Average financial aid package:	$16,015

Where It's At

BSC's 192-acres are located just three miles from downtown Birmingham, Alabama's largest city. Among this city's many attractions are the International Motorsports Hall of Fame, Aldridge Gardens, the Five Points South entertainment district, the Ruffner Mountain Nature Center, the Alabama Jazz Hall of Fame, and the Birmingham Civil Rights Institute. Birmingham is renowned for its golf courses, which number around 20, in addition to its hunting and fishing spots, including the 25,000-acre Sipsey Wilderness Area. The minor-league Barons play baseball at the Hoover Metropolitan Stadium, while the Steeldogs play arena football at the Birmingham-Jefferson Convention Complex. Mobile and Memphis are both about four hours away by car.

What It's Like

Everybody at this friendly campus (known as the Hilltop) hangs out at the Cellar. Open every night except Fridays and Saturdays, it serves coffee and snacks and hosts weekly open-mike nights. There are about 80 organizations on the Hilltop, ranging from 13 fraternities and sororities to the Gospel Choir to the Southern Outdoor Adventure Club. As the Panthers, students compete on 14 Division I athletic teams, including baseball and women's air rifle.

Students must attend 40 cultural events . . . from a Broadway show to a Kwanza celebration.

About 90 percent of students live on campus in one of seven traditional residence halls. None of the halls are co-ed, and most of the rooms are doubles. Students play sports or just lounge around the Dorm Quad, a large grassy area between the halls.

BSC offers more than 35 majors in five academic divisions: fine and performing arts, business, science and mathematics, education, and the humanities. Everybody must take courses during the Interim Term, and the course taken during a student's senior year must relate in some way to the major.

As part of the Foundations requirement, students have to take classes in the arts and sciences, including one class from each of the five academic divisions, and they must show proficiency in math and writing. To graduate, students also have to attend 40 cultural events, ranging from a Broadway show to a Kwanza celebration.

In addition to the study abroad opportunities offered during Interim Term, BSC sponsors international programs that last for a summer, semester, or year. Another popular option is doing an internship or volunteering abroad, such as working on a newspaper in Argentina or in a library in Cuba.

The Leadership Studies program trains students to be effective leaders. To earn a Distinction in Leadership at graduation, students take certain classes, such as Group Dynamics and Contemporary Southern Politics. And at the multimillion-dollar Stephens Center, student scientists get access to the same high-tech equipment used by the faculty.

Carroll College

1601 North Benton Avenue **(406) 447-4300**
Helena, MT 59625 **http://www.carroll.edu/**

Why It's Cool

Chatterers, storytellers, speakers, and debaters—motormouths of all sorts will find a home at Carroll. If you like to argue, join the Talking Saints forensics team, a speech and debate group recently ranked third in the United States. If you like discussions, you'll love the required Alpha Seminar, which lets you jabber with fellow first-years about what it means to be at a Catholic liberal arts college. And if you're into chitchat of the electronic variety, post your heart out on the online Carroll Boards, which list information about study groups, parties, and other activities. At Carroll, talk is anything but cheap.

KEEP ON GABBING. THE TALKING SAINTS DEBATE TEAM HAS BEEN CONSISTENTLY RANKED AMONG THE TOP FIVE IN THE COUNTRY.

The Details

Campus setting:	urban
Degrees:	bachelor's
Calendar:	semesters
Public/Private:	private religious
Number of full-time faculty:	77
Student-to-teacher ratio:	14:1

Admissions requirements:

- **Options:** common application, deferred entrance, electronic application
- **Application fee:** $35
- **Required:** essay or personal statement, high school transcript, letter of recommendation, SAT or ACT
- **Application deadlines:** 6/1 (freshmen), 6/1 (transfer)
- **Early decision:** —
- **Notification:** continuous (freshmen), continuous (transfer)

Average high school GPA:	3.45
Average freshman SAT verbal/math score:	557 / 552
Average freshman ACT score:	24
Number of applicants:	1,049
Number of applicants accepted:	844
Percentage of students from out of state:	41%
Total freshman enrollment:	356
Total enrollment:	1,461
Percentage of students who live in campus housing:	58%
Total tuition fee:	$16,778
Total cost with fees & expenses:	$23,924
Average financial aid package:	$14,376

Where It's At

Carroll is located in Helena, Montana's small state capital. A walking path connects Carroll to Helena's downtown area, which features restaurants, specialty stores, the Holter Museum of Art, the Grandstreet Theater, and the Last Chance Gulch, where gold was discovered in 1864. At the Myrna Loy Center, students receive discounted tickets to musical performances and movies. The local Montana Historical Society displays more than 50,000 historical artifacts. Outdoor activities include hiking, backpacking, skiing, and rafting at the Helena National Forest and ten nearby state parks. Yellowstone and Glacier National Parks are each about four hours away. Billings, the largest city in Montana, is also about four hours away.

What It's Like

As a Catholic college, Carroll stresses Christian values in campus and academic life. Nevertheless, Carroll accepts students from all spiritual traditions, and more than a third of the student body is not Catholic. The interdisciplinary Alpha Seminar introduces students to college-level reading and writing, and students must also take Theological Foundations, an introduction to Roman Catholic theology and traditions, as part of the CORE requirements.

Cheering crazies and opinionated voices . . .

Courses in four areas make up the other CORE requirements: writing, foundations, diversity, and areas of knowledge. Foundations classes cover such subjects as composition and communication. To fulfill the diversity requirement, students may study abroad or take classes that examine other cultures. For areas of knowledge, students take courses in such subjects as math, history, philosophy, theology, literature, and the natural sciences.

Majors range from public administration to nursing. Engineering students may participate in a cooperative dual degree program, in which they major in math at Carroll for three years and then transfer to such schools as Columbia University or the University of Southern California to study engineering for two years. Upon graduation, each school awards students a degree. Six preprofessional programs allow students a chance to prepare for graduate study in veterinary medicine, optometry, or dentistry, among other areas.

Generally, students here hit the books before the parties, but everybody makes time for something fun once in a while. There are 12 men's and women's athletic teams, including the NAIA–champion football squad. Carroll also has its own professional dance troupe, Artisan Dance, which performs regularly. Notable alumni appear on *Saints and Scholars*, a student-run interview program on Carroll TV. Other student activities include Pep Band, the Carroll Crazies sports fans, and Carroll Voices, an electronic forum for opinions. Students at this treasure school are totally glad to be there: Close to 70 percent of students who go to Carroll are attending their first choice.

Centenary College

400 Jefferson Street
Hackettstown, NJ 07840
(908) 852-1400
http://www.centenarycollege.edu/

Why It's Cool

Come to Centenary. Get a free laptop. That's right: As a full-time undergrad, you'll receive an IBM laptop, complete with wireless technology, so you can access the web anywhere, anytime. Plus, a lot of technologically savvy profs broadcast their lectures online, which means you can master the material without ever leaving your bed. Talk about incredible. But you'll also get a personal academic tutor, a bucolic campus, and a college town recently named by CNNMoney one of the top 100 places to live in the United States. What else can we say? Centenary rules.

CENTENARY REQUIRES ITS STUDENTS TO DO COMMUNITY SERVICE, WHICH MIGHT INCLUDE GROOMING DOGS AND CATS FOR THE WINTER SOLSTICE PET PHOTOS FUND-RAISER.

The Details

Campus setting:	suburban
Degrees:	bachelor's, master's
Calendar:	semesters
Public/Private:	private religious
Number of full-time faculty:	53
Student-to-teacher ratio:	15:1

Admissions requirements:

- **Options:** common application, deferred entrance, electronic application
- **Application fee:** $30
- **Required:** essay or personal statement, high school transcript, letter of recommendation, SAT or ACT
- **Application deadlines:** continuous (freshmen), continuous (transfer)
- **Early decision:** —
- **Notification:** continuous (freshmen), continuous (transfer)

Average high school GPA:	2.7
Average freshman SAT verbal/math score:	465 / 468
Average freshman ACT score:	15
Number of applicants:	698
Number of applicants accepted:	674
Percentage of students from out of state:	12%
Total freshman enrollment:	258
Total enrollment:	2,600
Percentage of students who live in campus housing:	58%
Total tuition fee:	$18,450
Total cost with fees & expenses:	$27,860
Average financial aid package:	$12,579

Where It's At

Centenary's 42-acre campus is located in Hackettstown, New Jersey. Hackettstown is a safe, suburban town just an hour from the bright lights of New York City. Among the town's attractions are Allamuchy Mountain State Park, with 2,400 acres of fishing and hiking, and the Waterloo Village, which re-creates nineteenth-century life through preserved houses and a general store. Donaldson Farms offers regular cider-tasting events and "pick-your-own" fruit excursions, while the Centenary Stage Company hosts musical performances and plays. Six Flags New Jersey and Philadelphia are both about two hours away, and Atlantic City is about three.

What It's Like

Centenary's commitment to putting students first is totally sincere. As soon as first-years arrive on campus, they get assigned a faculty mentor, an academic tutor, and a learning associate—an upperclass student who gives advice on anything from time management and study skills to the best places to get pizza.

The Centenary Wireless Experience not only means that every student gets a free laptop but also that professors are committed to incorporating technology into their classes. As part of the yearlong First-Year Experience, newbies choose from among 18 writing-intensive seminars, including *The Simpsons*: An American Family and The Sociology of Reality TV. Every seminar links to the wireless network, which means students don't always have to be in the classroom in order to learn.

A free laptop and your very own academic tutor

Among the many majors offered are fashion merchandizing, sports management, and aquatic biology. Centenary also has a program in equine studies, as well as a 65-acre Equestrian Center. All students must fulfill core requirements in the liberal arts, including courses in history, American studies, composition, and math.

Students are required to perform at least ten hours of community service each year. And all first-years participate in the Community Plunge, one Saturday during the fall semester devoted to volunteering at a local agency or park. Another popular service opportunity is the Midnight Run, during which students spend a night in New York City, distributing food and supplies to the homeless.

Activities range from writing for the literary magazine *Prisms* to hosting a show on the campus radio station to working with SIFE (Students in Free Enterprise). As the Cyclones, students compete on 14 Division III athletic teams.

There are seven residence halls, including the co-ed Washabaugh Hall, which features walk-in closets, and the apartments at Bennett-Smith Hall. First-years live in the co-ed singles and doubles of Reeves and Smith Halls.

Centre College

600 West Walnut Street **(859) 238-5200**
Danville, KY 40422 **http://www.centre.edu/**

Why It's Cool

Afraid to commit? Don't be. At this school, commitment rocks. The Centre Commitment guarantees that you'll get to go abroad, do an internship, and graduate within four years (or your fifth year is free). You'll choose from more than 25 majors and minors on campus, and Centre's got international programs throughout the world, ranging from three weeks to a full year. Picture yourself studying volcanoes in New Zealand or primates in Barbados, then jetting back to the United States for an internship at Toyota or the Centers for Disease Control. And, in some cases, Centre will even *pay* you to work off campus.

A PORTRAIT OF DECEASED ALUM FRED VINSON ATTENDS EVERY CENTRE FOOTBALL GAME, AS WELL AS OTHER IMPORTANT EVENTS. THE PORTRAIT IS KNOWN AS "DEAD FRED."

The Details

Campus setting:	small town
Degrees:	bachelor's
Calendar:	4-1-4
Public/Private:	private religious
Number of full-time faculty:	92
Student-to-teacher ratio:	10:1

Admissions requirements:

- **Options:** common application, deferred entrance, early admission, early action, electronic application
- **Application fee:** $40
- **Required:** essay or personal statement, high school transcript, letter of recommendation, SAT or ACT
- **Application deadlines:** 2/1 (freshmen), 6/1 (transfer)
- **Early action:** 12/1
- **Notification:** 3/15 (freshmen), 7/1 (transfer), 1/15 (early action)

Average high school GPA:	3.70
Average freshman SAT verbal/math score:	653 / 629
Average freshman ACT score:	26
Number of applicants:	1,604
Number of applicants accepted:	1,099
Percentage of students from out of state:	30%
Total freshman enrollment:	297
Total enrollment:	1,069
Percentage of students who live in campus housing:	95%
Total tuition fee:	$21,800
Total cost with fees & expenses:	$29,900
Average financial aid package:	$18,053

Where It's At

Centre's 115-acre campus is located in Danville, a large town in the Bluegrass region of central Kentucky. Danville has five historical districts and several landmark buildings. Visitors can tour the oldest post office in the West at Constitution Square or learn about Kentucky's role in the Civil War at the Perryville Battlefield. Other area attractions include the Pioneer Playhouse, an outdoor dinner theater, and the 14,000-acre Bernheim Arboretum and Research Forest. About an hour away, Louisville is home to the Kentucky Derby, the Kentucky Derby Museum, Six Flags Kentucky Kingdom, and the Louisville Slugger Museum.

What It's Like

Greek life dominates Centre's social scene. Prepare to rush a fraternity or sorority or, at the very least, to spend your weekends partying. All told, about 55 percent of students belong to a Greek house. But Centre students don't just go Greek, they go just about everywhere. In fact, 75 percent of students spend some time abroad. Centre offers semester-long study opportunities in France, England, and Mexico. Another option is going abroad during CentreTerm, a three-week term in January. Students head to Fiji or Bulgaria, among other locations.

Improve your GPA by seeing a Dolly Parton concert.

Although there are more than 25 majors from which to choose, students are encouraged to design their own specializations. Recent self-designed majors include European studies and religion and the performing arts. Preprofessional programs range from prepharmacy to pre-MBA.

All students must fulfill requirements in writing, math, and foreign language. To meet Centre's Convocations requirement, students attend roughly 12 cultural events per year. In return, they get an A, which then factors into their GPA. Centre usually designates about 30 events as Convocations, from comedy shows to a Dolly Parton concert at the on-campus Norton Center for the Arts to hearing a Nobel Prize winner debate with a professor.

As part of the Centre Commitment, anyone who applies for an internship gets an internship. Every student automatically gets assigned a career counselor, and the Career Services office keeps lists of potential jobs.

The new College Centre offers students the opportunity to work out, check out a library book, and attend class all in one multimillion-dollar, high-tech complex. The Old Quad has traditional dorms for first-year men and upperclass students. About 94 percent of students live on campus.

Centre might be small, but it has more than 100 clubs and hosts more than 2,000 events per year. There are 19 Division III athletic teams. Other groups include the Culinary Arts Club and the co-ed, service-oriented Alpha Pi Omega.

Chaminade University of Honolulu

3140 Waialae Avenue **(808) 735-4711**
Honolulu, HI 96816 **http://www.chaminade.edu/**

Why It's Cool

CSI has nothing on CUH. If you long to catch bad guys, then this university is the place for you. Through the forensic science department, you'll study everything from the role of insects in solving murders to cutting-edge molecular technology used to analyze crime scenes. If you'd rather work in the courtroom, there's a major in criminology and criminal science, with a prelaw concentration. Courses in psychology will help you unlock the secrets of evil masterminds, while behavioral science will teach you to discover the hidden meanings of gestures. Did we mention that CUH is just two miles from the beach?

CUH'S STUNNING CAMPUS OVERLOOKS DIAMOND HEAD, AN INACTIVE VOLCANO THAT AFFORDS 360-DEGREE VIEWS OF OAHU.

The Details

Campus setting:	urban
Degrees:	bachelor's, master's
Calendar:	semesters
Public/Private:	private religious
Number of full-time faculty:	77
Student-to-teacher ratio:	11:1

Admissions requirements:

- **Options:** common application, deferred entrance, electronic application
- **Application fee:** $50
- **Required:** high school transcript, SAT or ACT
- **Application deadlines:** continuous (freshmen), continuous (transfer)
- **Early decision:** —
- **Notification:** continuous (freshmen), continuous (transfer)

Average high school GPA:	3.07
Average freshman SAT verbal/math score:	476 / 482
Average freshman ACT score:	20
Number of applicants:	791
Number of applicants accepted:	765
Percentage of students from out of state:	43%
Total freshman enrollment:	248
Total enrollment:	1,783
Percentage of students who live in campus housing:	—
Total tuition fee:	$14,330
Total cost with fees & expenses:	$23,920
Average financial aid package:	$12,846

Where It's At

CUH is located in the historic district of Kaimuki, in Honolulu, Hawaii. Located on Oahu, Honolulu is home to Waikiki, a stretch of shops, beaches, hotels, and restaurants; the Ala Moana Center, the largest open-air market in the world; a symphony and opera house; the Iolani Palace, once home to the Hawaiian royal family; and several museums, including the USS *Arizona* Memorial, dedicated to the memory of the Pearl Harbor attack in World War II. Every February, NFL teams compete at the Pro Bowl, held in Aloha Stadium. Locals and tourists alike enjoy hiking Diamond Head, a volcanic crater and former U.S. military outpost with spectacular views; surfing and snorkling at the North Shore; and year-round fabulous weather.

What It's Like

CUH has ocean breezes and liberal arts. General education requirements include writing-intensive courses, upper-division interdisciplinary courses, and courses that demonstrate global awareness. To meet these requirements, students might take such classes as Cultural Anthropology, Landscapes of Hawaii, and Visual Design.

Students choose majors from among more than 30 fields, including Hawaiian and Pacific studies, and can receive undergraduate certificates, which complement majors, in environmental studies and gender studies. The popular forensic science department has such classes as Forensic Photography and offers advice on careers in all areas of criminal justice, including prosecution, crime scene investigation, and forensic technology.

Surf's up—and so is your IQ.

As part of its commitment to educating the whole student, CUH offers 19 service-learning courses in religious studies and math, among other areas of study. In these courses, students combine community service with classroom work. Recent courses have worked with Project SHINE, in which students teach English to immigrants, and Paolo Pipeline, which pairs students with at-risk youths.

Each year, students put on the Pacific Island Review and the International Extravaganza to celebrate the multiple cultures and traditions at CUH. Welcome Week helps new and returning students acclimate to the academic year by hosting career and club fairs, concerts, and picnics. The "Be My Guest . . ." program lets students take their professors out for a free lunch.

There are ten Division II athletic teams, including men's water polo and women's volleyball. Intramural offerings range from billiards to a softball home-run derby. Commuter and residential students participate in such organizations as the American Society of Interior Designers, Delta Epsilon Sigma (a national Catholic honorary), and CJ Sleuths (for people interested in criminal justice).

Although CUH is affiliated with the Catholic Church, students of all faiths are welcome to partake of its intense academic and tropical atmosphere. At this treasure school, the surf is up—and so is your IQ.

Riding the Orient(ation) Express: Best First-Year Orientations

At most schools, orientations are dull affairs, consisting of a couple barbecues and a pile of brochures. Not so at these Treasure Schools. The orientations here are designed not only to make you feel comfortable on campus but also to get you totally psyched about college life. And there's not a brochure in sight.

Earlham College (P. 78)

Earlham's been doing the outdoor-orientation thing for a long, long time (since 1970, in fact). You'll choose either Mountain (backpacking in Utah) or Water (canoeing in Canada), then spend about three weeks having adventures in the great outdoors.

Green Mountain College (P. 102)

The five-day Wilderness Challenge will orient you to GMC's unique environmental-friendly philosophy from day one. You'll hike, camp, canoe, rock climb, and mountain bike through the Adirondacks.

Hendrix College (P. 112)

Forget about the standard meet-and-greet parties held at most schools. Sure, you'll meet-and-greet at Hendrix, but you'll be meeting other first-years while also rock climbing, hiking, camping, or building houses and volunteering throughout Arkansas.

Hiram College (P. 114)

During New Student Institute Week, you might sing in the talent show, take a language placement exam, do-si-do during a night of square dancing, go canoeing, meet your faculty adviser, and talk about making the transition from high school to college in informal discussion groups—just not all at the same time.

Lewis & Clark College (P. 124)

Orientation at this school is so special they hold it twice. There's the standard orientation in the fall, which introduces you to life on campus. But there's also the optional New Student Breakaway Adventures, an orientation that takes place before the official one. You'll choose from a bunch of weekend getaways, from rock climbing to backpacking to caving.

North Central College (P. 150)

The Ongoing Orientation pairs you up with an upperclass mentor, who will feed you, pet you, and make sure you get to bed on time. Well, not quite, but he or she will show you the North Central ropes.

Prescott College (P. 160)

You'll spend a month getting oriented at this school. Prescott's optional Wilderness Orientation teaches you the fundamentals of low-impact camping in the American Southwest. If the desert's not for you, you can spend a month kayaking and canoeing on Arizona's largest man-made lake or doing community service in the local Prescott community.

Rollins College (P. 178)

Spend your first weekend in college off campus—for free. Rollins sponsors the weekend trip to a fun location as part of its orientation activities for first-years.

Unity College (P. 200)

You'll find your inner crunchiness during the New Student Orientation Trip—a weeklong hiking, camping, or kayaking adventure.

The University of the South (P. 214)

Sewanee's Pre-Orientation includes ropes courses, volleyball, caving, canoeing, rock climbing, swimming, and hiking at Lake Cheston. The super-fun weekend ends with Casino Night.

Coe College

1220 1st Avenue, Northeast **(319) 399-8000**
Cedar Rapids, IA 52402 **http://www.coe.edu/**

Why It's Cool

There's more than corn at Coe. Sure, it's located in Iowa, but Coe emphasizes education over vegetables. In fact, the folks at Coe have a plan: to turn you from a bright-eyed college student into a confident citizen of the world, ready for any situation life might throw at you. The so-called Coe Plan combines community service with required residential life and small classes. Sound good? It gets better: All seniors must take a practicum, which puts students into the real world as interns, student teachers, or research assistants. That's a plan worth sticking to.

BOO! STUART HALL IS SAID TO BE HAUNTED BY THE GHOST OF A YOUNG CO-ED NAMED HELEN, WHO DIED IN THE INFLUENZA EPIDEMIC OF 1918.

The Details

Campus setting:	urban
Degrees:	bachelor's, master's
Calendar:	4-4-1
Public/Private:	private religious
Number of full-time faculty:	75
Student-to-teacher ratio:	13:1

Admissions requirements:

- **Options:** common application, deferred entrance, early admission, early action, electronic application
- **Application fee:** $30
- **Required:** essay or personal statement, high school transcript, letter of recommendation, SAT or ACT
- **Application deadlines:** 3/1 (freshmen), continuous (transfer)
- **Early action:** 12/10
- **Notification:** 3/15 (freshmen), continuous (transfer), 1/20 (early action)

Average high school GPA:	3.58
Average freshman SAT verbal/math score:	580 / 569
Average freshman ACT score:	24
Number of applicants:	1,177
Number of applicants accepted:	845
Percentage of students from out of state:	30%
Total freshman enrollment:	316
Total enrollment:	1,354
Percentage of students who live in campus housing:	84%
Total tuition fee:	$22,290
Total cost with fees & expenses:	$29,200
Average financial aid package:	$20,076

Where It's At

Coe's 50 acres are smack-dab in the middle of Cedar Rapids, Iowa's second-largest city. Students can join the website CulturalCorridor.org to find out about upcoming shows and exhibitions. The Paramount Theatre hosts a Broadway Series, which brings musicals to town, and the Cedar Rapids Museum of Art displays work by local and national artists. Cedar Rapids is also home to the RoughRiders, a professional hockey club, and the River Raiders, a professional basketball team. Bikers can kick up dirt at the local BMX track. Chicago and Minneapolis are just five hours away.

What It's Like

Coe's cool. Every student must participate in the Coe Plan. First-years complete five hours of community service and attend an Issue Dinner, in which they learn about a social issue from an expert. Sophomores focus on career planning by taking workshops in résumé writing and interviewing. Optional formal dinners give sophomores the chance to develop good business etiquette. There are also general education requirements, including courses in the fine arts and the quantitative and behavioral sciences.

Writing tutors and really cheap coffee

According to the Plan, juniors and seniors must take an academic practicum of their choice. The practicum, which might include performing an original musical composition or doing research abroad, gives students the chance to apply classroom learning to practical, real-world situations.

Students choose from more than 40 majors, ranging from athletic training to gender studies, theater arts, and the design-your-own interdisciplinary. All first-years take a writing-intensive seminar that introduces them to the rigors of academic essays. Recent seminars have included Introduction to Cinema Studies, Probability: A World of Chance, and Art and the Creative Process. Luckily, the Coe Writing Center offers students writing tutors and really cheap coffee.

Residential life is a big deal at Coe. All students are permitted to live on campus for all four years. Dorm choices include Murray Hall, which has astounding views of Cedar Rapids and is home to primarily international students and visual arts majors; the laid-back, male-only Greene Hall; and the air-conditioned Armstrong-Douglas Hall, which also has its own piano and Ping-Pong tables.

Among the many on-campus groups are the Rugcutters, devoted to dance; *The Pearl*, a literary magazine; and the Coe Walaroo Drum Line, which performs percussion pieces during football and basketball games. Students come from 33 states and more than 15 countries—and they leave Coe ready to live, work, and play anywhere.

College for Creative Studies

201 East Kirby
Detroit, MI 48202
(313) 664-7400
http://www.ccscad.edu/

Why It's Cool

For those of you born with a mouse in one hand and a pen in the other, check out the College for Creative Studies. You can major in animation or industrial design, take classes in photography and sculpture, and minor in art history or art therapy. It's a dream come true for Tim Burton wannabes. Plus, CCS doesn't just let you take creative courses, it also trains you for such careers as courtroom artist or furniture designer. You'll work with faculty to prepare a portfolio of your best work, and you'll find prospective employers through the CCS Job Book. Better watch your back, Tim.

THE BLUE MONKEY SIDESHOW KICKS OFF THE FALL SEMESTER WITH INTENSE CARNIVALESQUE ANTICS LIKE KNIFE-THROWING, FIRE-SWINGING, AND RECLINING ON BEDS OF NAILS.

The Details

Campus setting:	urban
Degrees:	bachelor's
Calendar:	semesters
Public/Private:	private nonprofit
Number of full-time faculty:	45
Student-to-teacher ratio:	10:1

Admissions requirements:

- **Options:** deferred entrance, electronic application
- **Application fee:** $35
- **Required:** essay or personal statement, high school transcript, letter of recommendation, SAT or ACT
- **Application deadlines:** continuous (freshmen), continuous (transfer)
- **Early decision:** —
- **Notification:** —

Average high school GPA:	3.22
Average freshman SAT verbal/math score:	—/—
Average freshman ACT score:	—
Number of applicants:	426
Number of applicants accepted:	340
Percentage of students from out of state:	17%
Total freshman enrollment:	175
Total enrollment:	1,265
Percentage of students who live in campus housing:	23%
Total tuition fee:	$21,990
Total cost with fees & expenses:	$25,116
Average financial aid package:	—

Where It's At

CCS's 10.5-acre campus is located in the cultural center of Detroit, across the street from the Detroit Institute of the Arts and next door to the Charles H. Wright Museum of African American History. The Renaissance Center and the Riverfront Promenade have helped revitalize Detroit's downtown area. Sports fans cheer on the Detroit Tigers (MLB) and the Detroit Lions (NFL) in newly renovated stadiums. As the birthplace of techno, Detroit hosts an annual electronic music festival. Music fans can also check out the Detroit Historical Museum, the Motown Historical Museum, or Young Soul Rebels Records and Tapes, a popular local store.

What It's Like

Creativity rules at CCS. A performance of the Blue Monkey Sideshow usually kicks off the fall semester, and students celebrate just about every holiday with some type of party or event. There's even a campus-wide festival each April to celebrate spring. Local bands frequently perform during lunch in the cafeteria, which also holds open-mike events and free massage sessions throughout the year. The Center Galleries host 16 exhibitions per year of work by faculty, alumni, and national artists. The U245 Student Gallery displays student art.

Free massage sessions throughout the year . . .

Students have two options for on-campus housing: the Art Centre Building (ACB) and the Palmer Court Townhomes. At ACB, students live in apartment suites, while residents of Palmer Court live in houses or lofts. At the Academic Resource Center, students take yoga, hold drum circles, and watch movies.

First-years take core courses in the arts, including basic drawing and design. From there, students specialize in one of 11 studio areas, all leading to the BFA: photography, interior design, fine arts, crafts, animation/digital media, advertising design, transportation design, product design, illustration, graphic design, and arts education. The arts education courses conclude with an internship in Detroit schools (students work as art teachers or aides). Everyone has access to the online CCS Job Book, which allows students to apply directly for jobs or internships.

All students must also complete coursework in the liberal arts. These courses often incorporate art or design into their curricula, as in Math and the Imagination, Psychology of Perception, or the History of Cities. Students who minor in art history or art therapy take more liberal arts courses than those who choose to focus on the studio arts. Through the Student Mobility program, students can spend the semester at participating institutions in New York City, Malaysia, and Ireland. At CCS, you're only limited by your imagination.

College of Charleston

66 George Street
Charleston, SC 29424
(843) 953-5507
http://www.cofc.edu/

Why It's Cool

Sweet tea and southern charm—the College of Charleston has plenty of both, plus outstanding academics, a gorgeous campus, and innovative programs. Try hospitality and tourism management, for example. Offered through the School of Business and Economics, this program thrusts students into a $4.5 *trillion* worldwide business, with roughly 212 million jobs. Y'all will definitely graduate marketable and ready-to-be-hired from this school. As for on-campus hospitality, the college has an extensive meal plan and a cafeteria that includes a delectable waffle station. CofC will be your *first* resort.

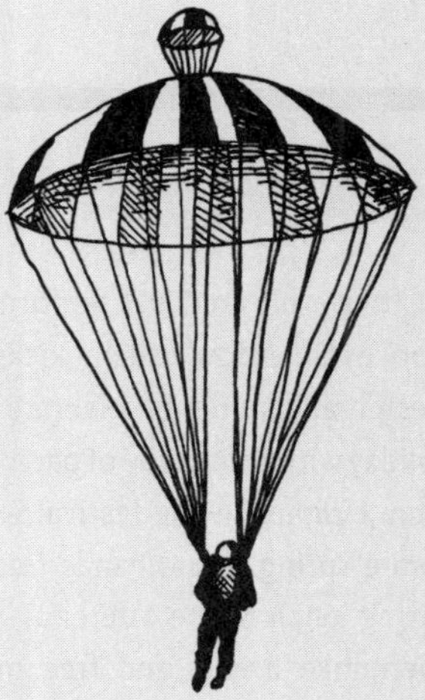

MEOW! COFC STUDENTS SEEKING A THRILL CAN TAKE THE PLUNGE AND JOIN THE COUGAR SKYDIVING CLUB.

The Details

Campus setting:	urban
Degrees:	bachelor's, master's
Calendar:	semesters
Public/Private:	public state
Number of full-time faculty:	499
Student-to-teacher ratio:	14:1

Admissions requirements:

- **Options:** common application, deferred entrance, early admission, early action, electronic application
- **Application fee:** $45
- **Required:** essay or personal statement, high school transcript, letter of recommendation, SAT or ACT
- **Application deadlines:** 4/1 (freshmen), 4/1 (transfer)
- **Early action:** 11/1
- **Notification:** 5/15 (freshmen), continuous (transfer), 1/15 (early action)

Average high school GPA:	3.78
Average freshman SAT verbal/math score:	612 / 606
Average freshman ACT score:	24
Number of applicants:	8,076
Number of applicants accepted:	5,238
Percentage of students from out of state:	35%
Total freshman enrollment:	1,944
Total enrollment:	11,607
Percentage of students who live in campus housing:	29%
Total in-state tuition, fees & expenses:	$13,618
Total out-of-state tuition, fees & expenses:	$21,556
Average financial aid package:	$8,820

Where It's At

Located in Charleston's downtown historic district, the College of Charleston's campus reflects its standing as the 13th-oldest university in the country. Several buildings have preservation protection, including the Bishop Robert Smith House, which dates back to the school's founding in 1770. Each year, Charleston hosts the Spoleto Festival, a 17-day extravaganza that features artists from a variety of disciplines, but tourists flock here year-round to stroll streets lined with oak trees and Spanish moss, visit the harbor, tour preserved antebellum plantations, hang out in one of the city's many squares, or cheer the city's professional soccer team.

What It's Like

Recently, CofC has been reexamining all aspects of university life, with the goals of increasing merit scholarships, adding more courses, improving facilities, and creating programs that link classroom learning to real-world situations. Students take classes in five schools: education, the arts, science and mathematics, business and economics, and humanities and social sciences. Majors include arts preservation and planning, history, and geology. CofC also offers more than 20 interdisciplinary minors, including British studies, discovery informatics, and criminal justice.

Historic student houses with fireplaces and hardwood floors

The Center for Student Learning provides students with peer tutors in math, foreign languages, and writing, as well as individual sessions for other subjects and postgraduate test prep. Plus, the center hands out free daily, weekly, and monthly planners. Self-starters can apply to do research under a faculty member in any discipline under the Undergraduate Research and Creative Activities program.

More than 200 organizations target every possible personality or desire: Musicians can show off during the Thursday Noon Student Recital Series, and journalists can write for *The George Street Observer*. There are 19 varsity athletic teams, including sailing. The Halsely Institute of Contemporary Art; the Avery Research Center, devoted to African American history; and the Sottile Theatre are a few of the on-campus resources. Housing options include traditional dorms whose many rooms include mini-fridges and historic homes. These nineteenth-century houses often have hardwood floors, narrow staircases, and their very own working fireplaces.

All incoming students receive *The Growl*, a newsletter written by upperclass students about campus life. During orientation, first-years meet with a counselor who provides guidance until a major is declared. This treasure school might be old, but don't expect cobwebs: CofC's commitment to students and cool programs keep it super-fresh.

The College of New Jersey

PO Box 7718
Ewing, NJ 08628

(609) 771-1855
http://www.tcnj.edu/

Why It's Cool

If you're ready to take the lead, then this popular school might be perfect for you. Founded way back as a teacher's college, TCNJ's still got a strong education department. Not only can you get certified to teach just about any subject, but you can also do some of your student teaching abroad. Imagine being *el profesor* in Costa Rica or Venezuela. If kids aren't for you, consider the Leadership in Public Affairs program, specially designed to jump-start your career in government. You'll take classes like Citizen Democracy and tackle issues like urban sprawl. We'd vote for you, for sure.

A PICTURE IS WORTH A 1,000 PROSPECTIVE FIRST-YEARS: SINCE CHANGING ITS LOGO TO A SHIELD, TCNJ HAS SEEN A *BIG* INCREASE IN APPLICATIONS.

The Details

Campus setting:	suburban
Degrees:	bachelor's, master's
Calendar:	semesters
Public/Private:	public state
Number of full-time faculty:	331
Student-to-teacher ratio:	13:1

Admissions requirements:

- **Options:** deferred entrance, early admission, early decision, electronic application
- **Application fee:** $50
- **Required:** essay or personal statement, high school transcript, SAT or ACT
- **Application deadlines:** 2/15 (freshmen), 2/15 (transfer)
- **Early decision:** 11/15
- **Notification:** 4/1 (freshmen), continuous (transfer), 12/15 (early decision)

Average high school GPA:	—
Average freshman SAT verbal/math score:	628 / 642
Average freshman ACT score:	—
Number of applicants:	6,485
Number of applicants accepted:	3,113
Percentage of students from out of state:	5%
Total freshman enrollment:	1,231
Total enrollment:	6,812
Percentage of students who live in campus housing:	65%
Total in-state tuition, fees & expenses:	$17,817
Total out-of-state tuition, fees & expenses:	$22,758
Average financial aid package:	$8,897

Where It's At

TCNJ's 289-acre campus is located in the sleepy town of Ewing, a suburb of Trenton, New Jersey. Trenton is home to the New Jersey State Museum; the Contemporary Victorian Museum; the Old Barracks Museum, dedicated to the Revolutionary War; Grounds for Sculpture Art Park; and the Cybis Porcelain Galleries. The Trenton Thunder, affiliated with the New York Yankees, play baseball at Waterfront Park. Nearby Princeton has quaint stores; international restaurants, including Les Copains; and delicious ice cream at Halo Pub and Ricky's Candy, Cones & Chaos. Philadelphia is about 30 minutes away by train, and New York City is about an hour away.

What It's Like

Simply put: Students here like to party. The Lakeside Student Government and the 25 fraternities and sororities hold frequent formals and semi-formals, so bring your fancy shoes—and consider recycling your tux or dress from prom.

But TCNJ's no cakewalk. Here, academics are divided into seven schools: business; art, media, and music; science; culture and society; nursing; engineering; and education, the most popular school. The Liberal Learning program requires students to take interdisciplinary classes, such as Exploring Concert Music and the History of New Jersey.

Students here like to party.

TCNJ really prepares its students for life after college, which is why more than 400 companies recruit on campus each year. And the Global Student Teaching program places undergraduates at schools in Croatia and Ireland, among other locations. Other study abroad opportunities include TCNJ programs in Thailand and England.

All first-years and sophomores are guaranteed housing in one of 14 residence halls. As part of the First-Year Experience, first-years live with other members of their first-year seminars, which range from Earth Ethics to The Movie That Changed Your Life. These learning communities are housed in the large doubles of Travers and Wolfe high-rises or the suites of Cromwell Hall. Upperclass students compete in a lottery system for the swanky on-campus town houses or the off-campus Country Club Apartments.

As the New Jersey Lions, TCNJ has won more championships than any other Division III school in the country. In total, 21 teams, including lacrosse and field hockey, compete. Club and intramural offerings range from co-ed flag football to whitewater rafting. All told, about 66 percent of students play on a varsity or intramural team.

Among the more than 150 student organizations are five student-run publications, the All College Theater, and the Lions Paintball Club. Recently, TCNJ has tried to recruit a more diverse student body, and participation in such groups as the African American Cultural Awareness Association and the Multicultural Lecture Series has increased as a result.

College of Santa Fe

1600 Saint Michael's Drive
Santa Fe, NM 87505
(505) 473-6011
http://www.csf.edu/

Why It's Cool

When Hollywood calls, will you be ready? A degree from the College of Santa Fe will prepare you for your close-up. Strong academic programs in theater and music teach you everything you need to know about performing, while classes in the visual arts and creative writing teach you the principles of design and dialogue. If you'd rather be behind the camera, you can major in the moving image arts or documentary studies. Best of all, the on-campus Garson Studios has two functioning sound stages—the perfect place for an internship. Imagine your name in lights. CSF can make it happen.

SEE CONTEMPORARY CLASSICS, OLD-FASHIONED FAVORITES, STUDENT-PRODUCED FEATURES, EXPERIMENTAL SHORTS, AND FIRST-RUN HITS AT THE SCREEN, CSF'S VERY OWN CINEMATHEQUE.

The Details

Campus setting:	urban
Degrees:	bachelor's, master's
Calendar:	semesters
Public/Private:	private nonprofit
Number of full-time faculty:	73
Student-to-teacher ratio:	8:1

Admissions requirements:

- **Options:** common application, deferred entrance, early admission, early decision, electronic application
- **Application fee:** $35
- **Required:** essay or personal statement, high school transcript, 2 letters of recommendation, SAT or ACT
- **Application deadlines:** continuous (freshmen), continuous (transfer)
- **Early decision:** 11/15
- **Notification:** continuous (freshmen), continuous (transfer), 12/15 (early decision)

Average high school GPA:	3.32
Average freshman SAT verbal/math score:	585 / 543
Average freshman ACT score:	23
Number of applicants:	434
Number of applicants accepted:	392
Percentage of students from out of state:	78%
Total freshman enrollment:	150
Total enrollment:	1,769
Percentage of students who live in campus housing:	62%
Total tuition fee:	$20,214
Total cost with fees & expenses:	$27,906
Average financial aid package:	$18,932

Where It's At

CSF's 90-acre campus is ten minutes from downtown Santa Fe, New Mexico. The cultural center of the Southwest, Santa Fe has many museums and galleries and a world-famous opera house. Popular restaurants include La Casa Sena and Tiny's, both right off the Plaza, a large, grassy gathering area. Roughly 320,000 acres of undeveloped nature and 31 state parks border Santa Fe. This land offers visitors white-water rapids, hiking and biking trails, and fishing holes. The ski resorts and celebrity residents of Taos are 90 minutes away, and Albuquerque, the state capital and home of CSF's second campus, is an hour away.

What It's Like

New students must take the first-year seminar, which introduces them to all aspects of college life. Students also have to take MAPs (short for "mapping knowledge"), interdisciplinary courses team-taught by professors from different departments. Recent MAP courses range from The Southwest: Matter, Memory, Imagination, which uses science, movies, and art to think about the Southwest region, to Living with the Bomb, which uses politics and poetry to examine the cold war.

The cafeteria's got vegan, vegetarian, and organic options, plus homemade desserts.

CSF's 11 academic departments offer more than 20 majors, including conservation studies and elementary education. The extremely popular documentary studies department combines courses in film, history, and literature. Documentary students can spend the semester doing on-site research at the Instituto Terra in Aimores, Brazil. Another popular department, moving image arts, offers such classes as World Cinema and Dimensions of Creativity. Moving image students can intern at the Garson Studios, one of two on-campus, professional sound stages, or take classes at The Screen, an on-campus movie theater that shows films seven days a week.

Through CSF's exchange program with Universidad de La Salle, students can spend a semester in Mexico City. At the Center for Experiential Education, students can find internships, get a part-time job, and participate in service-learning programs, such as entertaining at-risk youths. Along with faculty advisers, CSF students teach Teen College, a free arts education program for junior high and high school students.

First-years and sophomores are required to live on campus in one of four residence halls, while juniors and seniors have the option of living in one of four on-campus apartment buildings. The Main Café, the campus cafeteria, offers locally grown food, vegetarian and vegan selections, and fresh-baked desserts. After hours, check out the Snack Bar, which has a smaller selection of the same great food.

Go Ahead . . . Make Our Day(s): Coolest Academic Calendars

The following schools have a whole new take on the semester, trimester, and quarter systems. At **Cornell** (p. 74), for instance, you can take one course at time. And **Hampshire** (p. 106) doesn't even have the usual first-year-sophomore-junior-senior thing; instead, students move from Division I to Division II to Division III.

Here are some other schools with new takes on the traditional academic year:

Alma College (P. 8)

Birmingham-Southern College (P. 38)

Hanover College (P. 110)

Hiram College (P. 114)

Knox College (P. 122)

Linfield College (P. 126)

North Central College (P. 150)

Prescott College (P. 160)

Randolph-Macon College (P. 164)

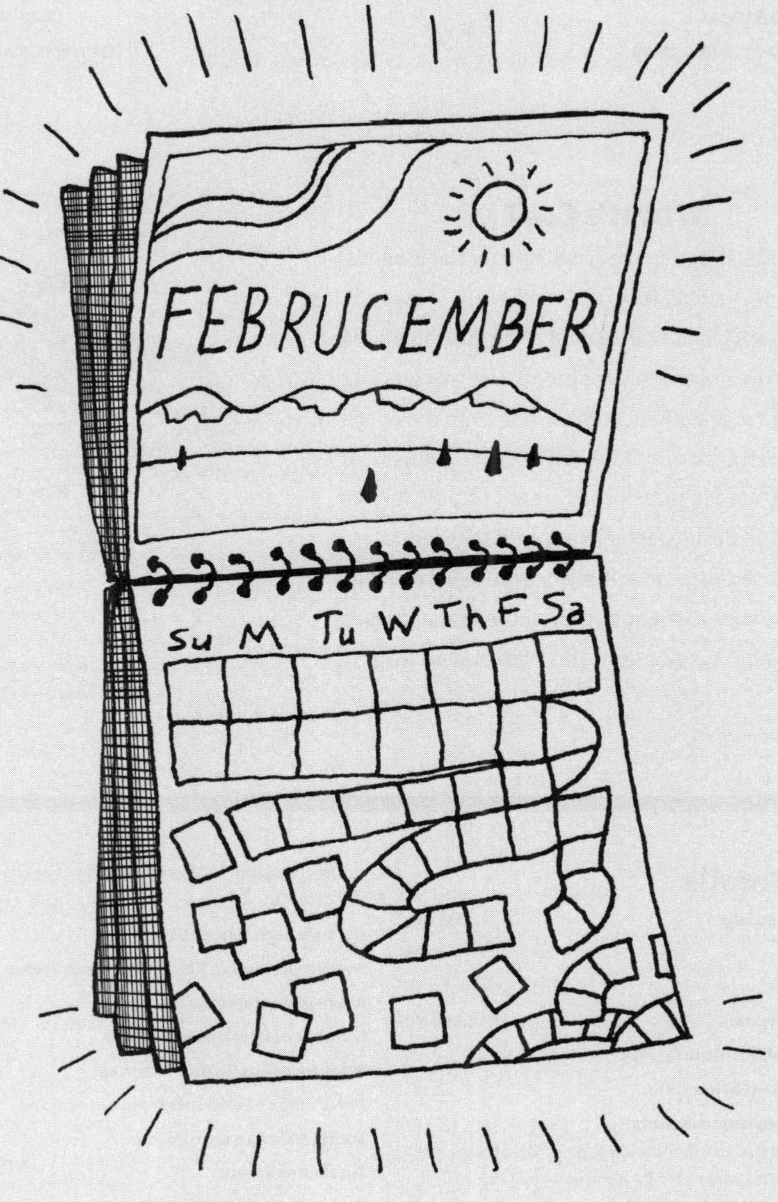
FEBRUCEMBER
Su M Tu W Th F Sa

College of the Atlantic

105 Eden Street **(207) 288-5015**
Bar Harbor, ME 04609 **http://www.coa.edu/**

Why It's Cool

At College of the Atlantic, one is *anything* but the loneliest number. This very small, very progressive school awards just one degree—a BA in human ecology (the interdisciplinary study of humans and the environment). But this school isn't a factory, and students here aren't drones. On the contrary. COA's all about freedom and flexibility. Each term, about 55 courses are offered in three broad areas of study: human studies, arts and design, and environmental science. You then choose classes as you wish, eventually picking a specialization, such as marine studies, the humanities, or landscape and building design. This one's a keeper.

CALL ME ISHMAEL. STUDENTS WORK WITH ALLIED WHALE TO CONDUCT RESEARCH ON WHALES UP AND DOWN THE NORTH AMERICAN COAST.

The Details

Campus setting:	small town
Degrees:	bachelor's, master's
Calendar:	three 10-week terms
Public/Private:	private nonprofit
Number of full-time faculty:	19
Student-to-teacher ratio:	9:1

Admissions requirements:

- **Options:** common application, deferred entrance, early admission, early decision, electronic application
- **Application fee:** $45
- **Required:** essay or personal statement, high school transcript, 3 letters of recommendation, SAT and SAT Subject Tests, or ACT (recommended)
- **Application deadlines:** 2/15 (freshmen), 4/1 (transfer)
- **Early decision:** 12/1
- **Notification:** 4/1 (freshmen), 4/25 (transfer), 12/15 (early decision)

Average high school GPA:	—
Average freshman SAT verbal/math score:	635 / 575
Average freshman ACT score:	23
Number of applicants:	255
Number of applicants accepted:	171
Percentage of students from out of state:	69%
Total freshman enrollment:	68
Total enrollment:	283
Percentage of students who live in campus housing:	40%
Total tuition fee:	$24,870
Total cost with fees & expenses:	$32,837
Average financial aid package:	$23,490

Where It's At

COA is located in Bar Harbor, Maine, a tiny town on Mount Desert Island. Here, you'll find unique, upscale shops and restaurants; the Abbe Museum, devoted to American Indian artifacts; and Kebo Valley Golf Club, the eighth-oldest golf course in the United States. Although many cruises and whale-watching ships stop at Bar Harbor, the area's biggest draw is Acadia National Park, 47,000 acres of ocean shore, mountains, woodlands, and lakes. Bar Harbor is about three hours from Portland and six hours from Boston. The local airport offers frequent shuttle service to Boston too.

What It's Like

COA wants to change the world, one degree at a time. While earning the human ecology degree, students can work with Allied Whale or Beech Hill Farm, which consists of 70 acres of sustainable farms and orchards. Before graduating, all students must write an essay about a meaningful subject of their choice. Seniors also complete the ten-week comprehensive Final Project, which can range from recording an album to writing an article—just about anything goes as long as the project demonstrates intellectual engagement.

Changing the world, one degree at a time

During their first year, students take traditional liberal arts courses in human ecology, history, and writing. The second and third years are spent fulfilling the human studies, arts and design, and environmental science components through such courses as Anthropology of the Yucatan, Animation, and Biology in the News. In addition to letter grades, students receive written feedback from professors.

About 20 percent of COA graduates become teachers, and COA offers a selective educational studies track to prepare future educators. All students must also do at least one term of community service before graduation. The George B. Dorr Museum of Natural History lets students work and learn at a museum devoted to the history of Maine, and COA just happens to offer a specialization in museum studies.

Student organizations include the Outing Club, which sponsors outdoor forays, and World Citizens for Social, Environmental, and Economic Justice, as well as sports teams like volleyball and soccer. Just about everyone eats at Blair Dining Hall, known as "Take-A-Break," which offers vegan and vegetarian options at every meal. First-years live in one of the seven on-campus apartments or three houses, which accommodate between six and 22 students. Seafox and Ryles, two of the smaller houses, are located on the water. COA gives you rooms—and an education—with a view.

College of the Ozarks

PO Box 17
Point Lookout, MO 65726
(417) 334-6411
http://www.cofo.edu/

Why It's Cool

Welcome to "Hard Work U." In return for a free education, you have to work. A lot. You'll toil 15 hours per week during each semester at one of 90 stations, which include the stained glass studio, dairy, and agricultural feed mill. Once you've decided on a major, you can gain real-world experience by adapting your work to fit your studies: Pre-engineers can work at the airport, while teachers can choose child care. All students get subsidized by C of O scholarships, so tuition costs you nothing. C of O really puts the *work* back into work-study.

YOU SPATULA OR MINE? STUDENT WORKERS HELP BAKE THE FAMOUS C OF O FRUITCAKE, 40,000 OF WHICH ARE PRODUCED EACH YEAR.

The Details

Campus setting:	small town
Degrees:	bachelor's
Calendar:	semesters
Public/Private:	private religious
Number of full-time faculty:	71
Student-to-teacher ratio:	16:1

Admissions requirements:

- **Options:** electronic application
- **Application fee:** —
- **Required:** high school transcript, 2 letters of recommendation, ACT
- **Application deadlines:** 2/15 (freshmen), 2/1 (transfer)
- **Early decision:** —
- **Notification:** continuous (freshmen), continuous (transfer)

Average high school GPA:	3.5
Average freshman SAT verbal/math score:	—/—
Average freshman ACT score:	22
Number of applicants:	2,393
Number of applicants accepted:	300
Percentage of students from out of state:	33%
Total freshman enrollment:	268
Total enrollment:	1,723
Percentage of students who live in campus housing:	84%
Total tuition fee:	—
Total cost with fees & expenses:	$4,930
Average financial aid package:	$11,775

Where It's At

C of O's 1,000-acre campus is located in Point Lookout, Missouri, close to the shores of Lake Taneycomo. Nearby Branson, often called the "Live Music Capital of the World," provides several attractions, including the Strip, seven miles of theaters hosting 90 shows a day; the Silver Dollar City and Celebration City theme parks; and the Imax Entertainment Complex. With close to 7,500 miles of shoreline, the Ozarks area attracts hikers, hunters, anglers, and campers. Springfield, just 40 minutes away, is home to the Juanita K. Hammons Hall for the Performing Arts and the Springfield Cardinals, a minor league baseball team.

What It's Like

Campus life revolves around Christianity. C of O nurtures a Christian worldview in its students by offering Bible studies and the Focus on the Family Institute, at which students explore the role of the church in society and their lives. To discourage debt, C of O rejects all federal and state loan programs and instead offers its students the opportunity to use work-study to pay for their liberal arts education. Curfews and dress codes are stressed, and the campus is completely dry.

Learn, live, and grow at the C of O.

The many majors include computer information science, communications, graphic arts, and conservation and wildlife management. Student workers tend to the exhibits on the history of the Ozarks region at the Ralph Foster Museum, as well as the more than 7,000 plants at the C of O greenhouses. Most students live on campus, in one of seven residential halls.

At the Keeter Center for Character Education, students can hear such speakers as Colin Powell and Benjamin Netanyahu as part of the Community Convocation Series. Students can also learn about the C of O's Citizens Abroad program and help plan the annual Honor America Day. Since 1934, students have been making the school's Famous C of O Fruitcake.

Student organizations range from the Baptist Student Union to the Students in Free Enterprise, which teaches its members to develop business projects that help community groups earn money. Five Division II varsity teams compete. Intramural teams include sand- and hard-court volleyball, Nerf football, and basketball.

The learning-and-living mentality at C of O encourages students to grow in five key areas: patriotism, academics, spirituality, vocation, and culture. Students take these life lessons to heart: 90 percent of C of O students move on to jobs, graduate school, or professional school within a year of graduation. The hard work definitely pays off.

The College of Wooster

1189 Beall Avenue
Wooster, OH 44691

(330) 263-2000
http://www.wooster.edu/

Why It's Cool

Wooster's take on the liberal arts is totally inimitable. You'll take a first-year seminar designed to change the way you think—literally. Then you'll take core courses that will radically alter your perspective on yourself and the world. Finally, your education will culminate in the three-semester Independent Study project. You'll spend about a year and a half working with a faculty mentor on an original paper, performance, work of art, or research experiment. After handing in your I.S. project, you'll get a yellow-and-black I DID IT button and a Tootsie Roll to mark the sweet occasion. And to top it all off? You'll head outside for a raucous parade. *Woo-hoo,* indeed.

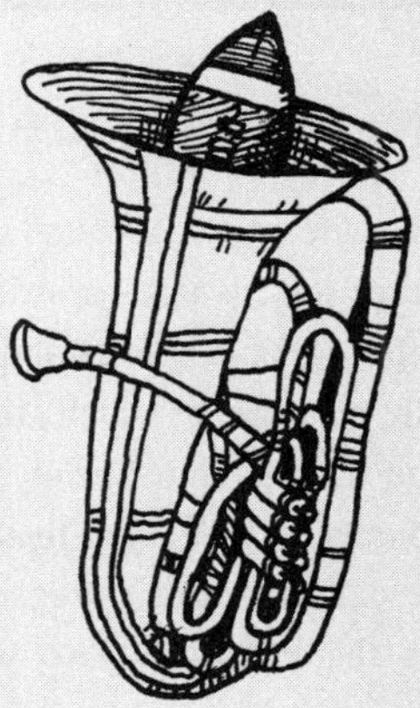

AN OLD TRADITION REQUIRES THE HEAD FOOTBALL COACH TO CONDUCT THE SCOT MARCHING BAND DURING ITS FALL CONCERT.

The Details

Campus setting:	small town
Degrees:	bachelor's
Calendar:	semesters
Public/Private:	private religious
Number of full-time faculty:	137
Student-to-teacher ratio:	12:1

Admissions requirements:

- **Options:** common application, deferred entrance, early admission, early decision, electronic application
- **Application fee:** $40
- **Required:** essay or personal statement, high school transcript, 2 letters of recommendation, SAT or ACT
- **Application deadlines:** 2/15 (freshmen), 6/1 (transfer)
- **Early decision:** 12/1
- **Notification:** 4/1 (freshmen), continuous (transfer), 12/15 (early decision)

Average high school GPA:	3.55
Average freshman SAT verbal/math score:	612 / 604
Average freshman ACT score:	24
Number of applicants:	2,523
Number of applicants accepted:	1,827
Percentage of students from out of state:	45%
Total freshman enrollment:	477
Total enrollment:	1,827
Percentage of students who live in campus housing:	99%
Total tuition fee:	$26,380
Total cost with fees & expenses:	$33,900
Average financial aid package:	$21,570

Where It's At

Small Wooster, Ohio, hosts a farmers' market, an art and jazz festival, and frequent concerts. Nearby Cuyahoga Valley National Park and Mohican State Park offer trails and picnic spots, while Cedar Point, the self-styled Roller Coaster Capital of the World, boasts 68 different rides. South of Wooster, the world's largest Old Order Amish community has restaurants, shops, and museums. A 30-minute drive gets students to Canton and the Pro Football Hall of Fame. Home to the Rock and Roll Hall of Fame, the Metroparks Zoo, the historic West Side Market, the Browns (NFL), and the Indians (MLB), Cleveland is just an hour away.

What It's Like

Wooster students share a love of academics, athletics, and traditions. Just about everybody lives on the 240-acre campus, in one of 12 residential halls, including some first-year–only dorms. The administration considers the Independent Study project to be so important that all seniors have the option of living in singles just so they can work on their projects in peace—and so they can plan life after graduation as part of the Senior Program.

Shuttlecocks and hot-sauce packets at graduation

Sophomores and juniors often live in theme houses, including Bontrager House, devoted to organic farming, and the Kennedy Apartments, devoted to the service organizations Homework for Hoops and Habitat for Humanity. Another option for these upperclass students is going abroad to such locations as Ireland, Costa Rica, Australia, and Senegal.

About 30 percent of the Wooster student body plays on one of the 22 Division III varsity teams, the Fighting Scots. For the less hard-core, there are many intramural and club teams for such sports as badminton and billiards. The campus also has its own nine-hole golf course, free to faculty, students, and staff. Some of the 100-plus activities include the Jenny Investment Club, the Juggling Club, the Personal Foul Dance Team, five fraternities, six sororities, and 37 community service groups. Each fall, campus groups participate in Scot Spirit Day to recruit new members.

The multitudinous majors and minors range from urban studies to communication sciences and disorders to Chinese. Students can choose from 11 preprofessional programs, including premedicine and preveterinary. But regardless of major, all students have to take courses that help broaden their awareness of other cultures and religions.

Tradition plays a big part in campus life. Graduating seniors, for instance, give the president a token of their appreciation upon receiving their diploma; past gifts have included shuttlecocks and hot-sauce packets. And every fall, the school hosts the Party on the Green, which includes bands. But the most appreciated Wooster tradition is probably the *two-week* spring break in March.

Colorado School of Mines

1500 Illinois Street **(303) 273-3000**
Golden, CO 80401 **http://www.mines.edu/**

Why It's Cool

Energy makes the world—and the Colorado School of Mines—go round. Upon embarking on their education in math and science, all CSM students receive a hard hat to wear and cherish for the next four years. Graduating students all receive a bachelor of science, as well as a job-placement rate of more than 70 percent. Here, even classes in the humanities touch on issues from electrical engineering, mining, geology, and the other nine majors. If you're into English, this school probably isn't for you. But if you're into the earth's resources and thinking about how the world works, then get ready to rock out at CSM.

ACCORDING TO CSM TRADITION, GRADUATING SENIORS WEAR SPECIAL SENIOR STETSONS AS THEY GO OFF TO BEGIN THEIR ENGINEERING CAREERS.

The Details

Campus setting:	small town
Degrees:	bachelor's, master's, doctoral
Calendar:	semesters
Public/Private:	public state
Number of full-time faculty:	193
Student-to-teacher ratio:	14:1

Admissions requirements:

- **Options:** deferred entrance, electronic application
- **Application fee:** $45
- **Required:** high school transcript, letter of recommendation, SAT or ACT
- **Application deadlines:** 6/1 (freshmen), 6/1 (transfer)
- **Early decision:** —
- **Notification:** continuous (freshmen), continuous (transfer)

Average high school GPA:	3.65
Average freshman SAT verbal/math score:	603 / 648
Average freshman ACT score:	25
Number of applicants:	3,120
Number of applicants accepted:	2,641
Percentage of students from out of state:	21%
Total freshman enrollment:	747
Total enrollment:	3,666
Percentage of students who live in campus housing:	25%
Total in-state tuition, fees & expenses:	$15,124
Total out-of-state tuition, fees & expenses:	$28,284
Average financial aid package:	$13,300

Where It's At

CSM's 373-acre campus is located in the small suburban town of Golden, only 13 miles from Denver. Golden lives up to its name: The town averages 300 sunny days per year. Local attractions include the Splash Aquatics Park, Buffalo Bill's Gravesite and Museum, and the Coors Brewery. Every winter, the town celebrates with candlelit walks and activities during the Olde Golden Christmas. The nearby American Mountaineering Center has the largest mountaineering library in North America, and Rocky Mountain National Park is just 90 minutes away. Skiers and snowboarders revel in Colorado's many winter resorts, such as Telluride and Aspen.

What It's Like

Every fall, first-years traditionally climb Mt. Zion with a ten-pound rock in hand to make a contribution to the M, a mountainside monument that overlooks CSM. Every spring, seniors repaint the M in a farewell gesture. Everyone wears their hard hats, and the paint splatters that cover the hats by the end of the day become marks of pride.

CSM offers just 12 majors in five fields: engineering, science, geosciences and resource engineering, economics and business, and mathematical and computer sciences. Students choose from such minors as humanities, international political economy, and a self-designed minor. Ten percent of the professors hold endowed chairs, which means that they've been recognized as being among the very best in their fields.

Engineering with a side of liberal arts

Even the required core courses in the Liberal Arts and International Studies (LAIS) program deal with math and science. All students must take Nature and Human Value, a writing-intensive course that explores ethical issues in science, economics, and engineering. Another required course is Human Systems, which studies how communities and institutions function. LAIS gives students a background in the humanities, social sciences, physical education, and writing.

Almost 10 percent of all students participate in the CSM Music Program, which includes courses and such activities as concert choir and an a cappella jazz octet. Some of the more than 100 student organizations are ten Greek houses, six honor societies, and Students for Creative Anachronism, a medieval and renaissance reenactment group. There are also 16 Division II varsity athletic teams.

First-years can choose to live together in apartment-style housing at Mines Park or in traditional dorms, which have the usual amenities. Through the school's Love from Home catering program, parents and friends can send students cakes and other goodies. Keep that hard hat handy: With CSM's high job-placement rate, you're sure to be dynamiting into the real world.

The Cooper Union
for the Advancement of Science and Art

30 Cooper Square **(212) 353-4100**
New York, NY 10003 **http://www.cooper.edu/**

Why It's Cool

The coolest thing about Cooper Union? It's free. Students pay zero, zilch, nada for a rigorous education in engineering, architecture, or the fine arts right in the heart of New York City. Who says you can't get something for nothing? Here, every student gets a tuition scholarship. In return for the free ride, every student works hard. Very hard. So hard that academic lightweights need not apply. Cooper Union gives you tough classes, hallowed history, and an urban university experience—all for less than the price of a cup of coffee.

COOPER UNION FOUNDER PETER COOPER INVENTED THE GELATIN DESSERT, JELL-O, IN 1845.

The Details

Campus setting:	urban
Degrees:	bachelor's
Calendar:	semesters
Public/Private:	private nonprofit
Number of full-time faculty:	56
Student-to-teacher ratio:	7:1

Admissions requirements:

- **Options:** deferred entrance, early admission, early decision, electronic application
- **Application fee:** $50
- **Required:** high school transcript, letter of recommendation, SAT or ACT
- **Application deadlines:** 1/1 (freshmen), 1/1 (transfer)
- **Early decision:** 12/1
- **Notification:** 4/1 (freshmen), 5/1 (transfer), 12/24 (early decision)

Average high school GPA:	3.20
Average freshman SAT verbal/math score:	664 / 687
Average freshman ACT score:	—
Number of applicants:	2,414
Number of applicants accepted:	295
Percentage of students from out of state:	41%
Total freshman enrollment:	207
Total enrollment:	955
Percentage of students who live in campus housing:	19%
Total tuition fee:	—
Total cost with fees & expenses:	$16,200
Average financial aid package:	$26,000

Where It's At

Cooper Union's urban campus is located in the East Village, a hip, happening neighborhood in New York City. People call New York "the capital of the world" for good reason: You can do, see, eat, and experience *everything* here. From the Statue of Liberty to Pablo Picasso's *Les Demoiselles d'Avignon* to the Yankees-Mets baseball rivalry, this city of 8 million offers cultural and recreational opportunities unavailable anywhere else in the world. Should you tire of the urban life, you can always hang out on Central Park's 843 acres or take a short train trip up to the Adirondacks.

What It's Like

Cooper Union was founded in 1859 to give the working class access to a quality education. That tradition continues today: Each of the roughly 900 students at the private Cooper Union receives a full-tuition scholarship (you'll still be responsible for some fees and expenses, though). In return, students devote themselves fully to academic work. We're talking all-nighters, work weekends, and lots of Red Bull. As one of the most rigorous academic institutions in the United States, Cooper Union demands excellence from its students in return for its investment in them.

Do, see, eat, experience *everything* here . . .

For the first four semesters, students take a preset core curriculum in the liberal arts, which might include classes in Renaissance drama, eighteenth-century political essays, and *Alice in Wonderland*. Regardless of the topic, each core class stresses communication; papers, presentations, and independent projects hone listening, reading, writing, and speaking skills. As juniors and seniors, students specialize in one of three areas—art, engineering, or architecture—but can take electives in languages, the humanities, and the social sciences.

When not studying, Cooper Union students choose from over 85 school-sponsored activities, including an Ultimate Frisbee team, the Chinese Gamers Society, and the Ice Cream Club. Girls can pledge Delta Eta, while guys can go Greek at Tau Delta Phi and Zeta Psi. Students mouth off with the Void Where Prohibited sketch-comedy club, while literary types write for *Jello*, the literary arts magazine.

An education here includes access to an award-winning faculty and a library that holds 100,000 volumes, and students live in one dorm, the Student Residence. Most students elect to live off campus in the nearby neighborhoods of Manhattan or in one of New York's four other boroughs. Wherever they live, all Cooper Union students can consider New York City their living, learning campus.

Grades? We Don't Need No Stinkin' Grades! Best Alternative Grading Systems

Forget about your ABCs (and Ds and Fs). These schools don't do letter grades. But you won't get off easy: You'll still have to take exams and write papers.

College of the Atlantic (P. 62)

The Evergreen State College (P. 92)

Fairhaven College (P. 94)

Hampshire College (P. 106)

New College of Florida (P. 148)

Prescott College (P. 160)

Reed College (P. 166)

University of Redlands (P. 210)

REPORT CARD
A
Algebraic Basket
weaving.
B
Scuba
B
Studies.
Basket
C
literature of
Weaving.
Advanced Underwater
Basket Weaving.

Cornell College

600 First Street West **(319) 895-4000**
Mount Vernon, IA 52314 **http://www.cornellcollege.edu/**

Why It's Cool

Cornell students take it one course at a time. No, seriously. Under the One-Course-at-a-Time (OCAAT) plan, the academic year is divided into nine blocks. You'll take one course per block, and you'll get a whole semester's worth of material in just under four weeks. Because you're only taking one class, you'll never have to prioritize, and you'll never get distracted by other subjects. No doing chemistry homework when you should be studying for your Spanish exam. No stressing because you've got two papers due on the same day. Classes here are short, sweet, and comprehensive. Can you say "block party"?

IN 1889, CORNELL SENIORS DRAGGED A 5,000-POUND ROCK TO CAMPUS FROM A NEARBY PARK. SINCE THEN, THE ROCK'S BEEN PAINTED, BURNED, KIDNAPPED, GRAFFITIED, AND BURIED.

The Details

Campus setting:	small town
Degrees:	bachelor's
Calendar:	nine 3.5-week terms
Public/Private:	private religious
Number of full-time faculty:	85
Student-to-teacher ratio:	11:1

Admissions requirements:

- **Options:** common application, deferred entrance, electronic application
- **Application fee:** $40
- **Required:** essay or personal statement, high school transcript, letter of recommendation, SAT or ACT
- **Application deadlines:** 3/1 (freshmen), 3/1 (transfer)
- **Early decision:** —
- **Notification:** continuous (freshmen), continuous (transfer)

Average high school GPA:	3.49
Average freshman SAT verbal/math score:	619 / 623
Average freshman ACT score:	25
Number of applicants:	1,716
Number of applicants accepted:	1,102
Percentage of students from out of state:	67%
Total freshman enrollment:	292
Total enrollment:	1,155
Percentage of students who live in campus housing:	88%
Total tuition fee:	$22,490
Total cost with fees & expenses:	$29,490
Average financial aid package:	$20,975

Where It's At

Cornell is located in the tiny town of Mount Vernon, Iowa. The gorgeous 129-acre campus has the distinction of being the only college whose entire campus made it onto the National Register of Historic Places. Mount Vernon has antique stores and galleries, in addition to fine examples of Victorian architecture. Nearby Cedar Rapids and Iowa City offer the National Czech and Slovak Museum and Library, the Cedar Rapids Art Museum, and an IMAX theater. Hikers and anglers go to Wapsipinicon State Park and Palisades-Kepler State Park. Des Moines, the state capital, is about two hours away, and Chicago is about four hours away.

What It's Like

Intense, but unusual and totally worthwhile. Under OCAAT, there's a lot of pressure on the faculty to compress a great amount of material into such a short term, and there's a lot of pressure on the students to absorb the material and do the assignments in just three and a half weeks. Students take eight blocks per year, using the extra block to extend winter or spring break, start summer early, take an extra class, or go abroad.

Homemade pizza at the president's house

Students must take core courses in eight divisions: fine arts, foreign language, math, laboratory science, nonlaboratory science, writing, social science, and the humanities. Physical education, physics, and philosophy are among the more than 40 majors. Students might also elect to skip some general education requirements in favor of designing their own interdisciplinary major; these students receive the BSS (Bachelor of Special Studies).

Students interested in the medical fields can take courses in Dimensions: The Center for Science and Culture in Health Care, designed to instill creativity and interpersonal skills in future health-care professionals. Off-campus programs take place in many cities and countries around the world, including Washington, D.C., Northern Ireland, Korea, and France.

About 75 percent of students do some type of volunteering through the Leadership and Service Office. All told, there are more than 100 student groups, including the Belly Dancing Club and the Star Wars Society. Many students belong to one of the 15 service-oriented, non-national Greek societies. There are 19 Division III athletic teams, known as the Rams.

Just about everyone lives in one of the ten residence halls on campus. An annual tradition gives first-years the chance to attend small parties at the house of the college president, Les Garner. There, they can pump the school's head honcho for information about classes, careers, and choices, while chomping on pizza made by Garner's wife. Sounds delicious to us.

Deep Springs College

HC 72, Box 45001	**(760) 872-2000**
Deep Springs, CA 89010	**http://www.deepsprings.edu/**

Why It's Cool

It's a man's world. OK, so that's not the real motto of Deep Springs, probably the most unusual school in the United States, but it could be. After all, this school's just for men. Smart men, who don't mind getting up before dawn to do the required chores and who willingly live without television. Sociable men, who can significantly contribute to the tiny campus community (just about 27 students) and its system of self-governance. Exceptional men, who have the stamina—and résumé—to get through a rigorous, über-selective admissions process (roughly 10 percent of applicants are accepted). But for the lucky few who do make it in, Deep Springs offers an unparalleled educational experience.

NO NEED TO BRING YOUR OWN STUFF— JUST GRAB WHAT YOU NEED FROM THE COMMUNAL BONEPILE, A HUGE STACK OF CLOTHES, SHOES, AND OTHER THINGS LEFT BEHIND BY FORMER STUDENTS.

The Details

Campus setting:	rural
Degrees:	AA
Calendar:	6 seven-week terms
Public/Private:	private nonprofit
Number of full-time faculty:	5
Student-to-teacher ratio:	3:1

Admissions requirements:

- **Options:** common application
- **Application fee:** —
- **Required:** essay or personal statement, high school transcript, letter of recommendation, SAT and SAT Subject Tests, or ACT
- **Application deadlines:** 11/15 (freshmen), 11/15 (transfer)
- **Early decision:** —
- **Notification:** 4/15 (freshmen), 4/15 (transfer)

Average high school GPA:	3.87
Average freshman SAT verbal/math score:	730 / 725
Average freshman ACT score:	—
Number of applicants:	147
Number of applicants accepted:	15
Percentage of students from out of state:	89%
Total freshman enrollment:	15
Total enrollment:	25
Percentage of students who live in campus housing:	100%
Total tuition fee:	—
Total cost with fees & expenses:	—
Average financial aid package:	—

Where It's At

Deep Springs College is located on Deep Springs Ranch. All students work the ranch, as cooks, as farmhands, as cowherds, or in some other capacity. Nearby Dyer, Nevada, and Big Springs, California, are small towns with little to do. About an hour away, Bishop, California, has restaurants, BMX tracks, a bowling alley, and a movie theater. The area's biggest draw, the eastern Sierra Nevada, affords ample opportunity for outdoor activities like horseback riding and hiking. Each May, Bishop hosts Mule Days, a celebration with food, entertainment, and a rodeo. Los Angeles and San Francisco are about six and eight hours away, respectively.

What It's Like

The only two-year school in this book offers students male bonding at its finest. Students work hard, but they don't party hard: Alcohol and drugs are banned from campus, and there's no cable TV. A school this different definitely isn't for everybody.

Life revolves around three pillars: labor, self-governance, and academics. In return for free tuition, students work the Deep Springs Ranch, growing alfalfa, raising cattle, and doing what needs to be done to keep the ranch running. Jobs range from cooking the meals to mending fences. Students democratically set all policies at the school, including whether drinking should be allowed and whether women should be accepted. Everybody lives together in one dorm.

Male bonding at its finest

The Curriculum Committee, composed jointly of students and professors, discusses which courses should be offered. CurCom also evaluates prospective teachers, because Deep Springs doesn't have a tenured faculty. Instead, professors hold teaching positions for varying lengths of time, ranging from one term (about six weeks) to six years.

There are no majors and no specialties—and only two courses are required: Composition and Public Speaking. Every Tuesday night, students and faculty get together for Public Speaking, at which students give speeches on any subject they choose for about ten minutes. In his two years at Deep Springs, a student will usually give around 20 graded speeches.

Aside from the required classes, students take whatever interests them, ranging from Fiction Writing to Energy and the Environment. In general, courses cover introductory material in the liberal arts, but with an average class size of four, any discussion can quickly become intense. Because the faculty lives on campus, professors will sometimes turn on their porch lights to encourage students to drop by in the evenings for more discussion.

Upon graduation, most students transfer to a four-year college. An astonishing one-third of alumni have become university professors, a testament to the long-lasting effects of a Deep Springs' education.

Earlham College

801 National Road West **(765) 983-1200**
Richmond, IN 47374 **http://www.earlham.edu/**

Why It's Cool

Imagine kicking off your college career by getting cozy with Mother Nature. Now picture yourself getting academic credit for courses in rock climbing and spelunking. Earlham can make it happen. August Wilderness takes you into the Great Outdoors for a 24-day orientation to college life. Through the Wilderness Program, you can minor in outdoor education or environmental studies. And you can always blow off steam on the 600-acre back campus: Its trails and obstacle courses will make you forget about the toughest test or nastiest essay. So go ahead and get wild at Earlham.

TENTS, NOT TESTS. AUGUST WILDERNESS GIVES YOU ACADEMIC CREDIT FOR GOING BACKPACKING IN UTAH OR CANOEING IN CANADA.

The Details

Campus setting:	small town
Degrees:	bachelor's, master's
Calendar:	semesters
Public/Private:	private religious
Number of full-time faculty:	91
Student-to-teacher ratio:	12:1

Admissions requirements:

- **Options:** common application, deferred entrance, early admission, early decision, early action, electronic application
- **Application fee:** $30
- **Required:** essay or personal statement, high school transcript, 2 letters of recommendation, SAT or ACT
- **Application deadlines:** 2/15 (freshmen), 4/1 (transfer), 1/1 (early action)
- **Early decision:** 12/1
- **Notification:** 3/15 (freshmen), 4/15 (transfer), 12/15 (early decision), 2/1 (early action)

Average high school GPA:	3.5
Average freshman SAT verbal/math score:	632 / 592
Average freshman ACT score:	25
Number of applicants:	1,518
Number of applicants accepted:	1,090
Percentage of students from out of state:	72%
Total freshman enrollment:	336
Total enrollment:	1,275
Percentage of students who live in campus housing:	88%
Total tuition fee:	$25,364
Total cost with fees & expenses:	$32,632
Average financial aid package:	$21,215

Where It's At

Earlham's 200-acre main campus nestles against 600 acres of hiking paths, farmland, and woodlands. Famous for its Antique Alley, a row of antique shops, the small city of Richmond, Indiana, is also home to the Joseph Moore Museum of Natural History and the Gennett Records Studio, at which some of the first jazz recordings were made. The Cope Environmental Center has 30 acres for hiking and research and holds frequent programs on such issues as sustainable farming and recycling. For a taste of urban life, students head to Dayton (about 40 minutes away), Indianapolis (about an hour away), or Cincinnati (also about an hour away).

What It's Like

Founded by Quakers in 1847, Earlham continues to emphasize its original values: honesty, intellectual endeavor, community, consensus, and respect. Student life centers around the Heart, a grassy area in the center of campus used for hanging out. It's an easygoing campus composed of mostly left-leaning, outdoorsy, laid-back folks.

Roughly 90 percent of students live on campus, in one of seven traditional residence halls or 12 theme houses, including Penn House (for students interested in the visual arts), Fry House (for students interested in interfaith issues), and Casa Hispana (for students interested in Spanish). Seventeen friendship houses allow groups to establish smaller residential communities within Earlham. This spirit of community extends to academics too: Students use first names when addressing their professors.

Student life revolves around the Heart.

Students compete on 14 Division III sports teams. Several recreational teams and clubs hold annual tournaments, such as the Climbing Wall Challenge, the Chess Tournament, and the Wiffle Ball Tourney. Among the many student organizations are *Sound and Sense*, the campus literary magazine, and the Student Filmmakers Guild. The super-popular Ultimate Frisbee team participates in tournaments throughout the United States.

More than 40 percent of all Earlham graduates continue on to graduate or professional school. Students must fulfill the school's general education requirements by taking liberal arts classes that emphasize reading, writing, and speaking. More than 25 percent of students choose interdisciplinary majors like peace studies and conflict resolution, over traditional majors like geoscience and biology.

Collectively, Earlham students have spent more than 50,000 hours performing community service, and full-tuition scholarships are offered to select incoming students with a demonstrated commitment to volunteering. Everybody's encouraged to participate in the Wilderness Program, which teaches leadership skills through such outdoor activities as ice climbing. We heart any school that lets you learn and lead.

Eckerd College

4200 54th Avenue South **(727) 867-1166**
St. Petersburg, FL 33711 **http://www.eckerd.edu/**

Why It's Cool

Don't let the white sands and palm trees fool you—Eckerd is all about intellectual labor. Beach bums need not apply. A rigorous set of liberal arts classes prepares you for the ultimate academic challenge: figuring out who you are and who you want to be. Combining heady self-analysis with community service, the required Quest for Meaning course makes you answer tough questions about how you want to live your life. Really. You even have to complete an original project called the Philosophy of Life. If you can't handle the truth, then Eckerd's not the place for you.

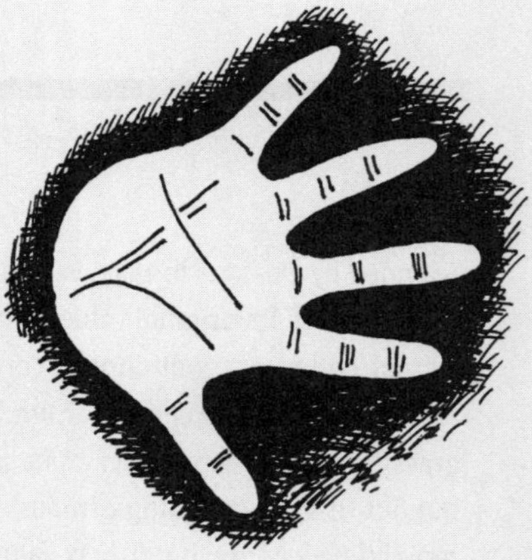

FIRST-YEARS TAKE THE HONOR PLEDGE, A PROMISE TO CONTRIBUTE TO THE COLLEGE COMMUNITY, BY LEAVING THEIR HANDPRINTS ON A COLORFUL RAINBOW.

The Details

Campus setting:	suburban
Degrees:	bachelor's
Calendar:	4-1-4
Public/Private:	private religious
Number of full-time faculty:	101
Student-to-teacher ratio:	13:1

Admissions requirements:

- **Options:** common application, deferred entrance, early admission, electronic application
- **Application fee:** $35
- **Required:** essay or personal statement, high school transcript, letter of recommendation, SAT or ACT, SAT Subject Tests (recommended)
- **Application deadlines:** continuous (freshmen), continuous (transfer)
- **Early decision:** —
- **Notification:** continuous (freshmen), continuous (transfer)

Average high school GPA:	3.30
Average freshman SAT verbal/math score:	583 / 569
Average freshman ACT score:	—
Number of applicants:	2,284
Number of applicants accepted:	1,696
Percentage of students from out of state:	69%
Total freshman enrollment:	468
Total enrollment:	1,688
Percentage of students who live in campus housing:	79%
Total tuition fee:	$24,116
Total cost with fees & expenses:	$31,688
Average financial aid package:	$18,961

Where It's At

Eckerd's 267-acre campus is located in St. Petersburg, a city on the small peninsula between Florida's Tampa Bay and the Gulf of Mexico. St. Pete, as the locals call it, has two major art museums, the Salvador Dalí Museum and the Museum of Fine Arts; the Pier Aquarium; and several performing arts centers. The Tampa Devil Rays (MLB) play here, and the first Grand Prix of St. Petersburg was held in 2005. Also nicknamed the Sunshine City, St. Pete has 35 miles of beaches. Tampa is about 30 minutes away by car, and Miami is about four hours away.

What It's Like

Upon arriving at Eckerd, all students must sign the Honor Pledge—and here "signing" means dipping your hand into colorful paint and adding your handprint to the rainbow formed by the several hundred "signatures" of your classmates. The Honor Pledge reminds students that together they form a community, and each person contributes to its health and success.

Most students live on campus in traditional dorms, apartment suites, and hotel-style accommodations. The majority of rooms have ocean views, and the Omega dorm features wraparound balconies. But the coolest feature of dorm living at Eckerd is the pet policy: Dogs are welcome at one on-campus residence.

Everybody fits in at this sunshiny school, from hippies to preppies, international students to native Floridians. The myriad student organizations include the Surf Club, the Earth Society, Marine Animal Rescue, and Palmetto Productions, a performance group. The Waterfront Program includes the Eckerd College Search and Rescue team, which helps patrol the waters of and provide assistance to people floating and boating in Tampa Bay.

Three weeks before the beginning of the fall semester, first-years head to Eckerd for the Autumn Term, an intense orientation. During this time, students take such classes as the Geology of Beaches and Health Psychology. They also meet with faculty mentors and begin doing college-level work.

All students must take the two-semester Western Heritage in a Global Context, an interdisciplinary course that explores the cultures of the world. The more than 35 majors include literature and marine science.

Can you handle the truth?

Eckerd's academic calendar has two 14-week fall and spring semesters separated by a four-week Winter Term. Independent study is encouraged during this short term, either on or off campus. Past projects have taken students to Greece and Mexico. About 50 percent of students study abroad, even though they may find Eckerd's tropical climate and waterfront campus difficult to leave.

Elmira College

One Park Place
Elmira, NY 14901
(607) 735-1800
http://www.elmira.edu/

Why It's Cool

Elmira helps you develop an appreciation for the finer things in life. As a first-year and again as a sophomore, you'll take Encore, the required performing arts appreciation course. You'll receive academic credit—and a grade—for attending eight arts performances per term. Events can range from a night of blues to selections from Elmira's own dance ensemble, Orchesis, to a one-man show about Mark Twain to a puppet show for grown-ups. You'll laugh, you'll cry, you'll write papers summarizing your thoughts and analyzing the shows you've seen. This school gets a standing ovation from us.

THIS MIGHT SOUND DORKY, BUT IT'S DEFINITELY NOT: ELMIRA FIRST-YEARS RECEIVE A PURPLE-AND-GOLD BEANIE DURING ORIENTATION, WHICH THEY THEN PROUDLY PUT ON.

The Details

Campus setting:	small town
Degrees:	bachelor's, master's
Calendar:	4-4-1
Public/Private:	private nonprofit
Number of full-time faculty:	86
Student-to-teacher ratio:	12:1

Admissions requirements:

- **Options:** common application, deferred entrance, early admission, early decision, electronic application
- **Application fee:** $50
- **Required:** essay or personal statement, high school transcript, 2 letters of recommendation, SAT or ACT
- **Application deadlines:** 4/15 (freshmen), — (transfer)
- **Early decision:** 11/15
- **Notification:** 4/30 (freshmen), continuous (transfer), 12/15 (early decision)

Average high school GPA:	3.50
Average freshman SAT verbal/math score:	558 / 552
Average freshman ACT score:	25
Number of applicants:	2,149
Number of applicants accepted:	1,446
Percentage of students from out of state:	48%
Total freshman enrollment:	326
Total enrollment:	1,853
Percentage of students who live in campus housing:	95%
Total tuition fee:	$26,130
Total cost with fees & expenses:	$36,010
Average financial aid package:	$21,331

Where It's At

Elmira's campus, festooned with the school's purple and gold colors, is located in Elmira, a small town in the Finger Lakes region of western New York State. As Mark Twain's summer home for many years, Elmira has several attractions devoted to the author, including his study, now preserved on campus, and his final resting place at Woodlawn Cemetery. The Clemens Center features movies, musical acts, and other performances. At the National Warplane Museum, visitors can learn about the aircraft used by the Armed Forces. Hockey fans cheer on the Jackals, Elmira's United Hockey League team. New York City is about four hours away by car.

What It's Like

Everything's intimate at Elmira, but not in a creepy way. Teachers frequently give out their home phone numbers on the first day of classes. Each year, the administration cancels class for Mountain Day, a chance for everyone—staff, students, administrators, professors—to hang out informally. And during the annual Holiday Banquet, students ask their favorite faculty member to a semiformal Thanksgiving dinner.

Students really value the close campus community. Back in the day, Elmira students decided to get rid of fraternities and sororities, and they've been banned from campus ever since. There are even Saturday classes: during the fall term, all first-years have to take a writing class that meets on Saturdays. But think of Saturday classes not as punishment but as yet another way Elmira demonstrates its commitment to students. Professors here are so eager to help that they give up their weekends to teach. Elmira helps its students prepare for life after college by requiring juniors and seniors to do an internship of up to 240 hours.

Everything's intimate at Elmira.

In addition to Encore, which develops students' appreciation for the arts, first-years must also complete 60 hours of community service and take two interdisciplinary courses in Western civilization and international issues. Elmira offers more than 35 majors, including very strong programs in international studies, the sciences, and communication.

Elmira's academic calendar features two 12-week terms and one six-week term beginning in April. Many students use the short term to go abroad, studying in such places as the Bahamas and Turkey.

First-years live in doubles with other first-years, usually in the co-ed Alumni or Anderson Halls. These dorms include wall-to-wall carpeting, laundry facilities (no quarters required), and pool tables. Upperclass students live in traditional dorms or in the Cottages, on-campus apartments. The more than 80 organizations include the nation's oldest literary magazine (*Sibyl*), the intramural bocce team, and 16 Division III varsity athletic teams.

What's the Frequency, Ken(dra)? Most Popular Campus Radio Stations

College radio is like corporate radio's cooler, hipper little brother. Tune in to hear East River Pipe, Clap Your Hands Say Yeah, Cat Power, and a whole slew of other cutting-edge artists and soon-to-be-discovered megastars that you've probably never heard of, rather than the standard Mariah Carey–Fifty Cent–Kelly Clarkson rotation. The listening is always easy at the following colleges.

Bates College (P. 26) WRBC–91.5 FM

Centenary College (P. 42) WNTI–91.9 FM

Emerson College (P. 88) WERS–88.9 FM AND WECB–99.9 FM

The Evergreen State College (P. 92) KAOS–89.3 FM

Grinnell College (P. 104) KDIC–88.5 FM

Knox College (P. 122) WVKC–90.7 FM

North Central College (P. 150) WONC–89.1 FM

Reed College (P. 166) KRRC–97.9 FM

Ripon College (P. 172) WRPN–90.1 FM

Elon University

2700 Campus Box
Elon, NC 27244

(336) 278-2000
http://www.elon.edu/

Why It's Cool

Get ready to take the wheel, because Elon straps you into the driver's seat. The Business of NASCAR, a four-week class offered each January, takes you on a behind-the-scenes ride through the world of stock car racing. Interview owners and sponsors to learn how to put together and market a team. Visit drivers at race shops to uncover the psychology of the pole position and the groove. Watch aerodynamic drag in action from a seat inside the pit stall. You'll do practically everything but suit up for the Daytona 500. Talk about life in the fast lane.

THE WEEKLY COLLEGE COFFEE PROGRAM LETS STUDENTS, FACULTY, AND STAFF HANG OUT OVER FREE DRINKS AND SNACKS.

The Details

Campus setting:	suburban
Degrees:	bachelor's, master's, doctoral
Calendar:	4-1-4
Public/Private:	private religious
Number of full-time faculty:	261
Student-to-teacher ratio:	15:1

Admissions requirements:

- **Options:** common application, deferred entrance, early admission, early decision, early action, electronic application
- **Application fee:** $40
- **Required:** essay or personal statement, high school transcript, letter of recommendation, SAT or ACT
- **Application deadlines:** 1/10 (freshmen), continuous (transfer), 11/10 (early action)
- **Early decision:** 11/1
- **Notification:** 3/15 (freshmen), continuous (transfer), 12/1 (early decision), 12/20 (early action)

Average high school GPA:	3.63
Average freshman SAT verbal/math score:	586 / 593
Average freshman ACT score:	—
Number of applicants:	8,063
Number of applicants accepted:	3,311
Percentage of students from out of state:	70%
Total freshman enrollment:	1,230
Total enrollment:	4,796
Percentage of students who live in campus housing:	59%
Total tuition fee:	$17,310
Total cost with fees & expenses:	$24,465
Average financial aid package:	$11,364

Where It's At

Elon's 575-acre campus is located in the small town of Elon, in North Carolina's Piedmont region. Elon has several restaurants and clubs, including Morazi's Pizza and The Lighthouse. Nearby Burlington has the Paramount Theatre, which features concerts and plays; the Burlington Aquatics Center; the large City Park; and the Burlington Indians, a minor league baseball team. The city of Greensboro, about 30 minutes away, has more than 170 parks. Each year, Greensboro hosts the Eastern Music Festival and the African American Arts Festival. Raleigh is about an hour away by car, and Washington, D.C., is about five hours away.

What It's Like

Elon students consistently get ranked as "busiest" and "very involved" on all sorts of top-ten lists of colleges and universities. But students here don't just study—they play sports, they volunteer, they call their professors at home when they have questions about an assignment. NASCAR fans or not, students really love it here.

Residential options include traditional dorms, such as the all-women West Hall; co-ed apartment-style suites at the Jordan Center; and theme housing, such as the Isabella Cannon International Studies Pavilion for students majoring in international studies or foreign languages.

Busy students . . . beautiful campus . . .

Four undergraduate colleges make up Elon: the School of Education, the School of Communications, the Love School of Business, and the College of Arts and Sciences. Among the many majors are physical education, journalism, and human services. Students may complement their majors with one of several interdisciplinary minors, including nonviolence studies and multimedia authoring.

Winter Term gives students an opportunity to do four weeks of concentrated study between semesters. On campus, students choose from an array of cool courses, including the Business of NASCAR and Wealth and Poverty. But many students elect to study off campus, participating in such programs as Astronomy in Mexico and Ghana: West African History and Culture.

Among the myriad student organizations are ten fraternities, 11 sororities, 16 Division I athletic teams, and ESTV, the campus television station. The Kernodle Center offers information about service-learning projects, and just about everyone at Elon volunteers at school or in the community. The Elon Experiences transcript lists each student's extracurricular activities, and seniors can get a copy to show perspective employers or graduate schools.

Known for its beauty, Elon's entire campus is one big, spectacular botanical garden. Each plant is labeled, and the grounds feature not one but *two* lakes. Each week, the campus community gathers at Fonville Fountain for informal chats during College Coffee, one of Elon's oldest traditions.

Emerson College

120 Boylston Street
Boston, MA 02116
(617) 824-8500
http://www.emerson.edu/

Why It's Cool

Worship words? Love language? If you're into talking or writing, then you might be into Emerson. At this school, you've got to take three communication classes in order to graduate. But students here don't just talk—they also paint, write, act, sing, design, make movies, or do something equally creative at either the School of Communication or the School of the Arts. But unlike a lot of artsy colleges, Emerson also gives you great classes in the liberal arts like The Psychology of Personality and Love and Eroticism in Western Culture. You'll develop your imagination *and* your IQ. Hey, it worked for Denis Leary, Jay Leno, and Henry "the Fonz" Winkler.

IN BOSTON COMMON, A GORGEOUS PARK ACROSS THE STREET FROM EMERSON, SWAN BOATS FERRY PASSENGERS AROUND FROG POND.

The Details

Campus setting:	urban
Degrees:	bachelor's, master's, doctoral
Calendar:	semesters
Public/Private:	private nonprofit
Number of full-time faculty:	139
Student-to-teacher ratio:	15:1

Admissions requirements:

- **Options:** deferred entrance, early admission, early action, electronic application
- **Application fee:** $60
- **Required:** essay or personal statement, high school transcript, 2 letters of recommendation, SAT or ACT
- **Application deadlines:** 1/15 (freshmen), 3/15 (transfer)
- **Early action:** 11/1
- **Notification:** 4/1 (freshmen), 5/1 (transfer), 12/15 (early action)

Average high school GPA:	3.53
Average freshman SAT verbal/math score:	634 / 597
Average freshman ACT score:	25
Number of applicants:	4,584
Number of applicants accepted:	2,207
Percentage of students from out of state:	63%
Total freshman enrollment:	700
Total enrollment:	4,398
Percentage of students who live in campus housing:	45%
Total tuition fee:	—
Total cost with fees & expenses:	—
Average financial aid package:	$11,820

Where It's At

In the heart of Boston, Massachusetts, Emerson's urban campus abuts Boston Common and the Theater District. Several Emerson buildings are located on Boylston Street, known as Boston's "Grand Boulevard"; the street is also home to historic brownstones and hip restaurants. Other attractions include the New England Aquarium, the Museum of Fine Arts, the Isabella Stewart Gardner Museum, and the Quincy Market/Faneuil Hall shopping complex. The 2.5-mile Freedom Trail winds around the city, past such historic sites as the location of the Boston Massacre. Sports teams include the Red Sox (MLB), Celtics (NBA), Bruins (NHL), and the New England Patriots (NFL). Plus, Boston is the ultimate college town: One in five people there is a student.

What It's Like

Creative types, nonconformists, unconventional individuals . . . As far as Emerson's easygoing, nonjudgmental students are concerned, anything goes. Through the ProArts Consortium, Emerson students get access to the classes and resources at the Berklee College of Music, Boston Architectural Center, School of the Museum of Fine Arts, Boston Conservatory, and Massachusetts College of Art.

Emerson has two schools: the School of Communication and the School of the Arts. Majors range from theater design/technology to political communication to the very competitive bachelor of arts in writing, literature, and publishing.

Home to creative types, nonconformists, unconventional individuals . . .

Everybody has to take the general education curriculum, meant to give students different perspectives on the world. For example, History of Jazz and Dress Codes: American Clothes in the Twentieth Century both fulfill the aesthetic perspective, while Caribbean Imagination fulfills the global diversity requirement.

Through the New Pathways Program, first-years can choose to live in one of four learning communities: performing cultures, digital culture, leadership through service, and writers' block. These students take linked gen ed classes, such as Digital Culture and Visual Arts, and participate in informal, social activities, such as editing an anthology of writing.

The four residence halls range from a walk-up brownstone in the Back Bay to the very large Little Building (home to 750 students). An all-new residence hall and performance complex, with a restaurant and eight practice studios, is set to open in 2008.

The External Program takes students to Los Angeles, where they'll choose from more than 800 internships, and to the Netherlands, where they'll live in a twelfth-century castle while taking classes. There's also a four-week program in film offered during the summer in Prague.

As the Lions, students play on 13 Division III athletic teams, including lacrosse. There are three sororities, three fraternities, and one co-ed fraternity. Other activities range from the Chocolate Cake City comedy troupe to EC Dance.

Eugene Lang College
The New School for Liberal Arts

65 West 11th Street
New York, NY 10011

(212) 229-5600
http://www.lang.edu/

Why It's Cool

Lang loves New York. The so-called Capital of the World has everything you could ever dream of, and as a Lang student, you'll have access to it all: internships at *The Daily Show*, *Teen Vogue*, Capitol Records, and Miramax, as well as free or cheap admission to the Museum of Modern Art and Broadway shows. But you'll also get checkout privileges at Cooper Union, New York University, and the Humanities and Social Sciences Library (whose collection includes the first published edition of Shakespeare), plus classes like Evil in the Twentieth Century and Global Hip-Hop. There's a lot to love about this city—and this school.

FOR JUST $2, THE SUBWAY WILL TAKE YOU ANYWHERE YOU WANT TO GO IN NEW YORK CITY, INCLUDING MADISON SQUARE GARDEN, THE BROOKLYN BRIDGE, AND THE MUSEUM OF THE CITY OF NEW YORK.

The Details

Campus setting:	urban
Degrees:	bachelor's
Calendar:	semesters
Public/Private:	private nonprofit
Number of full-time faculty:	35
Student-to-teacher ratio:	12:1

Admissions requirements:

- **Options:** common application, deferred entrance, early admission, early decision
- **Application fee:** $40
- **Required:** essay or personal statement, high school transcript, 2 letters of recommendation, SAT or ACT
- **Application deadlines:** 2/1 (freshmen), 5/15 (transfer)
- **Early decision:** 11/15
- **Notification:** 4/1 (freshmen), 6/1 (transfer), 12/15 (early decision)

Average high school GPA:	2.99
Average freshman SAT verbal/math score:	629 / 566
Average freshman ACT score:	23
Number of applicants:	862
Number of applicants accepted:	560
Percentage of students from out of state:	55%
Total freshman enrollment:	187
Total enrollment:	742
Percentage of students who live in campus housing:	36%
Total tuition fee:	$25,470
Total cost with fees & expenses:	$36,280
Average financial aid package:	$17,793

Where It's At

Lang's campus consists of a group of buildings and brownstones in New York City's Greenwich Village. Nearby Washington Square and Union Square Parks are popular spots in which to hang out, as are French Roast (open all day and all night), Caffe Reggio, and other neighborhood coffeehouses. This city of 8 million people has top-notch museums (the Metropolitan Museum of Art, the Museum of Modern Art), terrific sports teams (the Yankees, the Knicks), magnificent shopping (Bloomingdale's, Bergdorf Goodman), and restaurants to suit every budget and taste ($2 falafel, $500 sushi). Central Park is an 843-acre urban oasis right in the center of the city.

What It's Like

The diverse, liberal, eccentric souls who make up Lang share one characteristic: a great love for New York City. Lang students would rather go out and find their own entertainment than participate in organized institutional activities. If you're not into the big city, Lang's probably not the school for you. But don't worry about finding a place to live: There are six residence halls available.

Diverse, eccentric souls who share a great love for New York City

Lang in the City lets students attend Broadway shows, the Metropolitan Opera, and other events for only five dollars, and they always get in free to the Museum of Modern Art. There are no sports teams, no fraternities, and no sororities. Instead, students come together through such groups as Shades of Urban Life and the Theater Collective.

Rather than traditional majors, Lang offers concentrations in several interdisciplinary areas, including urban studies and writing. Juniors and seniors frequently take graduate-level courses through Milano: The New School for Management and Urban Policy, and anyone can apply to take courses at the New School for Drama (which houses the famous Actors Studio) or the other colleges that make up the New School University. An agreement with Cooper Union lets Lang students take science classes there.

First-years take two writing courses organized around such topics as The Beat of the Fifties and Love in the Western World. A First-Year Workshop helps students adjust to the pressures and responsibilities of college life in the city. Seniors must complete the Senior Experience Project, ranging from a thesis to a museum installation to a video.

More than a third of students do at least one internship, for which they earn academic credit, and many do two or more. Students have interned for magazines like *Spin* and television shows like *Saturday Night Live*.

The Evergreen State College

2700 Evergreen Parkway, Northwest
Olympia, WA 98505
(360) 867-6000
http://www.evergreen.edu/

Why It's Cool

Evergreen wants you . . . to take responsibility for your education. You won't get grades here, but you will get written feedback from your teachers. You won't take regular classes, but you will sign up for coordinated studies programs—groups of interdisciplinary seminars, labs, and lectures team-taught by between two and four faculty members that last all year. You can even get academic credit for life experience. But before you can graduate, you'll have to discuss what you learned as an undergrad—and your future learning goals. Maybe you'll even have to hum Evergreen's fight song, which ends, "Let it all hang out."

EVERGREEN'S FAMOUS ALUMNI INCLUDE MICHAEL RICHARDS, WHO PLAYED KRAMER ON *SEINFELD*, AND MATT GROENING, CREATOR OF *THE SIMPSONS*.

The Details

Campus setting:	urban
Degrees:	bachelor's, master's
Calendar:	quarters
Public/Private:	public state
Number of full-time faculty:	160
Student-to-teacher ratio:	21:1

Admissions requirements:

- **Options:** early admission, electronic application
- **Application fee:** $37
- **Required:** high school transcript, SAT or ACT
- **Application deadlines:** 3/1 (freshmen), 3/1 (transfer)
- **Early decision:** —
- **Notification:** 4/1 (freshmen), 4/1 (transfer)

Average high school GPA:	3.12
Average freshman SAT verbal/math score:	594 / 548
Average freshman ACT score:	22
Number of applicants:	1,534
Number of applicants accepted:	1,459
Percentage of students from out of state:	23%
Total freshman enrollment:	480
Total enrollment:	4,410
Percentage of students who live in campus housing:	20%
Total in-state tuition, fees & expenses:	$10,620
Total out-of-state tuition, fees & expenses:	$21,234
Average financial aid package:	$10,547

Where It's At

Located in Olympia, the capital of Washington State, Evergreen sits on 1,000 acres. The campus includes tree-lined trails, a private beach on Puget Sound, an organic farm, and a community garden. Students craving urban life can head downtown for free via the Intercity Transit. Each year, this small city hosts a marathon and the Dixieland Jazz festival, and students can always shop at the farmers' market, see plays at the Olympia Little Theater, hear concerts by the Olympia Symphony Orchestra and Masterworks Choral Ensemble, or just stroll through one of the many waterfront parks. Seattle is about an hour away.

What It's Like

Founded in the early 1970s as an experimental college, Evergreen retains a liberal, "it's all good" atmosphere. But taking responsibility for your education is a major tenet of Evergreen's philosophy. With the help of faculty advisers, every student creates an individualized specialization by taking several coordinated studies programs.

Rather than individual classes, Evergreen offers coordinated studies programs, in which students examine one theme, event, or phenomenon through several disciplines. For example, students in Art's Sources spend one quarter reading literature about art and one quarter creating their own art in the fine metals studio. The two-quarter program Consuming Utopia: From Wilderness to Wal-Mart draws on readings from philosophy, film studies, and history to examine the idea of "utopia."

A unique school for unique students

The course catalog lists the academic areas covered by and the possible career options stemming from every program. At the end of each quarter, students get written feedback from professors (not letter grades). Students also write up their own evaluations of their performance. The lack of emphasis on grades lets students learn for learning's sake, without worrying about GPA or class rank. It also makes for a less competitive classroom environment.

Campus life is equally cooperative and noncompetitive. Housing includes traditional dorms and apartment-style buildings. First-years can elect to live in theme areas, such as Community Action House. Students can work together in the community garden, take a kayaking class through the Wilderness Resource Center, or play on one of the varsity athletic or intramural teams, including volleyball, soccer, and Ping-Pong.

Evergreen recognizes more than 50 student organizations—from the Electronic Music Collective to the Chemistry Club. There's also an on-campus FM radio station, as well as several public service centers that allow students, faculty, and staff to give back to the community by volunteering.

Fairhaven College
Western Washington University

516 High Street
Bellingham, WA 98225
(360) 650-3680
www.wwu.edu/depts/fairhaven

Why It's Cool

Fairhaven gives you the best of both educational worlds: the individual attention, intimacy, and seminar-style classes of a tiny liberal arts college combined with the access to research facilities, diverse campus, and huge range of courses at a big university. Students choose from doing either a traditional major at Western Washington University (WWU) or a self-designed interdisciplinary major at Fairhaven, called the Fairhaven Concentration. And while WWU gives out letter grades, Fairhaven has both students and teachers write narrative evaluations of student performance. Who says you can't have it all?

ROCK OUT. WWU'S OUTDOOR SCULPTURE COLLECTION MEANS THAT STUDENTS PASS BY COOL STRUCTURES ON THEIR WAY TO CLASS.

Note: The following statistics apply to Western Washington University.

The Details

Campus setting:	small town
Degrees:	bachelor's, master's
Calendar:	quarters
Public/Private:	public state
Number of full-time faculty:	160
Student-to-teacher ratio:	21:1

Admissions requirements:

- **Options:** early admission, electronic application
- **Application fee:** $37
- **Required:** high school transcript, SAT or ACT
- **Application deadlines:** 3/1 (freshmen), 3/1 (transfer)
- **Early decision:** —
- **Notification:** 4/1 (freshmen), 4/1 (transfer)

Average high school GPA:	3.12
Average freshman SAT verbal/math score:	594 / 548
Average freshman ACT score:	22
Number of applicants:	1,534
Number of applicants accepted:	1,459
Percentage of students from out of state:	23%
Total freshman enrollment:	480
Total enrollment:	4,410
Percentage of students who live in campus housing:	20%
Total in-state tuition, fees & expenses:	$10,620
Total out-of-state tuition, fees & expenses:	$21,234
Average financial aid package:	$10,547

Where It's At

WWU has 73 buildings on 215 acres in Bellingham, Washington, a small city on Bellingham Bay. Community events include the Bellingham Farmers' Market and Literature Live at Village Books. Each August, Bellingham hosts a music festival; every fall, the Lynden Craft and Antique Show returns to the nearby fairgrounds. The American Museum of Radio and Electricity and the Lynden Pioneer Museum are among the many local museums. Hikers and skiers head to Mount Baker, while anglers and whale watchers travel to the San Juan Islands. Seattle is just 90 minutes south, and Vancouver, British Columbia, is about 60 minutes north.

What It's Like

Founded as an experimental college in 1967, Fairhaven's spirit of innovation lives on. Interdisciplinarity, personal responsibility for learning, and the development of a sense of interconnectedness to the world are emphasized in every aspect of academic and social life. As one of seven undergraduate colleges at WWU, Fairhaven has a distinct identity as the university's progressive liberal arts school.

Roughly 65 percent of Fairhaven students complete the Fairhaven Concentration, a self-designed major that combines classes from several departments. A faculty committee must approve the majors, which culminate in senior projects. The Fairhaven Law and Diversity Program lets juniors and seniors concentrate on a prelaw curriculum.

Experimental college, experiential learning

Students also have the option of doing a traditional major, such as economics/political science, through WWU. All students must complete core classes in three areas: humanities and the expressive arts, society and the individual, and science and our place on the planet. At the end of the quarter, students write self-evaluations and receive written feedback from their teachers in lieu of letter grades.

On-campus resources include the Outdoor Experiential Learning Site, five acres of undeveloped land with a greenhouse, three cabins dating from the 1920s, and herb gardens. WWU also has a large outdoor sculpture collection. The many libraries on campus include the Center for Pacific Studies and the Map Library. Fairhaven students can live in WWU dorms, which range from traditional halls to apartments.

Fairhaven students participate in WWU activities, including volunteering at the Peace Resource Center and developing programs for the Underground Coffeehouse Concert Series. Sponsored by Associated Students (a special events group), the High Street Music Fair brings bands to campus for an all-day celebration on two stages. Fairhaven students can study or do internships on six continents and across the United States.

See the World: Best Study Abroad Programs

These schools will really take you places.

LONDON/SCOTLAND PREVIEW:

Arcadia University (P. 16)

First-years can spend their spring break in the United Kingdom for just $245.

JAN TERM TRAVEL COURSES:

Austin College (P. 22)

Through the monthlong January Term at Austin, you might study gender in South India, cities in West Africa, or culture in Fiji, New Zealand, and Australia.

INTERNATIONAL STUDIES:

Goucher College (P. 100)

Everybody here is required to go abroad. Plus, Goucher will give you $1,200 toward your travel expenses.

TROPICAL ECOLOGY AND ETHNOBIOLOGY IN COSTA RICA:

Tuskegee University (P. 198)

Get up close and personal with the rainforest on this semester-long trip through one of the most ecologically diverse places in the world.

OTHER SCHOOLS WITH PHENOMENAL STUDY ABROAD PROGRAMS:

Agnes Scott College (P. 2)

Antioch College (P. 10)

Centre College (P. 44)

Elon University (P. 86)

Kalamazoo College (P. 116)

Lewis & Clark College (P. 124)

Linfield College (P. 126)

Loyola University Chicago (P. 128)

Presbyterian College (P. 158)

The University of Tampa (P. 212)

Goshen College

1700 South Main Street **(574) 535-7000**
Goshen, IN 46526 **http://www.goshen.edu/**

Why It's Cool

Pack your bags and bring your work ethic. Goshen's unusual Study-Service Term combines studying abroad with volunteering. For the first half of the semester, you'll master the language and customs of the host country (SST programs currently run in seven countries, including China, Peru, and Senegal). You'll then spend the next six weeks volunteering, perhaps teaching English or building houses with Habitat for Humanity. But you won't only be doing good deeds; you'll get a chance to see the sights too. Bon voyage, do-gooder.

GOSHEN HAS A HISTORY OF PRANKS, INCLUDING ONE IN WHICH A COW WAS RELEASED ON THE TOP FLOOR OF A BUILDING.

The Details

Campus setting:	small town
Degrees:	bachelor's
Calendar:	semesters
Public/Private:	private religious
Number of full-time faculty:	64
Student-to-teacher ratio:	10:1

Admissions requirements:

- **Options:** common application, deferred entrance, early action, electronic application
- **Application fee:** $25
- **Required:** essay or personal statement, high school transcript, 2 letters of recommendation, SAT or ACT
- **Application deadlines:** 8/15 (freshmen), 8/15 (transfer)
- **Early action:** 12/1
- **Notification:** continuous (freshmen), continuous (transfer), 12/15 (early action)

Average high school GPA:	3.46
Average freshman SAT verbal/math score:	580 / 560
Average freshman ACT score:	23
Number of applicants:	410
Number of applicants accepted:	315
Percentage of students from out of state:	47%
Total freshman enrollment:	168
Total enrollment:	908
Percentage of students who live in campus housing:	67%
Total tuition fee:	$19,300
Total cost with fees & expenses:	$26,550
Average financial aid package:	$17,181

Where It's At

Goshen's 135-acre campus is located in Goshen, a small town in northern Indiana. Students can get their caffeine fix at the Electric Brew and see avant-garde dramatic and musical performances at the Creative Enterprise Center. They can swim in Lake Michigan at the Warren Dunes State Park, kayak on the St. Joseph River, and canoe on the Elkhart River. Every year, nearby Elkhart hosts the County 4-H Fair. South Bend, just 40 minutes away by car, has Notre Dame College (and its legendary football team), an art museum, a zoo, an orchestra, the Morris Performing Arts Center, and the College Football Hall of Fame. Chicago is about two hours away.

What It's Like

Goshen welcomes students of all religious faiths and spiritual traditions to its Christ-centered education. Anabaptist-Mennonite values dominate campus life, from Goshen's commitment to nonviolent resolution of all conflicts to its motto, "Culture for Service," and its Bible and religious studies requirement.

The college also emphasizes diversity: 10 percent of students come from countries other than the United States, and Goshen requires everybody to fulfill an international education component, through SST, through traditional study abroad, or by demonstrating significant familiarity with another society.

Study, serve, sightsee . . .

Students choose from more than 30 majors, 35 minors, and nine preprofessional programs. One option is the peace, justice, and conflict studies program. This major emphasizes the peaceful resolution of all conflicts, whether global, local, social, or personal. Goshen is also strong in premed: in recent years, Goshen students have had a 100 percent acceptance rate to medical school.

Career Services has a four-year plan to help students use their liberal arts education to achieve their professional goals. Each year focuses on a different mission: awareness, exploration, experience, and transition. During their first year, students become aware of their interests by joining campus groups or taking self-assessment tests. As sophomores, students explore career paths through research and by meeting with the folks at Career Services or a mentor. Juniors gain experience by doing an internship. Finally, seniors transition from college to the work force by attending job fairs and networking with Goshen alumni.

There are 14 Division II athletic teams, including baseball and basketball, and nine intramural teams, including volleyball and softball. Other student organizations include EcoPax, the Amateur Boxing Club, and *Broadside*, a poetry journal. Each year, Goshen hosts a Celebrate Service Day, in which students skip classes to volunteer around the community.

Goucher College

1021 Dulaney Valley Road
Baltimore, MD 21204
(410) 337-6000
http://www.goucher.edu/

Why It's Cool

Goucher really, really wants you to see all there is to see and do all there is to do around the world. In fact, Goucher was the first college to require its students to study abroad—and now they'll even give you a $1,200 voucher to help you start your journey. Look at stars in Spain, analyze economics in England, watch opera in Italy, study marine biology in Honduras . . . the options are almost endless. We think that alone is pretty great, but get this: In 2004, Goucher students were named the happiest in the United States. So go on and get happy.

RIGHT BEFORE FINALS, GOUCHER HOSTS WINTER MELTDOWN, AT WHICH STUDENTS CAN USE A SLEDGEHAMMER TO BANG OUT THEIR STRESS ON AN OLD, DILAPIDATED CAR.

The Details

Campus setting:	suburban
Degrees:	bachelor's, master's
Calendar:	semesters
Public/Private:	private nonprofit
Number of full-time faculty:	104
Student-to-teacher ratio:	10:1

Admissions requirements:

- **Options:** common application, deferred entrance, early admission, early action, electronic application
- **Application fee:** $40
- **Required:** essay or personal statement, high school transcript, 3 letters of recommendation, SAT or ACT
- **Application deadlines:** 2/1 (freshmen), 5/1 (transfer)
- **Early action:** 12/15
- **Notification:** 4/1 (freshmen), 5/15 (transfer), 2/15 (early action)

Average high school GPA:	3.21
Average freshman SAT verbal/math score:	609 / 588
Average freshman ACT score:	24
Number of applicants:	2,870
Number of applicants accepted:	1,946
Percentage of students from out of state:	72%
Total freshman enrollment:	401
Total enrollment:	2,349
Percentage of students who live in campus housing:	80%
Total tuition fee:	$25,750
Total cost with fees & expenses:	$35,525
Average financial aid package:	$19,481

Where It's At

Goucher's 287-acre campus is located Baltimore, Maryland. To get to the restaurants and shops of downtown Towson, a nearby Baltimore suburb, students can walk or hop on the Collegetown shuttle, which also stops at Johns Hopkins University and Loyola College. Each year, Towson hosts the Spring Festival, one of the largest street fairs on the East Coast, featuring games, food, and entertainment. Baltimore is home to the Orioles (MLB) and the Inner Harbor, a renovated neighborhood on Chesapeake Bay that includes the Maryland Science Center and Harborplace, a huge mall. Washington, D.C., is about an hour away by car.

What It's Like

There may not be a typical Goucher student, but everybody here relishes the college's diversity. If you're into other people, other places, and other cultures, this might be the school for you. Just about everyone hangs out at the Gopher Hole, which offers free coffee when you bring your own mug on Wednesdays.

Goucher requires all students to study abroad for at least three weeks. Two popular options for fulfilling this requirement are the intensive courses abroad (ICAs) and the International Scholars Program (ISP). ICAs are three-week classes that usually take place during the winter, spring, or summer breaks. Recent offerings include China: Past, Present, and Future and in French in Avignon.

Free coffee, lots of culture

The ISP lets students of any major add an international component to their academic work. Participants take three courses known collectively as Perspectives on the Global Condition and the single-course Local/Global Connections on campus. Then, students go abroad to the country of their choice, including such destinations as Ghana and India.

Among the more than 30 majors are dance and sociology. Service-learning courses, in which students volunteer as part of the course requirements, include Academic Writing and Advanced Video Production. All students must take courses in a foreign language and math, among other liberal arts fields. Anyone can submit essays for publication in *Verge*, a prestigious on-campus journal that publishes research papers and nonfiction.

First-years take several special courses, including an introduction to college writing and Frontiers, the umbrella term for the first-year seminar. Frontiers seminars emphasize reading and thinking, and past offerings include Memoir and The Information Age: Do You Get It?

On-campus housing options range from the nonsmoking, co-ed (by room) Tuttle House to Robinson House, which requires residents to communicate in a language other than English at all times. The Hip-Hop Club and Sacred Ground, which combines dancing and Christianity, are two of the more than 60 clubs on campus.

Green Mountain College

One College Circle | **(802) 287-8000**
Poultney, VT 05764 | **http://www.greenmtn.edu/**

Why It's Cool

At Green Mountain College, green is good. Everything at GMC centers around the environment. You'll take a break from one of the required courses in the Environmental Liberal Arts Program (ELA) to milk the cows (on campus . . . really) or go caving with the Green Mountain Adventure Program (MAP). You can even major in adventure recreation, which includes such classes as Outdoor Living Skills and Essentials of Rock and Ice Climbing. If nature floats your boat, this is your school. You'll graduate a lean, mean, outdoor-expedition-leading machine.

EVERYBODY'S WELCOME AT THE ALL-NIGHT "LITERARY LOCKDOWN," AT WHICH STUDENTS TRY TO READ A NOVEL ALOUD FROM START TO FINISH IN ONE NIGHT.

The Details

Campus setting:	small town
Degrees:	bachelor's
Calendar:	semesters
Public/Private:	private religious
Number of full-time faculty:	41
Student-to-teacher ratio:	12:1

Admissions requirements:

- **Options:** common application, deferred entrance, electronic application
- **Application fee:** $30
- **Required:** essay or personal statement, high school transcript, letter of recommendation, SAT or ACT
- **Application deadlines:** continuous (freshmen), continuous (transfer)
- **Early decision:** —
- **Notification:** 8/1 (freshmen), 8/1 (transfer)

Average high school GPA:	3.01
Average freshman SAT verbal/math score:	530 / 499
Average freshman ACT score:	21
Number of applicants:	943
Number of applicants accepted:	765
Percentage of students from out of state:	87%
Total freshman enrollment:	—
Total enrollment:	639
Percentage of students who live in campus housing:	85%
Total tuition fee:	$20,614
Total cost with fees & expenses:	$29,004
Average financial aid package:	$17,867

Where It's At

GMC and its 155-acre farm are located in the small town of Poultney, in Vermont's Southwestern Lakes region. Poultney has a library, post office, and small strip of shops on Main Street. At the Lake St. Catherine State Park, students can take in amazing views of the water and the Adirondacks. A free shuttle takes students into Rutland, home to the Chaffee Art Center and the New England Maple Museum. Skiers and snowboarders head to nearby Killington and Stratton. Boston is just over three hours away, and New York City is a little less than five hours away.

What It's Like

More than just the mountain is green at GMC. This outdoorsy school draws outdoorsy students. Everybody here is committed to learning about the natural, social, and political climates that shape the world, and everybody tries to live peacefully with one another and with the environment. Not surprisingly, recycling, natural fibers, jam bands, and hiking boots are big on campus.

Recycling, jam bands, and hiking boots are big.

To help students become responsible citizens, Green Mountain requires everyone to take ELA electives. These classes combine environmental themes with the critical thinking skills stressed in the liberal arts. For example, students can take Environmental Algebra or American Views of the Environment to 1945. The more than 25 majors range from the traditional (business, hospitality management) to the nontraditional (adventure recreation, commercial recreation).

Everybody must take four core courses: Images of Nature, A Delicate Balance, the writing-intensive Voices of Community, and Dimensions of Nature. Images of Nature, a small seminar taken during the first year, introduces GMC's eco-friendly philosophy and teaches writing. In the seminar A Delicate Balance, juniors and seniors hear presentations about key environmental issues from professors and professionals. At the end of the term, students give their own presentations on topics of their choosing.

Close to 20 percent of GMC students play on one of the 14 Division III athletic teams. Other student activities include the *Reverie* literary magazine and the Pre-Law Club. The Bozen Wellness Center offers yoga and other fitness classes. The optional Wilderness Challenge takes first-years on a five-day trip into the Adirondacks a few weeks before school starts.

The six residence halls, home to 90 percent of students, have theme floors so that those with common interests can live together. Everyone hangs out in the Gorge, watching television or meeting with study groups held in the giant room. At this school, the indoors are as great as the outdoors.

Grinnell College

1121 Park Street
Grinnell, IA 50112
(641) 269-4000
http://www.grinnell.edu/

Why It's Cool

At Grinnell, you'll never have to take a class you dislike: The open curriculum allows you to choose courses based on your academic interests, not on distribution requirements. Say *buh-bye* biology and *adiós* Spanish. But slackers, beware: You can't major in something random like basket weaving. Grinnell's intellectual environment is not for wimps. The required First-Year Tutorial prepares you for the academic rigors to come. You'll write papers, give presentations, and regularly meet with the professor. But the classes, including Baseball: Its Literature, Science, and Societal Impact and Elvis Everywhere, are so cool, you'll forget you're in school.

ONCE A STOP ON THE UNDERGROUND RAILROAD, GRINNELL WAS ALSO ONE OF THE FIRST SCHOOLS TO ADMIT AFRICAN AMERICANS AND WOMEN.

The Details

Campus setting:	small town
Degrees:	bachelor's
Calendar:	semesters
Public/Private:	private nonprofit
Number of full-time faculty:	150
Student-to-teacher ratio:	9:1

Admissions requirements:

- **Options:** common application, deferred entrance, early admission, early decision, electronic application
- **Application fee:** $30
- **Required:** essay or personal statement, high school transcript, 3 letters of recommendation, SAT or ACT
- **Application deadlines:** 1/20 (freshmen), 5/1 (transfer)
- **Early decision:** 11/20
- **Notification:** 4/1 (freshmen), 5/20 (transfer), 12/20 (early decision)

Average high school GPA:	—
Average freshman SAT verbal/math score:	683 / 686
Average freshman ACT score:	26
Number of applicants:	2,970
Number of applicants accepted:	1,501
Percentage of students from out of state:	75%
Total freshman enrollment:	434
Total enrollment:	1,556
Percentage of students who live in campus housing:	75%
Total tuition fee:	$25,200
Total cost with fees & expenses:	$33,090
Average financial aid package:	$22,426

Where It's At

The diversity of the students—who come from 50 states and 50 countries—make the 130 acres of Grinnell College a hip enclave within the cornfields of central Iowa. Fewer than 10,000 people live in Grinnell, although the small town boasts a recently renovated downtown and the Strand, a movie theater with its original 1916 facade. Each fall, the Happy Days Festival features food, carnival rides, and an old-car parade. Students can escape the rural life to Des Moines and Iowa City, both about an hour away, or to Chicago and Minneapolis, both about four hours away.

What It's Like

Josiah B. Grinnell founded the town of Grinnell in 1854, after Horace Greeley told him to "Go west, young man." Notable alumni who have gone west and graduated from Grinnell include Herbie Hancock and Gary Cooper. The alumni of today tend to do more than just go west—they tend to go really, really far. Grinnell produces more Peace Corps volunteers per capita than any other school: More than 300 alumni have entered the corps. Socially committed graduates can also enter the Grinnell Corps, where they devote a year to domestic and international volunteer work.

A hip enclave within the cornfields of Iowa

Under the open curriculum, students take any course that interests them, from Making Documentary Films to Japanese Comics and War, as long as they take a certain number of credit hours, complete the First-Year Tutorial, and fulfill the requirements for the major. Students choose their majors from departments within three broad divisions—humanities, social sciences, and science—or from ten interdisciplinary concentrations, including global development studies and American studies. Grinnell also offers courses through seven special programs, each of which has a specific focus, such as the Center for Prairie Studies.

After the first year, students can create a mentored advanced project (MAP), working closely with at least one professor on a highly focused academic project. Summer MAP students even receive a stipend so that they can focus on their studies without having to worry about money.

Students choose from more than 140 organizations, from deejaying at the campus radio station, KDIC, to spelunking through the Grinnell Outdoor Recreation Program and writing for the student newspaper, *The Scarlet and Black*. Unlike a lot of other U.S. colleges, Grinnell offers need-blind admission, which means that a student's ability to pay does not factor into whether he or she is offered admission. This school ensures that its applicants are judged on merit, not wallet size.

Hampshire College

893 West Street **(413) 549-4600**
Amherst, MA 01002 **http://www.hampshire.edu/**

Why It's Cool

Rumor has it that Hampshire lets you major in anything from basket weaving to Ultimate Frisbee. The truth is . . . you can, sort of. With the help of a faculty adviser, you'll design your own course of study, taking classes in five schools: natural science; social science; interdisciplinary arts; cognitive science; and humanities, arts, and cultural studies. Go ahead and combine your love of environmental design, sculpture, and dance, or film and neuroscience. Specialize in invention and innovation, animal science, or peace and world security studies . . . you're only limited by the breadth and depth of your own interest.

GOT A LIGHT? CREATIVE LAMP CONSTRUCTION IS ONE OF THE MANY CLASSES OFFERED DURING HAMPSHIRE'S OPTIONAL JANUARY TERM.

The Details

Campus setting:	rural
Degrees:	bachelor's
Calendar:	4-1-4
Public/Private:	private nonprofit
Number of full-time faculty:	114
Student-to-teacher ratio:	11:1

Admissions requirements:

- **Options:** common application, deferred entrance, early admission, early decision, early action, electronic application
- **Application fee:** $55
- **Required:** essay or personal statement, high school transcript, 2 letters of recommendation
- **Application deadlines:** 1/15 (freshmen), 3/1 (transfer), 12/1 (early action)
- **Early decision:** 11/15
- **Notification:** 4/1 (freshmen), 4/15 (transfer), 12/15 (early decision), 1/15 (early action)

Average high school GPA:	3.28
Average freshman SAT verbal/math score:	658 / 609
Average freshman ACT score:	25
Number of applicants:	2,180
Number of applicants accepted:	1,282
Percentage of students from out of state:	84%
Total freshman enrollment:	370
Total enrollment:	1,352
Percentage of students who live in campus housing:	93%
Total tuition fee:	$30,418
Total cost with fees & expenses:	$39,591
Average financial aid package:	$25,660

Where It's At

Hampshire's rural, 800-acre campus is in Amherst, a small town in western Massachusetts. Several groups, including the National Yiddish Book Center and New England Wetlands, have offices on campus as part of Hampshire's Cultural Village. Students can take a free bus ride into Amherst or Northampton, which include such attractions as the Emily Dickinson Museum, Thornes Marketplace, Look Park, and the Iron Horse Music Hall. Each fall, the Three County Fair, the longest running agricultural fair in the country, hosts a week of horse-racing, food, and fireworks. Boston is less than two hours away by car, and New York City is about three hours away.

What It's Like

Kooky, crazy, creative. Hampshire students are as idiosyncratic as their majors. We hear there's a clothing-optional dorm, and the two most popular social events are "Trip or Treat" around Halloween and the Drag Ball in the spring. Hampshire alumni include Elliot Smith and Ken Burns.

Hampshire is part of the Five Colleges consortium, along with Smith, Mount Holyoke, Amherst, and the University of Massachusetts–Amherst. A free bus system links the schools, making it easy to take one of the 6,000 courses offered each year. Through the consortium, students can earn certificates in such programs as African studies and logic.

Three words: clothing optional dorm

Study at Hampshire is divided into divisions—not class years. During Division I, students take eight courses from the five schools. Division II students begin planning and working on their concentration. Finally, Division III students complete a comprehensive project on a specific idea or theme. Hampshire runs more like a graduate school than a college: Students work closely with faculty to develop their own interests and do their own projects.

Professors give students written feedback rather than letter grades. And Hampshire does not require standardized tests for admission, focusing instead on transcripts, recommendations, student essays, and optional submissions. In recent years, 100 percent of students with health and premed concentrations were accepted to medical school.

Just about everyone lives on campus in one of five residential houses. First-years usually live in the singles and doubles of Merrill or Dakin. Upperclass students live in two- or three-story apartments known as "mods." Eating options range from the Tavern, a student-run café and performance space that sells baked goods, to the Mixed Nuts Food Co-Op.

The optional January Term lets students take an in-depth class on campus or abroad. Recent offerings include Writing for Television and Rock Climbing in Greece. At the Outdoor Program and Recreation Athletics, students can rent equipment for hiking, climbing, and camping.

No Shame in Not Being the Same: Most Diverse Campuses

We at SparkCollege believe that uniqueness is good. In other words, only milk should be homogenous. *Viva la difference!*

KUM - BA - YA!

Hanover College

PO Box 108	**(812) 866-7000**
Hanover, IN 47243	**http://www.hanover.edu/**

Why It's Cool

Hanover helps you get on to get off. Once you're on campus, Hanover encourages you to leave and get a job, study abroad, or do an internship in nearby Cincinnati. Just about every major at Hanover has an off-campus, real-world component, such as the chance to do physics research in Brazil. And if you can't find what you're looking for, you can always propose your own off-campus plan. The unique academic calendar—four courses in the fall, four courses in the winter, and a monthlong spring term—means you'll have plenty of time to be here, there, and everywhere in between.

ACTOR WOODY HARRELSON, STAR OF *CHEERS* AND ADVOCATE FOR MARIJUANA-LAW REFORM, GRADUATED FROM HANOVER IN 1983.

The Details

Campus setting:	small town
Degrees:	bachelor's
Calendar:	4-4-1
Public/Private:	private religious
Number of full-time faculty:	86
Student-to-teacher ratio:	11:1

Admissions requirements:

- **Options:** common application, deferred entrance, early admission, early action, electronic application
- **Application fee:** $30
- **Required:** essay or personal statement, high school transcript, letter of recommendation, SAT or ACT
- **Application deadlines:** 3/1 (freshmen), continuous (transfer)
- **Early action:** 12/1
- **Notification:** continuous (freshmen), continuous (transfer), 12/20 (early action)

Average high school GPA:	—
Average freshman SAT verbal/math score:	594 / 589
Average freshman ACT score:	24
Number of applicants:	1,659
Number of applicants accepted:	1,237
Percentage of students from out of state:	30%
Total freshman enrollment:	380
Total enrollment:	1,062
Percentage of students who live in campus housing:	96%
Total tuition fee:	$20,150
Total cost with fees & expenses:	$27,600
Average financial aid package:	$14,751

Where It's At

Hanover's 650-acre campus is located in Hanover, a small town in southeastern Indiana, along the Ohio River. At the 50,000-acre Big Oaks National Wildlife Refuge, visitors can bird-watch, hunt, hike, and roam around 52 caves. Golfers tee up at Spring Hills Golf Course, while the mini-golfers head to the Clifty Golf Range. Popular local wineries include Lanthier Winery, the Ridge Winery, and Madison Vineyards. About two hours away by car, Cincinnati has numerous attractions, such as the Cincinnati Art Museum, the Bengals (NFL), the Reds (MLB), and the Krohn Conservatory.

What It's Like

At Hanover, school is always in session. Be prepared to continue class discussion informally over a snack at the Shoebox, an on-campus eatery, or a shake from Hinkle's Sandwich Shop in nearby Madison. Students very much live out Hanover's slogan, "Powered by Thought."

Although affiliated with the Presbyterian Church, Hanover accepts students from all religious backgrounds. About 90 percent of students work, research, or study off campus, and Hanover encourages everyone to add practical, professional experience to his or her academic experience.

Powered by thought

During the four-week Spring Term, students take one in-depth class on or off campus. Students might study Shakespeare in London or examine rock formations in New Mexico. Most majors offer internships, such as the opportunity for art history majors to spend a summer at the Indianapolis Art Center. Other majors include medieval-renaissance studies and theological studies.

All students participate in the First-Year Experience, which eases the transition from high school to college. First-years begin with a week-long orientation in August, then take Great Works, which studies literary masterpieces, and Human Nature, an interdisciplinary course on what it means to be human, once the fall semester starts. Other degree requirements include courses in a foreign language, philosophy/theological studies, and physical education.

More than 90 percent of students receive some type of aid. Most students live on campus in Greek houses (there are five fraternities and four sororities); the recently constructed, air-conditioned, apartment-style Greenwood Suites; or traditional halls. Theme housing, in which the residents bond over a shared interest, such as safe sex or music appreciation, is another on-campus residential option.

Hanover sponsors 16 varsity athletic teams (the Panthers), including cross-country and golf. Among the many student organizations are Anime, a club for those interested in Asian animation, and Best Buddies, which pairs students with people with intellectual disabilities.

Hendrix College

1600 Washington Avenue
Conway, AR 72032
(501) 329-6811
http://www.hendrix.edu/

Why It's Cool

Step aside, Homer. Hendrix has a whole new Odyssey. In Homer's classic poem, Odysseus spends 20 years wandering around and having adventures. At Hendrix, you'll have life-altering experiences in one-fifth the time. You'll choose at least three options from six broad categories: special projects, artistic creativity, service to others, global awareness, professional and leadership development, and undergraduate research. Earn Odyssey credit through such adventurous activities as studying abroad in India to taking Mathematical Problem-Solving to being the captain of a Division III varsity athletic team to running the on-campus chapter of Rock the Vote. Homer would be impressed.

EACH FALL, THE CAMPUS CELEBRATES THE *ELIMINATION* OF THE GREEK SYSTEM.

The Details

Campus setting:	suburban
Degrees:	bachelor's, master's
Calendar:	semesters
Public/Private:	private religious
Number of full-time faculty:	83
Student-to-teacher ratio:	11:1

Admissions requirements:

- **Options:** common application, deferred entrance, early admission, electronic application
- **Application fee:** $40
- **Required:** essay or personal statement, high school transcript, letter of recommendation, SAT or ACT
- **Application deadlines:** 8/1 (freshmen), 8/1 (transfer)
- **Early decision:** —
- **Notification:** continuous (freshmen), continuous (transfer)

Average high school GPA:	3.60
Average freshman SAT verbal/math score:	649 / 610
Average freshman ACT score:	25
Number of applicants:	1,027
Number of applicants accepted:	875
Percentage of students from out of state:	42%
Total freshman enrollment:	295
Total enrollment:	1,049
Percentage of students who live in campus housing:	97%
Total tuition fee:	$21,336
Total cost with fees & expenses:	$28,546
Average financial aid package:	$14,675

Where It's At

A small suburban town near the Ozark Mountains in Arkansas, Conway is home to Hendrix, in addition to the University of Central Arkansas; six public parks and sports complexes, including Wooly Hollow State Park; Riddle's Elephant Farm; and several antique stores. Anglers and sunbathers head to the 6,700-acre Lake Conway, while hikers and history buffs visit the Cadron Settlement Park, which memorializes the Cherokee Trail of Tears. Every year in May, Conway hosts the Toad Suck Daze Festival, a celebration of music, food, and art. Little Rock is only 30 minutes away by car, and Memphis is about three hours away.

What It's Like

A long-standing affiliation with the Methodist Church influences campus life, but Hendrix welcomes students of all faiths. Many students choose to spend their breaks volunteering on missions to Costa Rica, the Bahamas, and elsewhere. About half of all students come from Arkansas; the rest come from 35 states and 11 countries.

Academic life at Hendrix revolves around the Odyssey program. Every student must also fulfill general education requirements in three categories: Learning Domains, which features the social sciences, humanities, and natural sciences; Capacities, which teaches writing, foreign language, physical education, and quantitative reasoning; and the Collegiate Center, which deals with current affairs and cultures. The average size of all classes is 15 students.

DANGER: Nutshells underfoot at Pecan Court

Hendrix offers approximately 30 majors, 30 minors, and eight preprofessional programs, including preministry. Majors include philosophy, religion, and English. The sciences are strong here too, and 10 percent of Hendrix graduates go on to medical school. As part of its Experiential Learning Opportunities, Hendrix sponsors programs in environmental studies in Cape Cod, Massachusetts, and also in international-intercultural studies in locations around the world.

Most students live on campus, in one of seven residential halls. Housing options range from traditional dorms to apartments and houses. Each spring, the women-only Veasey Hall hosts a luau. Galloway Hall is listed on the National Register of Historic Places.

All first-years attend a weeklong Orientation Trip, led by an upperclass student. Small groups head out for an adventure, which might include canoeing on the Buffalo River or building a house with Habitat for Humanity.

More than 50 years ago, Hendrix abolished the Greek system on campus, and the Hendrix Olympix celebrates that anniversary each fall. Everyone competes in a series of activities, which culminate in the golden shoes award. Just about everybody lounges outside during downtime, especially at the Pecan Court, an area covered in pecan shells.

Hiram College

PO Box 96
Hiram, OH 44234
(800) 362-5280
http://www.hiram.edu/

Why It's Cool

At Hiram, you'll always be tuned to the right station—the James H. Barrow Field Station, that is. You'll get actual, nature-centered experience, conducting environmental science research, maintaining trails, and studying animal behavior. The field station includes ponds, crop fields (sorry . . . no circles), a nature trail, and an aquatics building with an experimental stream. The outdoors will be your classroom. Not to mention that the entire station—buildings, wildlife, and greenery—is taken care of by students, so it'll be your job to keep things up and living. With this kind of experience, you'll definitely graduate a good-*natured* adult.

RECEIVE AN OFFICIAL "BEER SCHOOL GRADUATE" T-SHIRT AT ONE OF HIRAM'S (IN)FAMOUS "NIGHT OUTS."

The Details

Campus setting:	rural
Degrees:	bachelor's, master's
Calendar:	special semesters
Public/Private:	private religious
Number of full-time faculty:	74
Student-to-teacher ratio:	11:1

Admissions requirements:

- **Options:** common application, deferred entrance, early admission, electronic application
- **Application fee:** $35
- **Required:** essay or personal statement, high school transcript, 2 letters of recommendation, SAT or ACT
- **Application deadlines:** 4/1 (freshmen), 7/15 (transfer)
- **Early decision:** —
- **Notification:** continuous (freshmen), continuous (transfer)

Average high school GPA:	3.39
Average freshman SAT verbal/math score:	574 / 549
Average freshman ACT score:	23
Number of applicants:	828
Number of applicants accepted:	715
Percentage of students from out of state:	—
Total freshman enrollment:	218
Total enrollment:	1,125
Percentage of students who live in campus housing:	88%
Total tuition fee:	$21,970
Total cost with fees & expenses:	$30,700
Average financial aid package:	$21,218

Where It's At

Hiram's 110-acre campus is located in Hiram, a village of 1,300 people in northeastern Ohio. Each year, Hiram hosts a Fourth of July celebration, and fans of the Insane Clown Posse get together to celebrate the band every summer. Northeastern Ohio offers Hiram students lots of other off-campus options: Nelson-Kennedy Ledges State Park has a variety of trails and picnic spots, while nearby Cleveland has the Rock and Roll Hall of Fame, the historic West Side Market, the Metroparks Zoo, the Museum of Natural History, and a world-renowned orchestra. Football fans tailgate at the Pro Football Hall of Fame in Canton, about an hour away.

What It's Like

The innovative Hiram Plan subdivides the 15-week academic semester into two chunks: a 12-week block, in which you take three classes, and a three-week block, during which you might go abroad, do an internship, or take one intensive class. You'll take eight classes in an academic year, but you'll take them according to whatever configuration works best for you.

Students choose from roughly 30 majors and 35 minors, ranging from biomedical humanities to environmental studies, and eight preprofessional programs. Hiram's strengths lie in the sciences, aided by Hiram's affiliations with the Shoals Maine Laboratory and the Northwoods Field Station in Michigan, as well as the on-campus Barrow Field Station.

Traditional semesters are for suckers!

The New Student Institute Week brings together first-years for an intense orientation to Hiram life. Activities include community-building athletic challenges like rope climbs and more intellectual gatherings like book discussions.

Community building doesn't stop after the first year. All students must live on campus in one of ten residential halls, some of which have unique setups: The second floor of Gray Hall functions as a co-op, whereby students get a discount on their housing costs in return for doing work around the dorm, and some of the floors of Peckham Hall are designated as "Create-Your-Own-Theme." There are also more than 70 social, academic, and athletic clubs that let students bond over a shared love of computers or scuba diving. Each year on Campus Day, Hiram gives students the day off from classes so they can spend the morning doing community service and then the afternoon hanging out.

More than 90 percent of all Hiram students receive some type of financial aid. Under the Tuition Guarantee, students pay the same amount annually for their years of study, regardless of any tuition increases that might occur or how long it takes to graduate.

Kalamazoo College

1200 Academy Street	**(800) 362-5280**
Kalamazoo, MI 49006	**http://www.kzoo.edu/**

Why It's Cool

This K's *really* special. Not only will you study on 60 lovely wooded acres, but you'll also get the specialized curriculum known as the "K" Plan. You'll take core courses in the liberal arts. You'll do the Senior Individualized Project, an intense research paper or performance in your major. You'll have access to a database of more than 2,100 internships. Best of all, the "K" Plan gets you into one of the best study abroad programs in the United States, where you'll choose from about 50 opportunities on six continents. But Kalamazoo, affectionately known as "K," is more than OK—it's *grrreat.*

AT THE ANNUAL MONTE CARLO EVENT, PROFESSORS AND ADMINISTRATORS ACT AS DEALERS WHILE STUDENTS GAMBLE FOR FUN PRIZES.

The Details

Campus setting:	suburban
Degrees:	bachelor's
Calendar:	quarters
Public/Private:	private religious
Number of full-time faculty:	100
Student-to-teacher ratio:	12:1

Admissions requirements:

- **Options:** common application, deferred entrance, early decision, early action, electronic application
- **Application fee:** $35
- **Required:** essay or personal statement, high school transcript, 2 letters of recommendation, SAT or ACT
- **Application deadlines:** 2/15 (freshmen), 2/15 (transfer), 12/1 (early action)
- **Early decision:** 11/15
- **Notification:** 4/1 (freshmen), 4/1 (transfer), 12/1 (early decision), 12/20 (early action)

Average high school GPA:	3.66
Average freshman SAT verbal/math score:	652 / 634
Average freshman ACT score:	26
Number of applicants:	1,852
Number of applicants accepted:	1,138
Percentage of students from out of state:	27%
Total freshman enrollment:	310
Total enrollment:	1,234
Percentage of students who live in campus housing:	75%
Total tuition fee:	$24,351
Total cost with fees & expenses:	$31,960
Average financial aid package:	—

Where It's At

K's approximately 60-acre campus is located in the city of Kalamazoo, in southwestern Michigan. Students can walk or ride the bus (free with ID) to Kalamazoo's happening downtown area, home to the coffeehouses Something's Brewing and Scone Zone, the Fandango Tapas Bistro, the Kalamazoo Mall, and the Whole Art Theatre, among other establishments. Western Michigan University and the Kalamazoo Institute of the Arts are also nearby. Markin Glen Park has 190 acres of trails, as well as spots for camping and fishing. Each year, Kalamazoo hosts the Gilmore International Keyboard Festival. Detroit is about two hours away by car.

What It's Like

Although students tend to come from somewhat similar backgrounds—most grew up in Michigan—they're really eager to try new things. About 80 percent go abroad to such destinations as Kenya, Trinidad, Ireland, and Ecuador. Opportunities abound for world travel.

As part of the "K" Plan, students take courses in such subjects as philosophy and the natural sciences. The Creative Expressions component requires students to take a fine arts class, such as Playwriting or Digital Art. K also mandates that students take five terms of physical education.

For fun, students run across the Quad. Naked.

First-years fulfill the writing requirement through an interdisciplinary seminar, a small class focused on an event or theme; past offerings include How Artists Become Themselves and Religion and Ecology. During the fall, first-years also take the First-Year Forum, which helps them adjust to the pressures of college life.

Among the more than 25 majors are health sciences and anthropology/sociology. The "K" Plan requires everyone to complete a Senior Individualized Project (SIP), a creative work, research paper, or another academic undertaking. In addition to the SIP, seniors take written or oral comprehensive exams given by their major department.

Doing an internship and studying abroad are the two optional components of the "K" Plan. Roughly 80 percent of students do an internship at such places as the British Broadcasting Company and the Sierra Club.

Seniors may live off campus, but everyone else must live in one of K's six residential halls, including the doubles of DeWaters and the large suites of Severn. The Living Learning Housing Units, in which residents with common interests live together in houses, are another residential option.

Popular student activities include Frisbee golf and Frelon, the dance group. We've heard that students sometimes strip naked and "streak" across the Quad for fun. Naked or not, K's a cool place to go to college.

Keene State College

229 Main Street
Keene, NH 03435
(603) 352-1909
http://www.keene.edu/

Why It's Cool

KSC helps you get centered. With eight academic centers on campus, you'll never have a question go unanswered again. There's tutoring at the Math Center, high-tech labs at the Science Center, term paper help at the Center for Writing, and academic advising at the Elliot Center. The Child Development Center gives teachers-to-be face time with kids at its preschool, while the Community Research Center lets budding sociologists conduct interviews. You can hear genocide survivors speak at the Cohen Center for Holocaust studies and see a show at the Redfern Arts Center. At KSC, you're the center of attention.

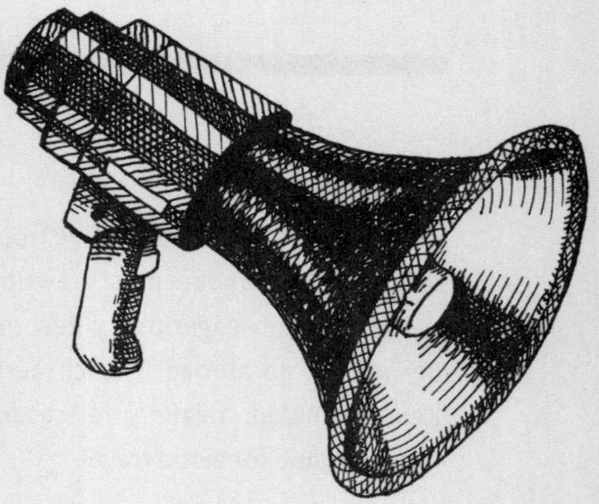

HEY, WHAT DO YOU SAY? TWICE A YEAR, KEENE STATE SPONSORS A SPEAKOUT CONFERENCE, A CHANCE FOR EVERYONE ON CAMPUS TO VOICE CONCERNS, TO VENT FRUSTRATIONS, AND TO SHARE OPINIONS.

The Details

Campus setting:	small town
Degrees:	bachelor's, master's
Calendar:	semesters
Public/Private:	public state
Number of full-time faculty:	184
Student-to-teacher ratio:	18:1

Admissions requirements:

- **Options:** deferred entrance
- **Application fee:** $25
- **Required:** essay or personal statement, high school transcript, letter of recommendation, SAT or ACT
- **Application deadlines:** 4/1 (freshmen), 5/1 (transfer)
- **Early decision:** —
- **Notification:** continuous (freshmen), continuous (transfer)

Average high school GPA:	2.99
Average freshman SAT verbal/math score:	505 / 499
Average freshman ACT score:	20
Number of applicants:	4,207
Number of applicants accepted:	2,997
Percentage of students from out of state:	47%
Total freshman enrollment:	1,072
Total enrollment:	4,937
Percentage of students who live in campus housing:	56%
Total in-state tuition, fees & expenses:	$13,466
Total out-of-state tuition, fees & expenses:	$19,906
Average financial aid package:	$7,258

Where It's At

KSC's 150-acre campus is located in Keene, New Hampshire. The National Trust for Historic Preservation has called the friendly, walkable town a "Currier and Ives landscape come to life," because of such eighteenth- and nineteenth-century buildings as Wyman Tavern and the Horatio Colony House. Each fall, during the Pumpkin Festival, Keene tries to set the world record for the greatest number of lit jack-o'-lanterns. Two of the area's biggest attractions are Mount Monadnock, the second-most-climbed mountain in the world, and the Colony Mill Marketplace, a group of restaurants and stores. Boston and Providence are both about two hours away by car.

What It's Like

At KSC, the administration really listens: Comments from SpeakOut are posted uncensored on a website, and administrators use the comments to make decisions about the future. Students and staff alike discuss such topics as "What does a twenty-first-century liberal arts education mean?"

It's OK to regress at the annual Children's Literature Festival.

Three schools make up KSC: the School of Sciences and Social Sciences, the School of Professional and Graduate Studies, and the School of Arts and Humanities. The more than 35 majors include management and film. Safety studies and education/early childhood development are two of the most popular specialties.

KSC's interdisciplinary minors include environmental studies and women's studies. Through the Cohen Center, students can work toward a minor in Holocaust studies. Other centers, such as the Math Center and the Center for Writing, let talented students work as tutors.

Housing options range from singles, doubles, triples, and quadruples in traditional dorms, such as Carle and Fiske, to the apartments of Pondside, Bushnell, and Tisdale. The all-you-can-eat menu at the new Zorn Dining Commons offers options for meat-eaters, picky eaters, pasta lovers, and vegetarians.

Among the many student organizations are the Art Collective, five sororities, two fraternities, the co-ed Greek house Delta Nu Psi, and the Architecture Club. There are 17 Division III athletic teams, including volleyball and men's and women's lacrosse.

Each winter, a group of KSC faculty, students, and staff head to Guatemala to build houses with Habitat for Humanity. The annual Children's Literature Festival features talks by illustrators, book signings, and readings. Several walking/running trails and cross-country skiing trails around campus are maintained by the recreational sports program. Intramural and club sport offerings include floor hockey, tennis, and rugby. We love schools where students are as keen as their college.

Easy Being Green: Most Environmentally Aware Schools

Reduce, Reuse, Recycle is more than a mantra at these schools—it's a lifestyle.

Bates College (P. 26)

College of the Atlantic (P. 62)

Earlham College (P. 78)

The Evergreen State College (P. 92)

Green Mountain College (P. 102)

Reed College (P. 166)

Sierra Nevada College (P. 184)

Unity College (P. 200)

Warren Wilson College (P. 220)

Willamette University (P. 226)

Knox College

2 East South Street
Galesburg, IL 61401
(309) 341-7000
http://www.knox.edu/

Why It's Cool

Be all that you can be. At Knox, you'll begin with a bold Educational Plan, an outline of courses you intend to take. Then, you'll choose two specializations from more than 60 academic areas. All the while, you'll maintain an ePortfolio, an online database all about you, including your activities and selections of your best academic work. If you're lucky, you'll take classes in the Old Jail, a former house of detention dating from 1874. The cell blocks—supposedly haunted—are frequently used to stimulate discussions about ghosts in the popular course Death and Dying. We salute your chilling innovation, Knox College.

GOBBLE, GOBBLE. THE WINNER OF THE ANNUAL KNOX-MONMOUTH FOOTBALL GAME GETS TO KEEP THE FAMOUS BRONZE TURKEY STATUE FOR ONE YEAR.

The Details

Campus setting:	small town
Degrees:	bachelor's
Calendar:	3 courses for each of 3 terms
Public/Private:	private nonprofit
Number of full-time faculty:	88
Student-to-teacher ratio:	12:1

Admissions requirements:

- **Options:** common application, deferred entrance, early admission, early action, electronic application
- **Application fee:** $35
- **Required:** essay or personal statement, high school transcript, 2 letters of recommendation, SAT or ACT
- **Application deadlines:** 2/1 (freshmen), 4/1 (transfer)
- **Early action:** 12/1
- **Notification:** 3/31 (freshmen), 4/30 (transfer), 12/31 (early action)

Average high school GPA:	—
Average freshman SAT verbal/math score:	631 / 616
Average freshman ACT score:	25
Number of applicants:	1,868
Number of applicants accepted:	1,352
Percentage of students from out of state:	46%
Total freshman enrollment:	363
Total enrollment:	1,205
Percentage of students who live in campus housing:	95%
Total tuition fee:	$24,960
Total cost with fees & expenses:	$32,238
Average financial aid package:	$21,390

Where It's At

Knox's 82-acre campus is located in Galesburg, a small town in western Illinois. Historic Seminary Street, the main thoroughfare, showcases the Galesburg Railroad Museum, Prairie Players Civic Theatre, and Uncle Billy's Bakery. Galesburg hosts events throughout the year, including Railroad Days in June, Community Day in November, and a holiday open house in December. The Carl Sandburg State House memorializes the childhood home of the American poet. Called the Jewel of Galesburg, the Orpheum Theatre shows movies and hosts musical performances. The 23 city parks have picnic spots, fishing holes, and hunting areas. Chicago is about four hours away by car.

What It's Like

Knox takes its motto, "Freedom to Flourish," seriously. Students relish the academic choices available, and more than 85 percent do an independent study or take a self-designed course. The academic calendar runs on a 3-3 system, which means that students take just three courses for each of the academic year's three terms. As part of the Educational Plan, students must complete two specializations, either two majors or a major and minor. The ePortfolio lets students keep a journal, amend their plans, and store their best work online.

Incoming students take the First-Year Preceptorial, an interdisciplinary seminar in which small groups discuss readings in the humanities and sciences. The seminar helps students think about what it means to study the liberal arts. As such, the course tries to answer questions like "What's the role of the individual in society?" and "What does it mean to be human?"

What does it mean to be human?

Close to 20 academic departments offer more than 35 majors, which include neuroscience and black studies. Ten preprofessional and cooperative programs let students prepare for advanced study in such subjects as architecture and optometry. Knox is also one of only eight colleges with a Peace Corps preparatory program.

The Repertory Theatre Term draws students from all majors and disciplines. Over a ten-week period, students mount productions of two full-length plays. Rep Term is the only undergraduate repertory theater program in the United States.

The student body is welcoming, free-spirited, and diverse: international and minority students make up close to 23 percent. Just about everyone lives on campus in one of the 15 residence halls. More than 100 student organizations focus on culture, politics, and sports.

To foster community, each year, on Pumphandle Day, everyone on campus—from students to faculty to administrators and staff—lines up. Each person then takes a turn moving down the line, shaking everyone's hands as they go. Knox is one friendly place.

Lewis & Clark College

0615 Southwest Palatine Hill Road **(503) 768-7000**
Portland, OR 97219 **http://www.lclark.edu/**

Why It's Cool

The spirit of exploration lives on at Lewis & Clark. At this school, you'll investigate, uncover, and discover—all before you've even set foot in a classroom. Each fall, College Outdoors sponsors an optional pre-orientation trip for first-years. Sign up, and you'll spend ten days rafting down the Deschutes River or hiking through a rain forest in the Cascade Mountains. Want to give back *and* do something adventurous? Try one of the Breakaway Service Trips—you'll build trails with the U.S. Forest Service or hoe a row at a local sustainable farm. We dig it here, and we bet you will too.

TAKE A HIKE! THE COLLEGE OUTDOORS PROGRAM TAKES STUDENTS ON TREKS THROUGH OREGON'S RAIN FORESTS.

The Details

Campus setting:	urban
Degrees:	bachelor's, master's, doctoral
Calendar:	semesters
Public/Private:	private nonprofit
Number of full-time faculty:	213
Student-to-teacher ratio:	12:1

Admissions requirements:

- **Options:** common application, deferred entrance, early admission, early action, electronic application
- **Application fee:** $50
- **Required:** essay or personal statement, high school transcript, 2 letters of recommendation, SAT, ACT, or academic portfolio
- **Application deadlines:** 2/1 (freshmen), 7/1 (transfer)
- **Early action:** 11/15
- **Notification:** 4/1 (freshmen), continuous (transfer), 1/15 (early action)

Average high school GPA:	3.65
Average freshman SAT verbal/math score:	652 / 636
Average freshman ACT score:	26
Number of applicants:	3,826
Number of applicants accepted:	2,468
Percentage of students from out of state:	80%
Total freshman enrollment:	537
Total enrollment:	3,259
Percentage of students who live in campus housing:	64%
Total tuition fee:	$26,154
Total cost with fees & expenses:	$34,284
Average financial aid package:	$24,380

Where It's At

Lewis and Clark's 137-acre campus is located in Portland, Oregon. Known as the "City of Roses," Portland boasts four public parks, including the International Rose Test Garden. An extensive light-rail system connects the city's neighborhoods, such as upscale Nob Hill and the Pearl District. Portland is also home to the Trail Blazers (NBA), filmmaker Gus Van Sant, and Powell's Books, one of the nation's largest bookstores. More than 300 vendors descend on Portland every weekend for the Saturday Market, the longest continuously running craft fair in the country. Students road trip to the Pacific Ocean (80 miles away) and Seattle (180 miles away).

What It's Like

Exploration is built into life at Lewis and Clark, as reflected by the school's motto: "To Explore, to Discover, to Work Together." All students must demonstrate a thorough understanding of another culture, either by taking a two-semester course about a culture or country or by studying abroad. More than 45 percent choose the latter option, selecting from among 25 destinations on six continents.

At the on-campus Oregon Center for Inquiry and Social Innovation, students can attend workshops and lectures on current events, led by the think-and-do-tank's experts. At the Rusty Nail, a student-run café, students can see local bands and participate in open mikes. But there's no excuse for not studying: Watzek Library is open 24 hours a day on weekdays. The student body—filled with hippies, outdoorsy folks, and brains—tends to lean to the left politically.

Lewis and Clark has three main academic divisions: arts and humanities, mathematical and natural sciences, and social sciences. Within the divisions are more than 20 departments and 25 majors, including biochemistry and East Asian studies. First-years take the two-semester Inventing America, a class that examines all aspects of society from the founding of the republic to contemporary times.

First-years and sophomores are required to live on campus in one of eight halls, which are either co-ed or women-only. Within some of these halls are theme floors, including Women in Math and Science and Outdoor Pursuits, so that students with similar interests can live together. Many juniors and seniors choose to live in the on-campus apartment complexes.

To explore, to discover, to work together

Among the several student organizations on campus are the Womyn's Center, the Environmental Affairs Symposium, and the Sailing Club. There are 19 Division III athletic teams. The New Student Breakaway Adventures take newbies on trips to exotic places, such as the Grand Canyon and Washington's Ancient Forest, before school starts.

Linfield College

900 Southeast Baker Street **(503) 883-2200**
McMinnville, OR 97128 **http://www.linfield.edu/**

Why It's Cool

Inquiring minds take the Linfield Curriculum. The curriculum begins with the Inquiry Seminar, which teaches you about college-level writing. Then, you'll take courses in five so-called Areas of Inquiry: ultimate questions; natural world; individuals, systems, and societies; images and arts; and vital past. You'll also take an Inquiry Seminar, an interdisciplinary class designed around a theme like creative lives. Sound good? It gets better. The required colloquium for new students will tell you everything you need to know about life at Linfield, from how to manage your time to how to major in economics to where to check your email.

BERNARD'S GARDEN CORN MAZE IS AMONG THE COOLEST THINGS ABOUT LIFE AT LINFIELD IN MCMINNVILLE, OREGON.

The Details

Campus setting:	small town
Degrees:	bachelor's
Calendar:	4-1-4
Public/Private:	private religious
Number of full-time faculty:	101
Student-to-teacher ratio:	13:1

Admissions requirements:

- **Options:** common application, deferred entrance, early action, electronic application
- **Application fee:** $40
- **Required:** essay or personal statement, high school transcript, letter of recommendation, SAT or ACT
- **Application deadlines:** 2/15 (freshmen), 4/15 (transfer)
- **Early action:** 11/15
- **Notification:** 4/1 (freshmen), 5/15 (transfer), 1/15 (early action)

Average high school GPA:	3.56
Average freshman SAT verbal/math score:	564 / 570
Average freshman ACT score:	24
Number of applicants:	1,864
Number of applicants accepted:	1,459
Percentage of students from out of state:	42%
Total freshman enrollment:	433
Total enrollment:	1,656
Percentage of students who live in campus housing:	74%
Total tuition fee:	$21,800
Total cost with fees & expenses:	$29,042
Average financial aid package:	$15,614

Where It's At

Linfield's 193-acre campus is located in McMinnville, a small town in northwestern Oregon nicknamed "Mac." In addition to the historic Third Street area, Mac is home to the Evergreen Aviation Museum; Shari's, a popular restaurant and hangout; and the Silver Falls State Park, featuring ten waterfalls. Every year, Turkey Rama celebrates the area's past connections to the fowl industry during three fun-filled days of dawn-to-dusk entertainment, food, and craft fairs. The Oregon coast and the 99W Drive In, which shows recent movies, are both an hour from campus. Salem, the state capital, is about 45 minutes away, and Portland is about an hour away.

What It's Like

Linfield's all about asking questions—and getting answers. Everybody must take two courses in each of the Five Areas of Inquiry, which emphasize writing, critical thinking, and in-depth understanding. Sample inquiry classes include Environmental Literature, Gender Issues in Education and Sport, and Electronic Media in the Arts. Many math and science classes hold optional weekly study sessions.

Linfield's all about asking questions.

Another big part of academics at Linfield is Experiential Learning. These courses emphasize hands-on education. Students get practical experience through internships, peer education, and paracurricular courses (classes in physical or creative activities, such as dance or working on the literary magazine).

Because most departments offer experiential courses, classes might include field trips to study local ecology with the environmental studies department; playing on the intercollegiate tennis team with the department of health, human performance, and athletics; and an individual program of reading with the English department. There are more than 40 majors, ranging from athletic training to music to finance.

The academic calendar features two semesters and an optional four-week January Term. Rather than heading home, students can get academic credit for taking American Sign Language at the American School for the Deaf in Salem, traveling to India to study its health-care system, or doing creative writing in Britain. Students can spend a semester abroad in cool places throughout the world, including Hong Kong and Ecuador. It's no surprise that 50 percent of students take advantage of this option.

Students live in one of 18 halls, co-ed and single-sex, and seven so-called suburb properties, houses and apartments owned by Linfield. The more than 80 clubs on campus include the Fishing Club, the Role-Playing Council, and the Vegan/Veggie Club. About 30 percent of students go Greek in one of four fraternities and four sororities. There are 16 Division III athletic teams.

Loyola University Chicago

820 North Michigan Avenue
Chicago, IL 60611

(773) 274-3000
http://www.luc.edu/

Why It's Cool

Pssssst. Loyola has got a deal for you. At this school, you'll get four campuses for the price of one. Yup, you read that right. You'll take classes at any of the three locations in Chicago. And you can spend a summer, semester, or year on the fourth campus, the Rome Center in Italy. From the manicured lawns and humanities classes at Lake Shore to the all-new apartments in Water Tower, from the top-notch library in Maywood to a room atop the highest hill in Rome . . . you'll get the best of four worlds at this school.

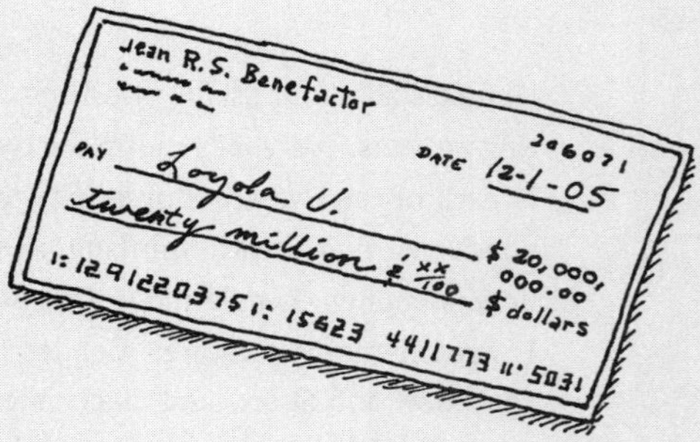

KA-CHING. IN DECEMBER 2005, LOYOLA RECEIVED A $20 MILLION GIFT FROM WEALTHY BENEFACTORS.

The Details

Campus setting:	urban
Degrees:	bachelor's, master's, doctoral
Calendar:	semesters
Public/Private:	private religious
Number of full-time faculty:	502
Student-to-teacher ratio:	13:1

Admissions requirements:

- **Options:** common application, deferred entrance, electronic application
- **Application fee:** $25
- **Required:** essay or personal statement, high school transcript, SAT or ACT
- **Application deadlines:** 4/1 (freshmen), 8/1 (transfer)
- **Early decision:** —
- **Notification:** continuous (freshmen), continuous (transfer)

Average high school GPA:	3.50
Average freshman SAT verbal/math score:	590 / 585
Average freshman ACT score:	24
Number of applicants:	11,296
Number of applicants accepted:	9,393
Percentage of students from out of state:	34%
Total freshman enrollment:	1,784
Total enrollment:	13,909
Percentage of students who live in campus housing:	29%
Total tuition fee:	$23,100
Total cost with fees & expenses:	$33,696
Average financial aid package:	$16,465

Where It's At

Loyola has three campuses in and around Chicago, Illinois. Located in residential northern Chicago, the Lake Shore campus is Loyola's main campus. Next door to the more urban Water Tower campus is the Magnificent Mile, featuring five shopping centers. Finally, the Maywood campus, home to the Medical Center, is in a primarily suburban area. Chicago has 54 museums, including the Art Institute and Museum of Science and Industry; the White Sox (MLB), Cubs (MLB), Bears (NFL), and Bulls (NBA); and the world's largest free public zoo, the Lincoln Park Zoo. Each summer, the gigantic Taste of Chicago features food, musical acts, and fireworks.

What It's Like

We hear Loyola's not as cliquey as some other schools, perhaps because a lot of students come from the Chicago area and commute. Loyola's Jesuit Catholic affiliation also helps foster the open-minded atmosphere. The Jesuits encourage diversity, so all faiths (or lack thereof) are not only welcomed but recruited. There's even a mosque inside the student center. All told, minorities make up almost 40 percent of the student body.

Preparing people to lead extraordinary lives

Lake Shore is the main campus, home to Cudahy Library, the College of Arts and Sciences, and several residential halls. The large singles and doubles of Mertz Hall have views of the city and Lake Michigan, and a lot of the newly renovated apartments in Georgetown Hall have fireplaces. Upperclass students have the option of living in the all-new high-rise at the Water Tower campus, just steps away from downtown Chicago.

Loyola's motto is "Preparing People to Live Extraordinary Lives." Everything on campus is geared toward helping students grow as individuals, from the core curriculum to the close relationship Loyola fosters with Chicago. The Center for Urban Research and Learning specializes in urban studies and encourages students to use Chicago as their classroom. Other courses offer service-learning components, such as the Homeless Clinic, staffed by nursing students.

Among the many majors are studio arts and biochemistry. Loyola also offers 16 combined bachelor's and master's degree programs, including a BS/MS in criminal justice. The high-tech Life Sciences Research and Education Center only helps strengthen an already amazing science program.

As part of the core curriculum, every student takes classes in ten "knowledge areas," including philosophical knowledge. Courses range from Photography to Business Ethics to War and War Experience, Ancient and Modern.

There are more than 125 student groups on campus, including the Aca'fellas singing group and Hip-Hop Congress. As the Ramblers, students compete on 11 Division I athletic teams.

Macalester College

1600 Grand Avenue
St. Paul, MN 55105

(651) 696-6000
http://www.macalester.edu/

Why It's Cool

Macalester puts the whole world in your hands. It's true. A plural, international outlook influences every aspect of college life: As you walk to class, you'll pass the United Nations flag, flown alongside the U.S. flag. You'll hang out with a diverse group of students (14 percent of students come from more than 80 countries). You might even live in one of six language houses, in which you'll speak a language other than English while at home. Or you can study abroad through the International Center. Given all this, it's no surprise that international studies is one of the most popular majors.

KOFI ANNAN, SECRETARY-GENERAL OF THE UNITED NATIONS, IS A NOTABLE MACALESTER ALUM.

The Details

Campus setting:	urban
Degrees:	bachelor's
Calendar:	semesters
Public/Private:	private religious
Number of full-time faculty:	151
Student-to-teacher ratio:	11:1

Admissions requirements:

- **Options:** common application, deferred entrance, early admission, early decision, electronic application
- **Application fee:** $40
- **Required:** essay or personal statement, high school transcript, 3 letters of recommendation, SAT or ACT
- **Application deadlines:** 1/15 (freshmen), 4/15 (transfer)
- **Early decision:** 11/15
- **Notification:** 4/1 (freshmen), 5/15 (transfer), 12/15 (early decision)

Average high school GPA:	—
Average freshman SAT verbal/math score:	688 / 665
Average freshman ACT score:	26
Number of applicants:	4,405
Number of applicants accepted:	1,706
Percentage of students from out of state:	75%
Total freshman enrollment:	486
Total enrollment:	1,900
Percentage of students who live in campus housing:	69%
Total tuition fee:	$28,642
Total cost with fees & expenses:	$37,473
Average financial aid package:	$23,461

Where It's At

Macalester's 53-acre campus is located in St. Paul, Minnesota. Grand Avenue, a strip of coffeehouses, bakeries, and art galleries, lies next to the campus. Minneapolis and St. Paul form the Twin Cities, one of the largest metropolitan areas in the United States. The area has professional sports teams, including the Minnesota Twins (MLB), Timberwolves (NBA), and Lynx (WNBA); two zoos and the Under Water Adventures Aquarium; the Circus Juventas, which trains kids in the circus arts; and the Chanhassen Dinner Theatres, the largest restaurant in Minnesota. Nearby attractions include the gargantuan Mall of America and the Museum of Questionable Medical Devices. At the Minnesota Landscape Arboretum, visitors can stroll through 1,000 lush, landscaped acres.

What It's Like

Multicultural isn't just a buzzword at Macalester. Students come from all over the world to attend this college, considered one of the coolest schools in the United States. Both students and administrators see the school as competitive with the Ivies—in admissions and academics. You'll work really hard, but you'll also be exposed to tons of new people, cultures, and experiences.

Everybody must take introductory-level classes in the liberal arts, including math and writing. To ensure an educational balance, students aren't allowed to take too many courses in any one area. Two diversity courses are required and can be fulfilled by such classes as Japanimation and Manga and Feminism/Representation/Film.

This is one cool school (and not just because it's located in Minnesota).

Macalester offers more than 35 majors and 30 minors. Several departments have classes with an international focus. Students may also specialize in Asian studies or Russian, Central, and East European studies. Additionally, students have access to study abroad programs in roughly 65 countries.

Each year, the Macalester International Roundtable invites several luminaries to contribute essays on a broad theme, such as nature and globalization. Both students and faculty are given an opportunity to publicly respond to the essays' arguments. Everything is then published in the *Macalester International*. Other annual events are Springfest, a campus-wide party with live music and dancing, and Midnight Breakfast, in which the president, faculty, and staff serve students breakfast before final exams begin.

Students live in one of ten residence halls, and first-years and sophomores are required to live on campus. At the six language houses, students speak Spanish, French, Chinese, Russian, Japanese, or Hebrew.

Bridges, which explores cross-cultural issues, and Fresh Concepts, a sketch comedy and improv group, are two popular student organizations. Macalester students get political by hosting protests and joining groups like Amnesty International. The college offers 19 Division III varsity teams, including fast-pitch softball.

It's All Greek to You: The Most Happening Fraternity/Sorority Scenes

Some say that going Greek is like buying your friends; others say that joining a fraternity or sorority means you instantly make hundreds of friends for life. We say the choice is yours—but at these schools Greeks are gods.

Manhattanville College

2900 Purchase Street
Purchase, NY 10577
(914) 694-2200
http://www.manhattanville.edu/

Why It's Cool

There may be a castle on campus, but Manhattanville's no elitist bastion. Here, you'll meet hordes of nice people from more than 50 countries and 35 states. You'll hang out together in four dorms and small classes (always fewer than 50 students). You'll go to socials where you can informally meet-and-greet with faculty. Each spring, the annual International Bazaar lets you sample food and watch performances from around the world. And anyone can apply to spend the semester studying in New York City, San Francisco, Madrid, or Oxford. Now, that's democratic.

MANHATTANVILLE'S QUADRANGLE, A POPULAR GRASSY HANGOUT IN FRONT OF THE CAMPUS CASTLE, WAS DESIGNED BY FEDERICK LAW OLMSTEAD, WHO ALSO DESIGNED CENTRAL PARK.

The Details

Campus setting:	suburban
Degrees:	bachelor's, master's
Calendar:	semesters
Public/Private:	private nonprofit
Number of full-time faculty:	90
Student-to-teacher ratio:	12:1

Admissions requirements:

- **Options:** common application, deferred entrance, early admission, early decision, electronic application
- **Application fee:** $50
- **Required:** essay or personal statement, high school transcript, 2 letters of recommendation, SAT or ACT
- **Application deadlines:** 3/1 (freshmen), 3/1 (transfer)
- **Early decision:** 12/1
- **Notification:** continuous (freshmen), continuous (transfer), 12/31 (early decision)

Average high school GPA:	3.0
Average freshman SAT verbal/math score:	538 / 526
Average freshman ACT score:	23
Number of applicants:	3,336
Number of applicants accepted:	1,875
Percentage of students from out of state:	28%
Total freshman enrollment:	438
Total enrollment:	2,608
Percentage of students who live in campus housing:	85%
Total tuition fee:	$23,620
Total cost with fees & expenses:	$35,500
Average financial aid package:	$20,888

Where It's At

Manhattanville's 100-acre campus is located in Purchase, New York, a small town in suburban Westchester County that offers more than 17,000 acres of parks. Other area draws include the Hudson River Museum and the scenic Ferncliff Cemetery, as well as art museums, performing art centers, and Sunnyside, the home of Washington Irving. Thoroughbred horses run the half-mile track—and compete for big purses—at Yonkers Raceway. Nearby Playland, an amusement park, features rides, picnic spots, mini-golf, and skating. New York City, just 30 minutes away, has the Metropolitan Museum of Art, the Knicks (NBA) and Liberty (WNBA) teams, the Statue of Liberty, and 18,000 restaurants, among other amazing attractions.

What It's Like

This campus cares. Putting politics aside, Manhattanville sponsors My Soldier, a unique program that pairs American soldiers with civilian pen pals who support the troops by sending packages. Volunteering is also big on campus, with students putting in close to 19,000 hours of community service per year.

All first-years must take the two-semester Preceptorial, an interdisciplinary course that develops communication and critical-thinking skills. Students read a variety of texts, from ancient to contemporary, all of which relate to abstract themes, such as love or knowledge. Other general education requirements include an introduction to using the library and courses in science, a foreign language, and the fine arts.

As sophomores, and again as seniors, students formally submit a portfolio of learning goals and writing samples, among other documents. This system ensures that each student actively participates in his/her education and that everybody gets individual attention from a panel of faculty.

Manhattanville offers 45 areas of study, plus a design-your-own interdisciplinary major. As part of the Semester in New York City, students live in Brooklyn and take classes or do an internship. Several study abroad programs allow students to earn Manhattanville credit while studying in such places as Ireland or Spain.

Spend a semester in New York City, and live in a Brooklyn brownstone.

The more than 50 campus clubs range from Students Against Animal Cruelty to Minds in Motion, a dance group, to deejaying at WMVL, the campus radio station. The 14 Division III athletic teams include men's and women's ice hockey.

First-years live in the co-ed Spellman Hall, while sophomores, juniors, and seniors choose from three traditional dorms: Founders Hall, Dammann Hall, and Tenney Hall. About 85 percent of students live on campus.

Every fall, campus leaders have their accomplishments recognized during a widely attended candlelight ceremony; every spring, the International Student Association puts on the super-popular International Bazaar.

Marlboro College

PO Box A, South Road
Marlboro, VT 05344
(802) 257-4333
http://www.marlboro.edu/

Why It's Cool

Marlboro's one smokin' school. No stodgy requirements. No preset curriculum. No classes for seniors. First, you'll take courses in whatever interests you—from Argentine Tango to Thinking Anthropologically. Then, you'll develop your own Plan of Concentration, which might involve a traditional specialization like astronomy or an interdisciplinary, individualized plan, which might combine subjects like art history, pottery, and chemistry. For your upperclass years, you'll switch to tutorials, working independently on your plan and regularly touching base with your advisers. If you're a free spirit looking for an intellectual challenge, then this might be the perfect place for you.

AT MARLBORO'S GRADUATE CENTER PROFESSORS HAVE BEGUN RECORDING THEIR LECTURES AND MAKING THEM AVAILABLE AS PODCASTS. SOME STUDENTS HAVE EVEN BEEN GIVEN FREE IPODS.

The Details

Campus setting:	rural
Degrees:	bachelor's, master's
Calendar:	semesters
Public/Private:	private nonprofit
Number of full-time faculty:	37
Student-to-teacher ratio:	8:1

Admissions requirements:

- **Options:** common application, deferred entrance, early admission, early decision, early action, electronic application
- **Application fee:** $50
- **Required:** essay or personal statement, high school transcript, 2 letters of recommendation, SAT or ACT, SAT Subject Tests (recommended)
- **Application deadlines:** 2/15 (freshmen), 4/1 (transfer), 1/15 (early action)
- **Early decision:** 11/15
- **Notification:** 4/1 (freshmen), 4/15 (transfer), 12/15 (early decision), 2/1 (early action)

Average high school GPA:	3.34
Average freshman SAT verbal/math score:	639 / 586
Average freshman ACT score:	27
Number of applicants:	367
Number of applicants accepted:	247
Percentage of students from out of state:	87%
Total freshman enrollment:	101
Total enrollment:	418
Percentage of students who live in campus housing:	82%
Total tuition fee:	$26,940
Total cost with fees & expenses:	$36,580
Average financial aid package:	$16,791

Where It's At

Marlboro's 360-acre campus is located on a former dairy farm in the tiny town of Marlboro, near the Green Mountains of southern Vermont. Classes are held in converted barns or structures built by students, staff, and faculty. Outdoor activities abound, from hiking the Appalachian Trail to skiing at Mount Snow or Bromley. During the summer, the campus hosts the renowned Marlboro Music Festival for classical music. About 20 minutes away, artsy Brattleboro offers the Brattleboro Museum and Art Center, the Vermont Theatre Company, and the Latchis Theater. Hartford is about 90 minutes away, and Boston is about three hours away by car.

What It's Like

This school is small, the politics are progressive, and the academic environment is tough. Classes average just ten students, so it's impossible to slack off and get away with it. Students here are proud of their fierce self-reliance and willingness to chart individual academic paths. Still, faculty members are totally accessible and always available for advice.

First-years begin formulating their Plans of Concentration by taking classes that interest them. As sophomores, students submit a preliminary plan that states what they intend to study. As juniors, they follow these plans and file a final plan at the end of the year. All seniors work independently, meeting frequently with their faculty advisers for one-on-one tutorials. Interdisciplinarity is encouraged.

Students here are proud of their fierce self-reliance.

Plans culminate in Plan Projects, which might range from a research paper to a photography exhibit. Seniors also sit for a lengthy oral examination given by at least two members of the Marlboro faculty and an outside evaluator (often a professor from another school).

All students must complete the Clear Writing Program. At the end of their first or second semester, students submit a 20-page portfolio of academic writing completed during a regular course or a writing seminar. Students whose portfolios don't make the grade must submit a new portfolio the following semester. The academic intensity works: Almost 70 percent of graduates go on to graduate or professional school.

The World Studies Program lets students specialize in international relations. Students in this field must do an internship in another country for at least six months. The nearby graduate School for International Training accepts Marlboro students on its 57 or so programs, including Development Studies in Uganda. Almost half of all students go abroad.

Most everyone lives on campus, in one of nine residence halls, two cabins, four apartments, six cottages, and three houses. There aren't any varsity teams, but the Outdoor Program sponsors all sorts of athletic activities, including Quidditch, a game from the Harry Potter series.

Miami University

501 East High Street
Oxford, OH 45056
(513) 529-1809
http://www.muohio.edu/

Why It's Cool

It's a high-tech world out there, and Miami shows you how to network your way through it. At the Center for Interactive Media Studies (IMS), you can put a high-tech spin on any major. If you're into English, sign up for Desktop Publishing. Econ majors might want to check out eBusiness, Entrepreneurship and Venture Capital. And anyone can join the IMS consulting firm, which designs websites and develops interactive programs for companies like Proctor and Gamble. The main IMS classroom even has a lava lamp, so you can zone out while you learn. Groovy *and* practical.

MANY MIAMI GRADUATES HAVE GONE ON TO SUCCESSFUL CAREERS AS ATHLETIC COACHES, LEADING SOME TO CALL THE SCHOOL "THE CRADLE OF COACHES."

The Details

Campus setting:	small town
Degrees:	bachelor's, master's, doctoral
Calendar:	semesters
Public/Private:	public state-related
Number of full-time faculty:	849
Student-to-teacher ratio:	17:1

Admissions requirements:

- **Options:** common application, deferred entrance, early decision, early action, electronic application
- **Application fee:** $45
- **Required:** high school transcript, letter of recommendation, SAT or ACT
- **Application deadlines:** 1/31 (freshmen), 5/1 (transfer), — (early action)
- **Early decision:** 11/1
- **Notification:** 3/15 (freshmen), continuous (transfer), 12/15 (early decision), — (early action)

Average high school GPA:	3.7
Average freshman SAT verbal/math score:	608 / 625
Average freshman ACT score:	25
Number of applicants:	14,977
Number of applicants accepted:	10,632
Percentage of students from out of state:	28%
Total freshman enrollment:	3,422
Total enrollment:	17,151
Percentage of students who live in campus housing:	45%
Total in-state tuition, fees & expenses:	$17,452
Total out-of-state tuition, fees & expenses:	$27,452
Average financial aid package:	$15,358

Where It's At

Miami's 2,000-acre campus is located in Oxford, an idyllic college town in southwestern Ohio. The Miami Metro bus takes students around town. Local attractions include 11 parks, the Fitton Center for the Creative Arts, and the OxAct theater group. Every year, local and national bands play in downtown Oxford as part of the Outdoor Summer Music Festival. Walking and biking are popular along stretches of the Miami-Erie Canal. Cincinnati, about 45 minutes away, is home to the Bengals (NFL) and Reds (MLB), the Krohn Conservatory, the Cincinnati Zoo and Botanical Gardens, and the National Underground Railroad Freedom Center. Dayton, about an hour away, has the RiverScape MetroPark, the Art Institute, and America's Packard Museum.

What It's Like

Greeks rule the social scene at Miami. Five fraternities were founded here, leading some to nickname the school "the Mother of Fraternities." More than 50 fraternities and sororities have chapters on campus. Still, Miami boasts more than 300 student groups and organizations, so there's plenty to do for Greeks and non-Greeks alike.

At any given moment, about 1,000 Miami students are studying around the world. Students at Miami's Luxembourg campus live with local families and take classes in a thirteenth-century castle. Another popular option is to take an international summer workshop; recent offerings include Biodiversity in Kenya and the People and Culture of Tibet.

Miami loves its broomball: There are more than 450 teams on campus.

Broomball is the most popular extracurricular activity. Based on ice hockey, broomball requires players to use sticks to move a big orange ball around the ice and score goals. But rather than wear pads or skates, participants dress in sweatpants and sneakers. At Miami alone, more than 6,000 students compete on 450 teams. There are also 16 Division I athletic teams.

Among the roughly 100 majors are public administration and architecture. The ten pre-professional programs range from podiatry to environmental management/forestry. With the Over-the-Rhine Design/Build Studio, architecture and interior design majors build and refurbish homes in the impoverished neighborhoods of Cincinnati.

As part of the Miami Plan, students take at least three courses outside of their major and do an intensive senior project, such as an experiment or performance, within their major. Other requirements include fine arts and natural science courses. First-years take a writing-intensive seminar, such as Coming of Age in America and Coffee and Globalization.

The 36 residence halls are organized around four quads—and there's not a single high-rise in sight. We hear that the most liberal halls are Clawson, Havinghurst, McKee, and Thomson on Western Quad. First-years choose residence halls based on their theme, including leadership, excellence, and community.

Millsaps College

1701 North State Street **(601) 974-1000**
Jackson, MS 39210 **http://www.millsaps.edu/**

Why It's Cool

Paging Doctor [insert your last name] . . . If you daydream about saving lives or finding the cure for cancer, then Millsaps has got the program for you: Medical Mentorship. You'll shadow MDs as they make their rounds in hospitals or check in with patients during office visits. Each week, you'll hang out with your mentor, a real-life health-care professional, and discuss issues related to the medical field. Couple this program with Millsaps's strong biology and chemistry departments, and you could be on your way to med school in no time flat or, as they say in the ER, *stat*.

THE OLDEST BUILDING ON CAMPUS, THE JAMES OBSERVATORY, IS A POPULAR SPOT FOR WATCHING COMETS, PICKING OUT CONSTELLATIONS, AND WISHING ON STARS.

The Details

Campus setting:	urban
Degrees:	bachelor's, master's
Calendar:	semesters
Public/Private:	private religious
Number of full-time faculty:	92
Student-to-teacher ratio:	12:1

Admissions requirements:

- **Options:** common application, deferred entrance, early admission, early action, electronic application
- **Application fee:** $25
- **Required:** essay or personal statement, high school transcript, letter of recommendation, SAT or ACT
- **Application deadlines:** continuous (freshmen), continuous (transfer)
- **Early action:** 12/1
- **Notification:** 8/1 (freshmen), continuous (transfer), 12/20 (early action)

Average high school GPA:	3.52
Average freshman SAT verbal/math score:	596 / 590
Average freshman ACT score:	24
Number of applicants:	1,007
Number of applicants accepted:	857
Percentage of students from out of state:	47%
Total freshman enrollment:	278
Total enrollment:	1,146
Percentage of students who live in campus housing:	82%
Total tuition fee:	$19,490
Total cost with fees & expenses:	$29,256
Average financial aid package:	$17,064

Where It's At

Millsaps's 100-acre campus is located in Jackson, the capital of Mississippi. Jackson boasts several attractions, including the antebellum Governor's Mansion and the Old Capitol building, Ballet Mississippi, the Mississippi Symphony Orchestra, the Jackson Zoological Park, the Mississippi Museum of Natural Science, and the New Stage Theatre, which offers musicals, plays, and other performances. Campers, hikers, and hunters haunt LeFleur's Bluff, a 305-acre park in Jackson. The park also hosts a variety of annual events, such as the Chimneyville Crafts Festival and the Canton Flea Market. New Orleans is about three hours away by car.

What It's Like

The United Methodist Church supports Millsaps through scholarship programs, but both the religious and the nonreligious student will find a home on campus. In fact, Millsaps is generally considered to be a liberal enclave within the more conservative state of Mississippi.

Perhaps the most distinctive aspect of life at Millsaps is the optional Faith and Work Initiative. Through lectures, discussions, and community service, students learn how their spiritual beliefs can inform their vocational choices. "Immersion" experiences allow students to explore their faith off campus, in such locations as San Francisco and New York City.

Find your faith in New York or San Francisco.

In addition to great programs in chemistry and biology, Millsaps offers undergraduate majors in business and classics; there are close to 30 majors in all. The competitive Millsaps Medical Mentorship gives aspiring doctors and premed students the chance to learn more about careers, as does Alpha Epsilon Delta, the prehealth honor society. Millsaps also offers preprofessional law, social work, teaching, and ministerial programs.

All students must take ten classes as part of the required core curriculum, including Introduction to Liberal Studies (which covers the basics of college-level reading and writing), as well as courses in such subjects as Western civilization and the natural sciences.

Eighty-two percent of students live on campus, drawn to the affordable dorms (mostly doubles) and the Campus Life Complex, at the heart of Millsaps. Both the new Physical Activities Center and renovated Campbell College Center (the student union) make up the complex.

Fourteen Division III athletic teams compete as the Majors, including the women's basketball team. Other student organizations range from the Cycling and Triathlon Club to Habitat for Humanity. There are 12 fraternities and sororities.

Through Millsaps's study abroad programs, students can learn Spanish in Costa Rica or examine archaeological findings in Albania. Each year, the huge festival known as Major Madness brings bands to campus for a spring celebration.

Mount Holyoke College

50 College Street
South Hadley, MA 01075
(413) 538-2000
http://www.mtholyoke.edu/

Why It's Cool

Sorry, boys, but Mount Holyoke College is all about girl power. Women come from all over the world to attend this highly selective school. One in three MHC students is from another country or belongs to a minority group. Smart thinking, ladies, because this choice pays off. Recent studies show that 94 percent of MHC students are employed or in graduate or professional school within a year of graduation. But students here don't just study; they also participate in more than 100 organizations. You go, girls.

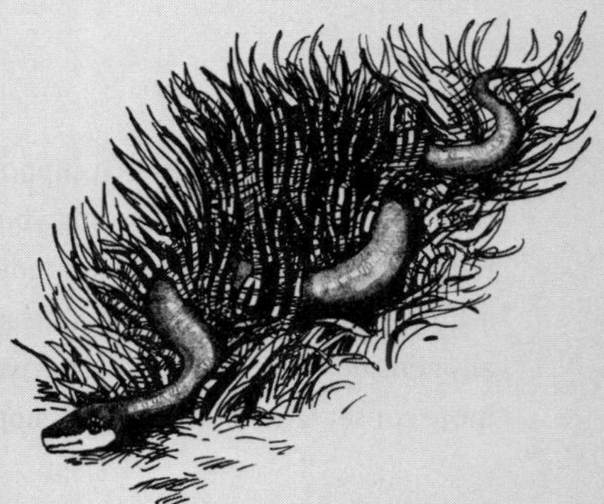

POET EMILY DICKINSON, WRITER OF SUCH WORKS AS "A NARROW FELLOW IN THE GRASS," SPENT A YEAR STUDYING AT MHC.

The Details

Campus setting:	small town
Degrees:	bachelor's
Calendar:	4-1-4
Public/Private:	private nonprofit
Number of full-time faculty:	209
Student-to-teacher ratio:	9:1

Admissions requirements:

- **Options:** common application, deferred entrance, early admission, early decision, electronic application
- **Application fee:** $55
- **Required:** essay or personal statement, high school transcript, 2 letters of recommendation
- **Application deadlines:** 1/15 (freshmen), 5/15 (transfer)
- **Early decision:** 11/15
- **Notification:** 4/1 (freshmen), 6/15 (transfer), 1/1 (early decision)

Average high school GPA:	3.59
Average freshman SAT verbal/math score:	652 / 628
Average freshman ACT score:	26
Number of applicants:	2,912
Number of applicants accepted:	1,643
Percentage of students from out of state:	74%
Total freshman enrollment:	556
Total enrollment:	2,073
Percentage of students who live in campus housing:	93%
Total tuition fee:	$30,770
Total cost with fees & expenses:	$40,748
Average financial aid package:	$26,176

Where It's At

MHC's 800-acre campus is located in South Hadley, a small town in western Massachusetts. Across the street from the school, the Village Commons shopping complex features movie theaters, restaurants, stores, and the Odyssey Bookshop, the largest independent bookstore in the region. Free buses run frequently to Amherst and Northampton, fun towns with funky stores and great places for ice cream, including Bart's and Herrell's. Nearby Springfield has the Basketball Hall of Fame. Skiers go to local Mount Tom or Vermont's Killington. Boston is only 90 minutes away by car, and New York City is about three hours away.

What It's Like

MHC is part of the Five Colleges consortium, so students are able to take classes at nearby Hampshire, Smith, and Amherst Colleges, as well as the University of Massachusetts–Amherst. A free bus system links the schools, enabling close to 30,000 students to use the resources of all five institutions. Students can receive Five College Certificates in several interdisciplinary programs, including Buddhist studies and logic. It's like five colleges for the price of one. The approximately majors at MHC include medieval studies, neuroscience and behavior, and critical social thought.

Like five colleges for the price of one

The women of MHC stay busy, penciling in countless activities to keep up with their fellow overachievers. On-campus activities range from riding at the third-largest equestrian center in the country to participating on one of the Division III athletic teams to writing for the Daily Jolt, a website devoted to everything about MHC.

When academics become too intense, students relax at the on-campus Japanese meditation garden and teahouse. The campus also features two ponds, a private golf course called the Orchards, an art museum, an amphitheater, and an observatory. MHC students live in one of 19 residence halls, each of which has a living room with a grandfather clock and piano. First-years may live together in doubles, triples, or quadruples or be paired with a sophomore or junior.

Roughly 40 percent of students study abroad, and MHC helps fund close to 80 percent of them. MHC sponsors programs in Japan, Senegal, and France, but, through the Center for Global Initiatives, students can find exchange programs in many other countries throughout the world.

Emily Dickinson studied here, as did Frances Perkins, the first female cabinet member, and Pulitzer Prize–winners Suzan-Lori Parks and Wendy Wasserstein. Today, MHC considers the whole applicant, not just numbers, and submission of standardized test scores is optional.

Call of the Wild: Coolest Outdoor Programs

Students at these colleges always heed the call of nature. Automatic membership in the Outing Club? Course credit for rock climbing or snowboarding? Done and done. We could hardly believe it ourselves, but there you go.

Bates College (P. 26)

Better polish those hiking boats. Everybody who gets into Bates automatically belongs to the Outing Club.

College of the Atlantic (P. 62)

What would you expect from a progressive, environmental college located on the water and next door to a gorgeous national park? How about hikes with the Outing Club, internships with Allied Whale, doing research in Salisbury Cove?

Eckerd College (P. 80)

Think *Baywatch*, only with liberal arts. Students in the Waterfront Program can join a real-life search and rescue team that patrols Tampa Bay. David Hasselhoff, eat your heart out.

Fairhaven College (P. 94)

Known as the "Outback," the five-acre Outdoor Experiential Learning Site lets students tend organic gardens; study 44 species of birds, deer, and other wildlife up close; and stay in two rustic cabins.

Green Mountain College (P. 102)

The Environmental Liberal Arts Program will let you have a cow—and milk it too. On the Wilderness Challenge, first-years trek through the Adirondacks. Sherpas not included.

Marlboro College (P. 136)

The Outdoor Program (OP) maintains the cross-country skiing, mountain biking, and hiking that cover Marlboro's 360-acre campus. As if the trails weren't enough, you can also spend part of your winter or spring break with the OP, having adventures and doing community service in such places as Costa Rica, Jamaica, and Canada.

Mount Holyoke College (P. 142)

Fore! At Mount Holyoke's very own golf course, you can play a quick nine holes, then head back to class. The 18-hole Orchards Golf Course is within walking distance from campus.

Reed College (P. 166)

The Reed College Canyon bisects campus—and provides 26 acres of undeveloped nature for your playing pleasure. When Reedies aren't putting wheels on furniture (don't ask), they might spend the weekend at Reed's very own ski cabin on Mount Hood or visit the Backpack Co-op to borrow all kinds of camping stuff for free.

Rollins College (P. 178)

Love the outdoors? Move into Lyman Hall, home of the ROC (Rollins Outdoor Club). It's all nature, all the time at this dorm.

University of Alaska Southeast (P. 202)

Are you a wrangler and an angler? Find out—and get certified in Outdoor Skills and Leadership by taking classes in rock climbing, backcountry navigation, wilderness first aid, and snowboarding.

The University of the South (P. 214)

Sewanee's gigantic campus is located on a mountain, so you know there's cool outdoor stuff going on. Borrow a bike from the Outing Program, rappel up (or down) the climbing wall, or take a 20-plus-mile hike through four different types of forests—all without leaving campus.

Warren Wilson College (P. 220)

Each year, everyone at Warren Wilson pitches in to give the campus a makeover on Service Day. OK, so your dorm room might be a mess, but your campus will be spotless.

Muhlenberg College

2400 Chew Street
Allentown, PA 18104

(484) 664-3100
http://www.muhlenberg.edu/

Why It's Cool

Bombed the SAT or the ACT? No worries: At 'Berg, as Muhlenberg is lovingly known, you can submit a graded high school paper and sit for a one-on-one interview with an admissions counselor in lieu of submitting standardized test scores. After all, this school's far more interested in the *whole* you—not just a part of you uncovered by some test. And this whole-you emphasis continues into 'Berg's curriculum, which focuses on teaching you both academic and life skills, helping you stay fit, improving your ability to communicate and express yourself, and altering your view of the world.

EACH SUMMER, THE MUHLENBERG SUMMER MUSIC THEATRE SPONSORS TWO FULL-LENGTH BROADWAY MUSICALS, ATTENDED BY MORE THAN 20,000. STUDENTS PARTICIPATE IN EVERY PART OF THE PROCESS.

The Details

Campus setting:	suburban
Degrees:	bachelor's
Calendar:	semesters
Public/Private:	private religious
Number of full-time faculty:	155
Student-to-teacher ratio:	12:1

Admissions requirements:

- **Options:** common application, deferred entrance, early admission, early decision, electronic application
- **Application fee:** $45
- **Required:** essay or personal statement, high school transcript, 2 letters of recommendation
- **Application deadlines:** 2/15 (freshmen), 6/15 (transfer)
- **Early decision:** 2/1
- **Notification:** 3/20 (freshmen), 7/1 (transfer), 2/15 (early decision)

Average high school GPA:	3.52
Average freshman SAT verbal/math score:	608 / 615
Average freshman ACT score:	—
Number of applicants:	4,040
Number of applicants accepted:	1,808
Percentage of students from out of state:	69%
Total freshman enrollment:	559
Total enrollment:	2,446
Percentage of students who live in campus housing:	91%
Total tuition fee:	$26,570
Total cost with fees & expenses:	$34,575
Average financial aid package:	$16,847

Where It's At

Muhlenberg's 81 green acres are just one of the attractions of the midsize city of Allentown, located in Lehigh Valley, Pennsylvania. Other area draws include Dorney Park and Wildwater Kingdom, a huge amusement and water park; a town symphony; the Crayola FACTORY®; and weekly farmers' markets. Each fall, the Allentown Fair arrives, complete with entertainment and agricultural shows. Outdoor activities include rides in hot-air balloons, rafting trips down the Lehigh River, and walking trails in 2,500 acres of county parks. Students craving concrete can head to Philadelphia in 90 minutes, New York City in two hours, and Baltimore in three hours.

What It's Like

'Berg's application requirements might be less intense than those at other schools, but students here don't slack—not with 14 honor societies and a 90 percent acceptance rate to law and medical schools. But a happening Greek scene, courtesy of eight fraternities and sororities, means you can hit the dance floor instead of the books once in a while.

Hug a tree at the Graver Arboretum, an outdoor classroom.

Everybody has to take classes in four big areas: academic skills, perspectives, exploration and integration, and physical education. Skills courses cover writing and researching. Perspectives help students expand their worldviews through classes in such subjects as history and the fine arts. An interdisciplinary, writing-intensive first-year seminar fulfills exploration and integration. Past offerings have ranged from Dark and Stormy Knights to On the Importance of Being Skeptical.

The more than 40 majors include African American studies and natural sciences. Academic resources range from the Raker Biological Field Station and Wildlife Sanctuary and the Graver Arboretum (40 undeveloped acres on which to conduct research on animal, plant, and aquatic life) to the Holocaust Resource Center and the Center for Ethics. If students can't find what they need at 'Berg, a cooperative program lets them take classes at nearby schools, including Lafayette College and Lehigh University.

Domestic study opportunities include a semester in Washington, D.C., during which students might do internships or take classes. International programs take students to Japan and Belgium, among other places.

First-years generally live in West Quad, in Walz, Prosser, and Brown Halls. Upperclass students might live in the apartments of MacGregor Village, the suites of Benfer Hall, and the Muhlenberg Independent Living Experience, small off-campus houses.

Students choose from more than 100 organizations, ranging from the HALO Club (devoted to Xboxes) to Knit Wits (devoted to fostering harmony through knitwear). The recently renovated Life Sports Center offers practice space for the 20 Division III teams and amateurs, including the air hockey club.

New College of Florida

5700 North Tamiami Trail
Sarasota, FL 34243

(941) 359-4700
http://www.ncf.edu/

Why It's Cool

New College helps you to *just say no*—to grades, to a preset curriculum, to a one-size-fits-all education. Each semester, you'll sign a contract with your faculty adviser, known as a "sponsor." Together, you'll decide which classes to take, which activities to pursue, and which experiences to have. At the end of the term, your profs will give you lengthy written feedback. You'll also meet with your sponsor to discuss how you might improve or how your goals have evolved. No GPA. No core classes. No factory-style learning. We say *yes* to Florida's public honors college.

THE PALM COURT IS A POPULAR CAMPUS SPOT, AND MOVIE SCREENINGS, PLAY PRODUCTIONS, AND IMPROMPTU GET-TOGETHERS HAPPEN THERE ALL THE TIME.

The Details

Campus setting:	suburban
Degrees:	bachelor's
Calendar:	4-1-4
Public/Private:	public state
Number of full-time faculty:	66
Student-to-teacher ratio:	10:1

Admissions requirements:

- **Options:** common application, deferred entrance, early admission, electronic application
- **Application fee:** $30
- **Required:** essay or personal statement, high school transcript, letter of recommendation, SAT or ACT
- **Application deadlines:** —
- **Early decision:** —
- **Notification:** 5/1 (freshmen), 5/1 (transfer)

Average high school GPA:	3.95
Average freshman SAT verbal/math score:	675 / 638
Average freshman ACT score:	26
Number of applicants:	716
Number of applicants accepted:	383
Percentage of students from out of state:	19%
Total freshman enrollment:	189
Total enrollment:	692
Percentage of students who live in campus housing:	68%
Total in-state tuition, fees & expenses:	$10,248
Total out-of-state tuition, fees & expenses:	$25,308
Average financial aid package:	$10,858

Where It's At

New College's 140-acre campus is located along Sarasota Bay on Florida's Gulf Coast. The city of Sarasota has numerous attractions and, in recent years, has become a winter haven for culture vultures looking for fun in the sun. Visitors head to the Ringling Museum of Art, the Marine Selby Botanical Gardens, the upscale shops of St. Armand's Circle, the Sarasota Film Festival, and Van Wezel Performing Arts Hall. Another big draw is the white sand of Sarasota's best beaches, including Lido Key and Siesta Key. Tampa—home to the Buccaneers (NFL), Busch Gardens, Ybor City entertainment district, and Lowry Park Zoo—is about an hour away by car.

What It's Like

A school this unusual tends to attract a particular type of student: an intellectually curious, self-motivated high achiever with good financial sense. After all, tuition here is substantially less than at the Ivies, and students are just as s-m-a-r-t. Maybe even smarter, because students at New College don't receive grades and therefore can keep their focus on learning—instead of worrying about class rank or GPA.

Intellectually curious, self-motivated high achievers with good financial sense . . .

New College became Florida's independent public honors college in 2001. But the school was founded in 1960 as a place committed to letting students pursue individual interests and to fostering close faculty-student collaboration on projects. Students take classes in four divisions: interdisciplinary studies, the natural sciences, the social sciences, and the humanities. Everybody does a monthlong independent study project (ISP) during January as sophomores, juniors, and seniors. All seniors complete a thesis and sit for a comprehensive exam in their area of concentration (AOC).

With the help of their sponsors, students write out goals for each semester in a contract. They also list internships, study abroad plans, or anything else that might contribute to a unique liberal arts education. Students have the freedom to do their own thing, which culminates in their AOC, similar to a traditional major. Students get Term Feedback, a long written evaluation, from professors and sponsors.

Residence hall options include the large Pei Complex and Viking Hall, a onetime motel that's now an "all-quiet" dorm. Organized around the spacious Palm Court, Pei rooms have private entrances, huge windows, and, in many cases, balconies. Dort and Goldstein Halls feature apartment-style suites.

Though there aren't any Greeks or varsity athletes, New College still has plenty of stuff to do. From an organized celebration of a great literary work to a student photography exhibit to an impromptu party at Palm Court, New College is one happening school.

North Central College

30 North Brainard Street, PO Box 3063
Naperville, IL 60566
(630) 637-5100
http://www.noctrl.edu/

Why It's Cool

Location, location, location. North Central College puts you at the heart of it all. You'll choose from among more than 50 majors and 12 "Distinctive Opportunities," each designed to help you uncover hidden talents. Want to research kinesiology? Apply for the Richter Fellowship and get $5,000 to attend spring training for the Chicago White Sox in Arizona. Like to talk? Work for the award-winning radio station WONC. Long to see the world? Take an international travel seminar to Southeast Asia or Cuba. North Central's Distinctive Opportunities let you go where you want to go and do what you want to do. How cool is that?

THE CAGE PROVIDES STUDENTS WITH A TASTY SELECTION OF SPECIALTY MEALS NOT OFFERED AT THE MAIN DINING HALL.

The Details

Campus setting:	suburban
Degrees:	bachelor's, master's
Calendar:	trimesters
Public/Private:	private religious
Number of full-time faculty:	125
Student-to-teacher ratio:	13:1

Admissions requirements:

- **Options:** common application, deferred entrance, early admission
- **Application fee:** $25
- **Required:** high school transcript, letter of recommendation, SAT or ACT, ACT (recommended)
- **Application deadlines:** continuous (freshmen), continuous (transfer)
- **Early decision:** —
- **Notification:** continuous (freshmen), continuous (transfer)

Average high school GPA:	3.49
Average freshman SAT verbal/math score:	577 / 600
Average freshman ACT score:	24
Number of applicants:	1,806
Number of applicants accepted:	1,245
Percentage of students from out of state:	9%
Total freshman enrollment:	379
Total enrollment:	2,377
Percentage of students who live in campus housing:	58%
Total tuition fee:	$20,160
Total cost with fees & expenses:	$28,147
Average financial aid package:	$18,447

Where It's At

North Central's 59-acre campus is located in the historic center of Naperville, a large suburb of Chicago, Illinois. *Money* magazine has ranked the suburb as one of the three best places to live in the United States. Along the Century Walk are several works by local artists that depict the history of Naperville. The Riverwalk is a five-mile, landscaped brick path, and the Riverwalk Amphitheater holds events and performances. Among the many museums is the Naperville Settlement, which re-creates nineteenth-century pioneer life. Each fall, Naperville hosts Oktoberfest. Each spring, the city holds reenactments of key Civil War battles and has a St. Patrick's Day parade. Students can take the 45-minute METRA train, just one block from campus, into Chicago.

What It's Like

The yearlong Ongoing Orientation Program helps first-years get used to college life. Newbies get an upperclass mentor and are divided into small groups called CREWs (which stands for "community, relationships, education, and wellness"), with whom they meet for the year for informal discussions. Residents usually live with their CREWs in tiny Geiger Hall, air-conditioned Rall Hall, or the doubles of Seager Hall.

Classes in the nearby Windy City will blow you away.

North Central runs on the trimester system: three ten-week terms. Between Thanksgiving and Christmas is an intense three-week block called the Interim Term. Students may elect to extend their winter break, go abroad, or take a class during this time. International Travel Seminars take students to multiple destinations over the three weeks. Each fall, students can travel to either China and Japan or London with a professor for a ten-week international class. There are also several exchange programs to such destinations as Sweden and Taiwan.

Before graduation, students fulfill requirements in three areas: academic major, exploration, and general education. Majors range from classical civilizations to international business. The exploration component allows students to earn a second major or a minor, or to take several upper-level electives. General education requires that students complete all sorts of introductory courses, including an interdisciplinary writing seminar and classes in life sciences, communication, and fine arts.

During the Chicago Term, a Distinctive Opportunity sponsored by the urban and suburban studies department, students take two courses and do an internship in downtown Chicago. Other Distinctive Opportunities include the Richter Independent Study Fellowship, which awards grants of up to $5,000 for independent projects, such as diabetes research in a laboratory or studying Creole in Jamaica; the highly successful Mock Trial and Model United Nations academic teams; and the honors program.

Occidental College

1600 Campus Road
Los Angeles, CA 90041

(323) 259-2500
http://www.oxy.edu/

Why It's Cool

Oxy's got everything you could possibly want in a college: a stunning campus that's often used as a movie location, easy access to a major metropolitan area, a multicultural student body, an emphasis on "global literacy," and incredible opportunities. If you're into money, help invest part of Oxy's six-figure endowment through the student-run Blyth Fund. If you're into international relations, spend a semester in New York City as part of Occidental-at-the-UN. You'll never take a class taught by a TA, and you'll get a student-to-faculty ratio of around 10 to 1. And here's another reason to love this school: a year-round average temperature of 72 degrees.

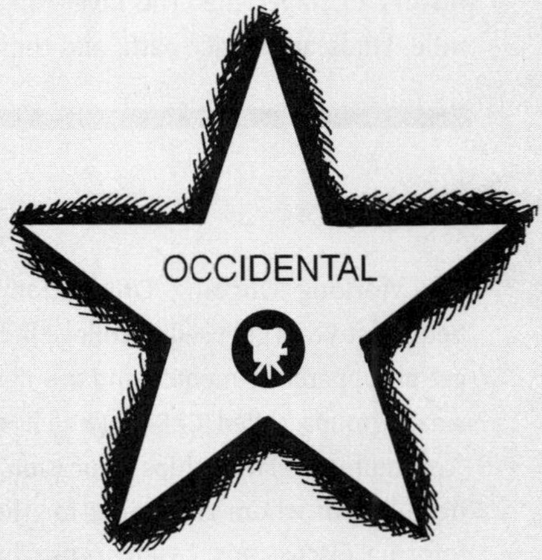

OCCIDENTAL'S GORGEOUS CAMPUS HAS BEEN THE SILENT STAR OF *BEVERLY HILLS 90210*, *CLUELESS*, AND *JURASSIC PARK III*, AMONG OTHER TELEVISION SHOWS AND MOVIES.

The Details

Campus setting:	urban
Degrees:	bachelor's, master's
Calendar:	semesters
Public/Private:	private nonprofit
Number of full-time faculty:	145
Student-to-teacher ratio:	10:1

Admissions requirements:

- **Options:** common application, deferred entrance, early admission, early decision
- **Application fee:** $50
- **Required:** essay or personal statement, high school transcript, 2 letters of recommendation, SAT or ACT, SAT Subject Tests (recommended)
- **Application deadlines:** 1/10 (freshmen), 3/15 (transfer)
- **Early decision:** 11/15
- **Notification:** 4/1 (freshmen), 5/1 (transfer), 12/15 (early decision)

Average high school GPA:	—
Average freshman SAT verbal/math score:	— / —
Average freshman ACT score:	—
Number of applicants:	4,836
Number of applicants accepted:	2,170
Percentage of students from out of state:	49%
Total freshman enrollment:	496
Total enrollment:	1,887
Percentage of students who live in campus housing:	70%
Total tuition fee:	$30,724
Total cost with fees & expenses:	$41,246
Average financial aid package:	$28,003

Where It's At

Oxy's 120-acre campus is located in Eagle Rock, recently described by the *Los Angeles Times* as "the latest 'it' neighborhood" of LA. The free Bengal Bus takes students to destinations around town, including the Glendale Galleria and the shops at historic Old Pasadena, on Thursdays, Fridays, and Saturdays. Other nearby attractions include Dodger Stadium, Chinatown, the open-air marketplace at Olvera Street, the Staples Center (home of the Lakers [NBA]), and the Rose Bowl Flea Market. Farther afield are Disneyland, the Museum of Contemporary Art, and the 650,000-acre Angeles National Forest. Venice Beach and Santa Monica are both about half an hour away.

What It's Like

While Oxy's not *The OC*, this school certainly has its share of wealthy, beautiful people. But you'll find students from every economic background and ethnicity here. Oxy's commitment to diversity also extends to its extracurricular and academic offerings. Through the Center for Community Based Learning, Oxy students teach the arts to young kids and help run farmers' markets, among other opportunities. And all students have to demonstrate a thorough understanding of several cultures, which Oxy calls "global literacy," by taking classes in various geographical regions of the world.

Courses like Stupidity will make you smarter.

First-years must take two classes: a seminar in cultural studies and an interdisciplinary colloquium. Recent seminars include Food Politics and The Taming of Infinity, and the choice of seminar determines where in the ten residence halls first-years live. In the colloquium, students trace a theme through several disciplines; the course Shades of LA: Contact and Conflict in Modern Los Angeles, for instance, draws on materials from English and political science.

There are approximately 30 majors at Oxy, nine of which are interdisciplinary, including diplomacy and world affairs. All students must pass a comprehensive exam during their senior year in their major. "Comps," as they are called, range from art exhibits to papers to performances. Every night, the tutors at the Center for Academic Excellence provide help in just about every subject.

Among the roughly 100 clubs are the Glee Club, the Bad Movie Club, and Live Poets Society. About 10 percent of students participate in one of the three fraternities and four sororities. There are 19 Division III athletic teams (the Tigers).

At the Marketplace, students dine on made-to-order pasta or home-style specials prepared on-site. The campus bookstore stocks more than 100 magazines. Just about everyone studies in Clapp Library and hangs out in the Tiger Cooler, a snack bar that will even deliver pizza to the dorms during the week.

Ohio Northern University

525 South Main Street
Ada, OH 45810
(419) 772-2000
http://www.onu.edu/

Why It's Cool

What happens when you cross practical job training with an extraordinary liberal arts foundation? You get an educated person perfectly prepared for the twenty-first century. In fact, you get an ONU graduate. Here, career planning begins on the very first day of your very first year. You can even get credit for taking a class on finding a job or applying to graduate school. And most majors require you to join a professional organization and attend academic conferences. But don't worry if you don't know what you want to do: ONU has a general studies program, which lets you learn a little about a lot.

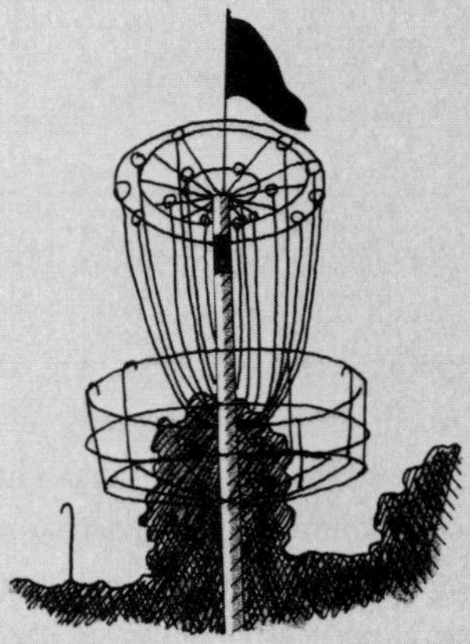

ONU HAS ITS OWN 18-HOLE DISC GOLF COURSE, AND THERE ARE ULTIMATE FRISBEE TEAMS FOR MEN AND WOMEN.

The Details

Campus setting:	small town
Degrees:	bachelor's, master's
Calendar:	quarters
Public/Private:	private religious
Number of full-time faculty:	207
Student-to-teacher ratio:	14:1

Admissions requirements:

- **Options:** common application, deferred entrance, electronic application
- **Application fee:** $30
- **Required:** high school transcript, letter of recommendation, SAT or ACT
- **Application deadlines:** 8/15 (freshmen), 9/1 (transfer)
- **Early decision:** —
- **Notification:** continuous (freshmen), continuous (transfer)

Average high school GPA:	3.65
Average freshman SAT verbal/math score:	572 / 597
Average freshman ACT score:	24
Number of applicants:	2,778
Number of applicants accepted:	2,156
Percentage of students from out of state:	16%
Total freshman enrollment:	753
Total enrollment:	3,495
Percentage of students who live in campus housing:	79%
Total tuition fee:	$25,605
Total cost with fees & expenses:	$33,075
Average financial aid package:	$21,922

Where It's At

ONU's 285-acre campus is located in the tiny town of Ada, Ohio. Known as "Tree City USA," rural Ada has few things to do but lots of community spirit. Each August, the Farmers and Merchants Picnic features food and entertainment, as does the Harvest and Herb Festival every September. Ada's Main Street has locally owned shops, such as Reichert's Clothing and Shoe Store, and restaurants, such as Regal Beagle. Other area attractions include shopping at the many antique stores in Hardin County, walking along the Old Sandusky Indian Trail, and visiting the Old Order Amish communities. Cincinnati is about three hours away by car.

What It's Like

More than 10 percent of the students at ONU were high school valedictorians, so be prepared for lots of smarties and go-getters. But when the dual emphasis on career planning and liberal arts gets too hectic, students relax by heading to the parties thrown by the 11 fraternities and sororities, watching the big-screen TV at Park Hall, or joining one of the 150 student organizations. As the Polar Bears, students compete on 18 Division III athletic teams, including wrestling.

Be prepared for lots of smarties and go-getters.

Four undergraduate colleges and one graduate school make up ONU: pharmacy, business administration, engineering, arts and sciences, and law. ONU lets students design a focus within their major called an "option"; for example, a biology major could have a business option, or a graphic designer might choose a multimedia option. Students who are not yet sure about their majors enroll in general studies or general sciences, which lets them fulfill general education requirements while learning about various majors and careers.

Each department dictates the graduation requirements for its majors. Most require students to attend cultural or professional events as part of an "enrichment" course, so an English major might receive credit for going to a poetry reading. Generally, departments also offer an "orientation" class, which introduces students to the personal and professional issues relating to a discipline or career. Students must also take courses in writing and history, among the other liberal arts. So-called freshman seminars help first-years adjust. And everybody has to join a professional organization related to his or her major.

International opportunities range from studying education in New Zealand or literature in Hungary to touring major European businesses. On campus, students live in one of 12 residence halls, including the traditional dorms of Northern House and the apartments of University Place and Campus Village. We adore you, ONU.

Picking Up the Signal: Most Tech-Savvy Schools

We searched all over (with our SparkCollege antennae, of course) for the biggest, baddest, most techie schools out there. And what do you know? We found some. Here they are, in real time.

Albertson College of Idaho (P. 4)

Berea College (P. 32)

Birmingham-Southern College (P. 38)

Centenary College (P. 42)

Keene State College (P. 118)

Miami University (P. 138)

Savannah College of Art and Design (P. 182)

Sierra Nevada College (P. 184)

Tuskegee University (P. 198)

University of Montevallo (P. 208)

University of Tulsa (P. 218)

Presbyterian College

503 South Broad Street **(864) 833-2820**
Clinton, SC 29325 **http://www.presby.edu/**

Why It's Cool

"PC" doesn't just stand for Presbyterian College. It also means *picturesque campus* (five buildings on the prestigious National Register of Historic Places), *plenty of chow* (the dining hall has ten all-you-can-eat food stations), *performances and culture* (students are required to attend ten events a year), *physics and computer science* (just one of the 17 academic departments), *professors who care* (faculty have won six South Carolina Professor of the Year awards), and *pleasantly competitive* (almost everybody plays a varsity or intramural sport). Most of all, PC means a *practical, challenging* education: here you'll expand your mind—and your career options. PC is *pretty cool.*

CYRUS THE SCOTSMAN, A 13-FOOT BRONZE STATUE, GUARDS THE ENTRANCE TO BAILEY STADIUM.

The Details

Campus setting:	small town
Degrees:	bachelor's
Calendar:	semesters
Public/Private:	private religious
Number of full-time faculty:	79
Student-to-teacher ratio:	13:1

Admissions requirements:

- **Options:** deferred entrance, early decision, electronic application
- **Application fee:** $30
- **Required:** essay or personal statement, high school transcript, letter of recommendation, SAT or ACT
- **Application deadlines:** 4/1 (freshmen), 7/1 (transfer)
- **Early decision:** —
- **Notification:** 6/1 (freshmen), — (transfer), — (early decision)

Average high school GPA:	3.37
Average freshman SAT verbal/math score:	567 / 574
Average freshman ACT score:	23
Number of applicants:	1,128
Number of applicants accepted:	876
Percentage of students from out of state:	39%
Total freshman enrollment:	344
Total enrollment:	1,187
Percentage of students who live in campus housing:	94%
Total tuition fee:	$19,740
Total cost with fees & expenses:	$28,987
Average financial aid package:	$19,217

Where It's At

PC's 240-acre campus is located in Clinton, a town in northwestern South Carolina. The historic downtown area is home to several locally owned stores and restaurants: Elaine's on the Square sells candles and gifts, as well as hosts weekly gospel singing, while Steamer's hot dogs have been voted the best in town. Each fall, the Clinton Fall Festival features live entertainment, food, and crafts. Outdoor activities range from playing 18 holes at the famous Musgrove Mill Golf Course to hunting at the Clinton House Plantation to strolling around Horseshoe Falls. Sometimes called the "Heart of the South," Columbia, the state capital, is about an hour away.

What It's Like

PC students love to join: About half the student body belongs to one of the eight fraternities and four sororities, while 80 percent of students play on an intramural team. As the Blue Hose, students compete on 16 Division II athletic teams. Community counts here, so be prepared to go Greek, lace up those sneakers, or just plain participate.

Almost everybody lives on campus, which helps foster a spirit of congeniality. Students choose from nine apartments, 11 residential halls, and 15 town houses. Two halls—Clinton and Barron—and two living/learning communities—Carol International House and Senior Hall—are co-ed. Available only to seniors, the town houses feature washers and dryers, dishwashers, and at least two full bathrooms.

Introduction to Inquiry teaches you to ask the right questions.

Among the 30 majors are sacred music and early childhood education. PC also has eight preprofessional programs, including preministry and predental. Every department sets the requirements for the Capstone, a big project, paper, or performance undertaken by seniors in their major. Each year, PC sponsors a giant fair for students in search of internships or jobs; past attendees have included American Express and Hyatt.

Other requirements include courses in the humanities, social sciences, and natural science. All students must take two religion classes: Survey of the Old Testament and Survey of the New Testament. First-years take either a special seminar or Introduction to Inquiry, both of which focus on easing the students' transition from high school to college.

As part of the Intercultural Education requirement, students are encouraged to study abroad. PC runs programs in roughly 50 places around the globe, including Russia and Argentina. The BorderLinks program lets students examine issues surrounding the U.S.-Mexico border by spending four weeks in Tucson, Arizona, and six weeks in Nogales, Mexico.

Over the school year, students have to attend five cultural events and five lectures, ranging from a showing of *Gattaca* to a performance by a Chinese dance troupe, as part of the Newton G. Hardie Cultural Enrichment Program.

Prescott College

220 Grove Avenue
Prescott, AZ 86301

(928) 778-2090
http://www.prescott.edu/

Why It's Cool

Forget about large lecture halls and fill-in-the-bubble exams. Forget about sitting in windowless rooms listening to profs drone on about algebra. Prescott's got a whole new take on education, and it's awesome. Welcome to experiential field-based classes. At Prescott, you'll learn by going out into the world. You'll focus on the liberal arts and the environment. Imagine getting course credit for researching marine biology in Mexico, examining rocks in the southwestern desert, or tending crops at the school's sustainable farm. No matter what you do or where you study, you'll get your hands dirty, your feet wet, and your mind rocked.

AVALANCHE FORECASTING IS JUST ONE OF THE MANY OFF-CAMPUS COURSES OFFERED BY PRESCOTT.

The Details

Campus setting:	small town
Degrees:	bachelor's master's, doctoral
Calendar:	quarters (4-week blocks followed by 10-week terms for each quarter)
Public/Private:	private nonprofit
Number of full-time faculty:	59
Student-to-teacher ratio:	12:1

Admissions requirements:

- **Options:** deferred entrance
- **Application fee:** $25
- **Required:** essay or personal statement, high school transcript, 2 letters of recommendation
- **Application deadlines:** 2/1 (freshmen), 2/1 (transfer)
- **Early decision:** —
- **Notification:** 3/15 (freshmen), 3/15 (transfer)

Average high school GPA:	—
Average freshman SAT verbal/math score:	564 / 536
Average freshman ACT score:	24
Number of applicants:	83
Number of applicants accepted:	70
Percentage of students from out of state:	87%
Total freshman enrollment:	41
Total enrollment:	1,036
Percentage of students who live in campus housing:	—
Total tuition fee:	$17,280
Total cost with fees & expenses:	$17,450
Average financial aid package:	$4,560

Where It's At

Prescott's campus is located in the town of Prescott, in north-central Arizona. Roughly 1.4 million acres of national forest surround the town, making such outdoor activities as hiking and rock climbing popular. The Smoki Museum primarily features objects from American Indian cultures, while the Sharlot Hall Museum holds art and artifacts of the West. Each summer, the World's Oldest Rodeo comes to Prescott as part of Frontier Days, a celebration of the Wild West; each December, Prescott townspeople build the World's Largest Gingerbread Village. Phoenix is about two hours away by car, and Tucson is about four hours away.

What It's Like

Prescott's philosophy is "learning by doing," but it might as well be "education in action" or "committed to the environment and to social justice." Students here are pretty laid back, but they definitely take their education seriously. In fact, they have to: Prescott makes you choose your advising committee, which then makes sure you're fulfilling all the requirements.

The remarkable academic calendar combines full-length terms with four-week blocks. Students take two terms (four classes per term) and two blocks (one in-depth class). Many students spend the blocks off campus, taking such courses as Sea Kayaking in Mexico or Backcountry Skiing in Idaho.

Totally and utterly hands-on

Students choose from among six interdisciplinary areas of study: arts and letters, adventure education, cultural and regional studies, human development, education, and environmental studies. Within those areas, students specialize in a particular competence (similar to a traditional major), such as agroecology in environmental studies or Spanish language and literature within culture and regional studies.

To earn a competence, Prescott students must fulfill various requirements. For instance, among the adventure education requirements are an environmental studies class and certification in wilderness first aid. Rather than give traditional grades, professors write long evaluations of student performance. Students also evaluate themselves, answering questions about how each class has developed their ethical commitments or increased their knowledge.

Writers can publish in the *Alligator Juniper*, Prescott's literary magazine, or *Raven Review*, the school paper. Although Prescott doesn't have any on-campus housing, the school provides several residential resources for students, including a comprehensive website. Notable campus features include the 30-acre Wolfberry Farm and the "green" roof garden atop the Crossroads Center (the student union).

First-years begin by taking part in a monthlong Wilderness Orientation. Small groups travel into the southwestern backcountry to learn about desert ecology and Prescott's self-directed, experiential learning philosophy. Sounds great—where can we sign up?

Purchase College
State University of New York

735 Anderson Hill Road **(914) 251-6000**
Purchase, NY 10577 **http://www.purchase.edu/**

Why It's Cool

Calling all culture vultures. If you love to sing and dance, paint, or make beautiful music, look no further. At Purchase, you can specialize in the liberal arts, visual arts, or performing arts. So go ahead and double-major in classical guitar and chemistry, printmaking and philosophy, or acting and art history. Take classes at the Conservatory of Music, the Conservatory of Dance, the Liberal Arts and Science School, and the School of Art+Design. This sweet combination helped propel these alumni to fame: Wesley Snipes, Parker Posey, and Stanley Tucci. You could be next.

ACTRESS EDIE FALCO, BETTER KNOWN AS CARMELA SOPRANO ON HBO'S *THE SOPRANOS*, IS A PURCHASE GRADUATE.

The Details

Campus setting:	suburban
Degrees:	bachelor's, master's
Calendar:	semesters
Public/Private:	public state
Number of full-time faculty:	136
Student-to-teacher ratio:	17:1

Admissions requirements:

- **Options:** deferred entrance, early admission, early decision
- **Application fee:** $50
- **Required:** high school transcript, letter of recommendation, SAT or ACT
- **Application deadlines:** continuous (freshmen), continuous (transfer)
- **Early decision:** 11/1
- **Notification:** 5/1 (freshmen), continuous (transfer), 12/15 (early decision)

Average high school GPA:	3.0
Average freshman SAT verbal/math score:	565 / 538
Average freshman ACT score:	—
Number of applicants:	6,899
Number of applicants accepted:	1,969
Percentage of students from out of state:	17%
Total freshman enrollment:	626
Total enrollment:	3,832
Percentage of students who live in campus housing:	64%
Total in-state tuition, fees & expenses:	$14,135
Total out-of-state tuition, fees & expenses:	$20,395
Average financial aid package:	$7,235

Where It's At

Purchase is located on 550 acres in a small town in Westchester County, a large suburb of New York City. In addition to the college, Purchase is home to Manhattanville College. Playland, a nearby amusement park, has rides, picnic spots, mini-golf, and skating. Westchester County has more than 17,000 acres of parks, as well as the Arts Exchange, Candace Perich Gallery, and Caramoor Center for Music and the Arts. The Purchase Loop, a free shuttle bus, takes students to local malls, grocery stores, movie theaters, and train stations with commuter service to New York City, which is only a 30-minute ride away. There, students can nosh at one of the 18,000 restaurants or hang out at the Museum of Modern Art.

What It's Like

Think of Purchase College as the perfect place to start anew. Forty percent of students transfer from other institutions, and they are a talented bunch. Everybody fits in, from straight-edgers to tattooed punks to do-gooders. About 65 percent major in the humanities and sciences, while the remaining 35 percent specialize at one of the conservatories. Combining the liberal arts with a conservatory-based arts program is the hallmark of a Purchase education.

Liberal arts, liberal politics, good parties . . .

Purchase, as a part of the State University of New York (SUNY), requires everyone to fulfill general education requirements, including courses in laboratory science and a foreign language. Plus, Purchase hosts summer study abroad programs in Italy, Spain, and France, as well as semester programs in the Netherlands, Australia, and the United Kingdom. On the whole, SUNY offers 260 programs abroad.

The 160,000-square-foot Art+Design building gives students space to create—and it stays open until 2 A.M. Students don't have to leave campus to see great works of art: The Neuberger Museum of Art exhibits works by Jackson Pollack and Ansel Adams. The Performing Arts Center draws people from all over to its renowned dance, music, and theater performances.

Not one, but *two* campus centers have meeting space for student organizations, including X-Stream Generation, a Christian group; the Socialist League; and the AIDS Task Force. At Campus Center North, students can relax in the fireside lounge, and they can play pool and video games at Campus Center South, which also runs special evening activities, from Jazz Club to Coffeehouse. After a decade-long hiatus, Purchase has recently reentered Division III competition, and there are 42 intramural offerings.

Some of the most popular annual events include the Gay/Lesbian/Bisexual/Transsexual Student Union's Striptease and Culture Shock, an annual event that features local and big-name bands. This treasure school's full of liberal arts, liberal politics, and good parties.

Randolph-Macon College

PO Box 5005
Ashland, VA 23005
(804) 752-7200
http://www.rmc.edu/

Why It's Cool

Go both ways at R-MC. As part of the First-Year Experience, you'll spend fall semester studying a theme or idea from one academic perspective, then you'll switch to another perspective for the spring semester. A little from column A, a little from column B. Take The Drug Trade, and you'll learn from professors in the chemistry and sociology departments. In God's Good Time compares the concept of time in physics with the concept of time in religious studies, while Six Billion Bodies and Souls uses readings from biology, sociology, and drama. It's interdisciplinary study at its finest.

EACH FALL, THE YELLOW JACKETS SUIT UP FOR THE ANNUAL FOOTBALL GAME AGAINST ARCHENEMIES HAMPDEN-SYDNEY; THEIRS IS THE OLDEST SMALL-COLLEGE RIVALRY IN THE SOUTH.

The Details

Campus setting:	suburban
Degrees:	bachelor's
Calendar:	4-1-4
Public/Private:	private religious
Number of full-time faculty:	88
Student-to-teacher ratio:	11:1

Admissions requirements:

- **Options:** common application, deferred entrance, early admission, early decision, electronic application
- **Application fee:** $30
- **Required:** essay or personal statement, high school transcript, letter of recommendation, SAT or ACT, SAT Subject Tests (recommended)
- **Application deadlines:** 3/1 (freshmen), 3/1 (transfer)
- **Early decision:** 11/15
- **Notification:** 4/1 (freshmen), 4/1 (transfer), 12/1 (early decision)

Average high school GPA:	3.33
Average freshman SAT verbal/math score:	566 / 561
Average freshman ACT score:	21
Number of applicants:	1,720
Number of applicants accepted:	1,327
Percentage of students from out of state:	33%
Total freshman enrollment:	325
Total enrollment:	1,127
Percentage of students who live in campus housing:	84%
Total tuition fee:	$21,990
Total cost with fees & expenses:	$30,135
Average financial aid package:	$16,629

Where It's At

R-MC's 110-acre campus is located in the small town of Ashland, a suburb of Richmond. Its location in central Virginia has led some residents to call Ashland "the Center of the Universe." The historic downtown is full of locally owned restaurants and shops, including Ashland Coffee and Tea, and it holds a farmers' market. Local attractions range from Monticello, Thomas Jefferson's estate, to the Museum of the Confederacy to Poplar Forest and the Danville Science Center. As the state capital, Richmond has lots of stuff to do and see, such as the Edgar Allan Poe Museum, the Fredegar Iron Works, and the scenic Canal Walk. Washington, D.C., is about 90 minutes away.

What It's Like

Connection is key at R-MC. Small classes mean lots of face time with professors (the student-to-faculty ratio hovers around 11:1, and the average class has 15 students). More than 60 clubs means there's something extracurricular for everyone, from the Franklin Society debating team to the *Yellow Jacket Weekly* newspaper. Plus, there are 15 Division II athletic teams. This social campus radiates friendliness: About half the student body belongs to a Greek house.

By far, the biggest connection made at R-MC is between students and academics. Everybody takes two required courses in seven areas: laboratory science, literature, composition, social science, religion or philosophy, math, and European history. Other requirements include demonstrating computer literacy and two semesters of physical education.

This social campus radiates friendliness.

The First-Year Experience emphasizes writing, researching, and speaking skills. To learn about how different disciplines work, first-years study an issue or phenomenon from two academic perspectives. At the end of the year, they do a big project that links the two perspectives. Students also take a seminar known as the "Writing Companion" that's affiliated with the yearlong class.

Among the 30 majors are international studies and women's studies. Minors range from Irish studies to speech communication to ethics. Prelaw and premed are two of the preprofessional programs. Through the Bassett Internship Program, students do 130 hours of work at an organization of their choice, including the United Nations and the Virginia Museum of Fine Arts, for academic credit.

Many students go off campus or abroad in January, during the four-week-long J-Term. Recent offerings include making wine in California, studying psychology and sociology in South Africa, and service learning in Guatemala.

On campus, students live in either of two complexes composed of ten residence halls and four town house–style buildings. Only one hall—Mary Branch—isn't air-conditioned, and all of them come with extra-long twin beds. There are also four special interest houses, including Multicultural and Macon Outdoors. Inside or outside—R-MC rocks.

Reed College

3203 Southeast Woodstock Boulevard
Portland, OR 97202
(503) 771-1112
http://www.reed.edu/

Why It's Cool

If you like your politics progressive and your academics demanding, then Reed just might be the school for you. As a first-year, you'll take the yearlong Humanities course, which covers the classics of Western civilization. Later, you'll do a comprehensive exam and thesis in your major. Classes here, known as "conferences," are run seminar-style, emphasizing discussions over lectures. It's no surprise that Reed sends more graduates on to PhD programs than all but two other schools in the United States. But Reedies aren't all work and no play: The Motorized Couch Collective (which attaches wheels to furniture) and the MLLL (a room that houses more than 40 years' worth of comic books) are but two of the more than 65 student groups on campus. Couches. Comics. Cool.

REED HAS THE ONLY NUCLEAR REACTOR IN THE COUNTRY OPERATED PRIMARILY BY UNDERGRADUATES.

The Details

Campus setting:	suburban
Degrees:	bachelor's, master's
Calendar:	semesters
Public/Private:	private nonprofit
Number of full-time faculty:	115
Student-to-teacher ratio:	10:1

Admissions requirements:

- **Options:** common application, deferred entrance, early admission, early decision, electronic application
- **Application fee:** $40
- **Required:** essay or personal statement, high school transcript, 2 letters of recommendation, SAT or ACT, SAT Subject Tests (recommended)
- **Application deadlines:** 1/15 (freshmen), 3/1 (transfer)
- **Early decision:** 11/15
- **Notification:** 4/1 (freshmen), 5/1 (transfer), 12/15 (early decision)

Average high school GPA:	3.80
Average freshman SAT verbal/math score:	703 / 668
Average freshman ACT score:	26
Number of applicants:	2,485
Number of applicants accepted:	1,180
Percentage of students from out of state:	86%
Total freshman enrollment:	337
Total enrollment:	1,341
Percentage of students who live in campus housing:	65%
Total tuition fee:	$30,670
Total cost with fees & expenses:	$39,920
Average financial aid package:	$24,122

Where It's At

Reed's 100-acre campus is located in southeastern Portland, Oregon. Students get cheap or free tickets to most of Portland's cultural events, and they hang out at the city's many coffeehouses, including the Daily Grind and the Pied Cow. Nearby Hawthorne Boulevard is home to eclectic restaurants, shops, and theaters. Yoko's and Queen of Sheba are two beloved local eateries. A light-rail system links Portland's many attractions, such as the Oregon Zoo and Powell's, one of the world's largest independent new-and-used bookstores. Sports fans cheer the Trail Blazers (NBA). Mount Hood, on which Reed maintains a ski cabin, is less than two hours away by car.

What It's Like

Reedies are a different breed. They study hard, they play hard, they have unique organizations, and they have cool traditions like the costume contest at the Halloween Social and an all-you-can-eat "feeding frenzy" held before finals. There are no varsity teams or Greek houses. Some students, known as "scroungers," don't buy food at the cafeteria: They wait for others to hand out leftovers. Unofficially, Reed's motto is "atheism, communism, free love.

Atheism, communism, free love

Reed's Honor Principle guides every facet of campus life: Not only are students forbidden from lying or cheating, but they must also think carefully about how every action affects the community. In return, many exams are take home, and a spirit of harmony pervades campus.

First-years take the yearlong Humanities 110, focusing on important works from Western civilization, such as the Bible and *The Odyssey.* Reed believes that this class will help ground students in the liberal arts, regardless of what they ultimately choose as a major. Other requirements include courses in math, physical education, and social sciences. Rather than fulfilling requirements randomly, students are urged to take at least two classes in any given department.

Among the close to 35 majors are the interdisciplinary history-literature and international and comparative policy studies. Undergraduates are given a lot of academic responsibility, including two sets of comprehensive exams and a long thesis done as a senior. As a result, they get to do rad stuff like perform graduate-level research with their professors and take care of Reed's nuclear reactor. Professors give both grades and written feedback. Unless a student receives a C, D, or F, the student will only see the feedback (not the letter grade).

Students live in one of 18 residence halls on campus. Theme dorms let students bond over similar interests, such as watching cartoons in Running with Scissors or being outdoors in Outhouse. Off campus, Reed sponsors programs in such locations as China and Ecuador.

Grabbing Life by the Balls: Most Athletic Campuses

Some people, including students at the following schools, just like getting sticky, smelly, and sweaty more than others.

Rhodes College

2000 North Parkway
Memphis, TN 38112
(901) 843-3000
http://www.rhodes.edu/

Why It's Cool

Rhodes knows how to show the love. Through Rhodes CARES, you can do it too by combining schoolwork and service in one of several programs. You might do research at a not-for-profit hospital, co-teach biology in the Memphis public schools, or present a paper at the Institute for Regional Studies' annual conference. You might even get a scholarship for your civic-mindedness. But it's not just the students who serve: Rhodes faculty also pitch in and volunteer their time and expertise as mentors, so they'll be working right alongside you. Ivory tower, schmivory tower. At Rhodes, *prestigious* never means *elitist*.

AIN'T NOTHIN' BUT A HOUNDDOG: MEMPHIS IS ALSO HOME TO GRACELAND, THE GRAND ESTATE OF ELVIS PRESLEY.

The Details

Campus setting:	suburban
Degrees:	bachelor's, master's
Calendar:	semesters
Public/Private:	private religious
Number of full-time faculty:	136
Student-to-teacher ratio:	11:1

Admissions requirements:

- **Options:** common application, deferred entrance, early admission, early decision, electronic application
- **Application fee:** $45
- **Required:** essay or personal statement, high school transcript, 2 letters of recommendation, SAT or ACT
- **Application deadlines:** 2/1 (freshmen), 2/1 (transfer)
- **Early decision:** 11/1
- **Notification:** 4/1 (freshmen), 4/1 (transfer), 12/1 (early decision)

Average high school GPA:	3.66
Average freshman SAT verbal/math score:	641 / 637
Average freshman ACT score:	26
Number of applicants:	3,429
Number of applicants accepted:	1,865
Percentage of students from out of state:	72%
Total freshman enrollment:	473
Total enrollment:	1,633
Percentage of students who live in campus housing:	76%
Total tuition fee:	$25,646
Total cost with fees & expenses:	$33,730
Average financial aid package:	$16,054

Where It's At

Rhodes's 100-acre campus is located in Memphis's historic district. Within walking distance from campus are the Memphis Brooks Museum of Art and the Memphis Zoo. As the birthplace of rock and roll and the unofficial home of the blues, Memphis, Tennessee, has several attractions devoted to music, including Beale Street, Graceland, and the Rock 'n' Soul Museum. Other draws include the Civil Rights Museum and the Grizzlies (NBA). Shelby Farms, the largest urban park in the United States, has more than 4,500 acres available for outdoor activities of all kinds. The sounds and sights of Nashville, the state capital, are just three hours away.

What It's Like

Students sweat off any academic stress at the Bryan Campus Life Center, home to the 19 Division III varsity teams (the Lynx). In addition to a gymnasium, racquetball courts, and an indoor track, the center also features the Lynx Lair food court, as well as the McCallum Ballroom, used for dances and other special events. Close to 25 percent of Rhodes students play a varsity sport, and popular teams include field hockey and soccer.

Where every student is a Rhodes scholar

First-years and sophomores must live on campus, in traditional dorms, town houses, and theme housing, including one that is substance free. All told, there are 90 organizations on campus, which sponsor upward of 250 events per year, from theater productions to mock trials to weekly outings with the film society.

More than 80 percent of Rhodes students do some type of community service. The Rhodes Center for Academic Research and Education through Service (CARES) offers students and faculty alike the opportunity to connect intellectual endeavor with service. Through the Kinney Program—founded more than 50 years ago—students lend a hand in the greater Memphis community, registering voters and doing other good deeds.

All Rhodes students take one of two four-semester courses. Search for Values explores important texts in Western history, while Life: Then and Now draws on religious and philosophical texts. Rhodes has more than 20 departmental majors, seven interdisciplinary majors, and close to 30 minors, including computer science. Foundation requirements develop communication skills; students fulfill the requirements by taking courses in such liberal arts subjects as literature and a foreign language.

Thirteen buildings have made the National Register of Historic Places, and Rhodes's groomed, gorgeous campus is a source of pride. Another source of pride is the Honor Code, signed by all students. With their signatures, students pledge to act honorably, to respect all members of the Rhodes community, and to appreciate diversity.

Ripon College

300 Seward Street, PO Box 248 **(920) 748-8115**
Ripon, WI 54971 **http://www.ripon.edu/**

Why It's Cool

Want to get a good job? Then you've got to talk the talk—and Ripon will show you how. The Communicating Plus program teaches you to speak, write, think, and solve problems. Ripon makes you marketable, hirable, and desirable. There's even a set of Principles and Practices of Business Communication. And to make sure that everyone on campus communicates with everyone else, Ripon cancels classes for 60 minutes every week for the Golden Hour—free time for you to hear a speaker, go to a lecture, attend a community fair, spend time in a peace circle, or just kick it with your friends. Right on, Ripon.

EACH YEAR, SUNFLOWERS BLOOM AT THE ON-CAMPUS CERESCO PRAIRIE CONSERVANCY, A 130-ACRE OUTDOOR CLASSROOM THAT'S ALSO HOME TO DEER, BIRDS, AND FOXES.

The Details

Campus setting:	small town
Degrees:	bachelor's
Calendar:	semesters
Public/Private:	private nonprofit
Number of full-time faculty:	51
Student-to-teacher ratio:	14:1

Admissions requirements:

- **Options:** common application, deferred entrance, electronic application
- **Application fee:** $30
- **Required:** high school transcript, letter of recommendation, SAT or ACT
- **Application deadlines:** continuous (freshmen), continuous (transfer)
- **Early decision:** —
- **Notification:** continuous (freshmen), continuous (transfer)

Average high school GPA:	3.43
Average freshman SAT verbal/math score:	558 / 552
Average freshman ACT score:	22
Number of applicants:	959
Number of applicants accepted:	783
Percentage of students from out of state:	24%
Total freshman enrollment:	202
Total enrollment:	927
Percentage of students who live in campus housing:	90%
Total tuition fee:	$20,490
Total cost with fees & expenses:	$27,090
Average financial aid package:	$17,891

Where It's At

Ripon's 250-acre campus is located in the small town of Ripon, Wisconsin. In 1854, radicals founded the Republican Party in Ripon, and the town has become a popular tourist destination for that reason. The historic downtown has restaurants and shops, and a farmers' market runs during the summer. The Pumpkin Fest Custom Car Show features souped-up automobiles, as well as a pet parade. About 200,000 migrating geese arrive at the Horicon National Wildlife Refuge twice yearly. Fond du Lac, the surrounding county, offers many outdoor activities, such as fishing and snowboarding. Green Bay and Milwaukee are both about two hours away.

What It's Like

Ripon combines a big education with small-town life. Regardless of their major or college year, students work closely with professors. In fact, 100 percent of Ripon faculty oversee independent study and research, which means that every single professor works with students one on one—that's an incredible statistic, and it demonstrates the faculty's devotion to helping undergrads.

Ripon students can choose from among 40 organizations, including three sororities, five fraternities, and one co-ed Greek house, Theta Sigma Tau. Other extracurricular options range from the Electronic Music Club to the Cultural Diversity Club to the Red Hawks Dance Team. Creative types join Photogenesis, the photography club; *Parallax*, the literary journal; or the *Crimson Journal*, the yearbook. Among the 14 intramural sports are dodgeball and bowling. Thirty-five percent of students participate on 18 Division III athletic teams known as the "Red Hawks," including swimming and indoor track and field.

Wookie lovers unite! Star Wars's own Han Solo studied here.

The Explore-Select-Connect Curriculum lets students create an academic plan that suits their interests. The Explore courses, taken in the first year, include introductory classes in the humanities and behavioral sciences, as well as one course in exercise science (a fancy way of saying "phys ed"). The Select courses fulfill the requirements of the majors and include electives. Majors range from the discipline-based economics to self-designed courses of study to the interdisciplinary global studies. Finally, the Connect courses include the senior-year capstone project, such as a performance or research paper.

About 90 percent of students live on campus. Housing options include traditional dorms, co-ed living groups, and apartment-style suites. The recently renovated Farr Hall of Science has state-of-the-art laboratories and a comprehensive science library, and the Rodman Center for the Arts has its own sculpture garden, gallery, and performance spaces. This school has a history of producing strong performers: Al Jarreau, Spencer Tracy, and Harrison Ford all studied at Ripon.

Rockford College

5050 East State Street
Rockford, IL 61108

(815) 226-4000
http://www.rockford.edu/

Why It's Cool

At Rockford, it's OK to act up. The revolutionary thinker and Nobel Peace Prize–winner Jane Addams graduated from Rockford back in the day, and today, the school keeps her spirit alive by encouraging social activism. So everybody gives back to the community in some way. Maybe you'll hold food drives or run fund-raisers at the Addams Center for Civic Engagement. You might spend your spring break building low-income housing. Even math classes have a volunteering component (plus, you'll get extra credit for tutoring youngsters). Feel free to be like Jane—you'll make the world a better place.

EACH APRIL, ROCKFORD CELEBRATES THE ARRIVAL OF SPRING WITH MUSIC, PARTIES, A PIE-EATING CONTEST, AND THE DUNK TANK, IN WHICH STUDENTS GET THE CHANCE TO DUNK THEIR PROFESSORS.

The Details

Campus setting:	suburban
Degrees:	bachelor's, master's
Calendar:	semesters
Public/Private:	private nonprofit
Number of full-time faculty:	75
Student-to-teacher ratio:	10:1

Admissions requirements:

- **Options:** common application, deferred entrance, early admission, electronic application
- **Application fee:** $35
- **Required:** high school transcript, letter of recommendation, SAT or ACT
- **Application deadlines:** continuous (freshmen), continuous (transfer)
- **Early decision:** —
- **Notification:** —

Average high school GPA:	3.03
Average freshman SAT verbal/math score:	543 / 536
Average freshman ACT score:	21
Number of applicants:	654
Number of applicants accepted:	384
Percentage of students from out of state:	4%
Total freshman enrollment:	119
Total enrollment:	1,280
Percentage of students who live in campus housing:	36%
Total tuition fee:	$22,460
Total cost with fees & expenses:	$30,641
Average financial aid package:	—

Where It's At

Rockford's 130-acre campus is located in Rockford, a midsize city on the Rock River in northern Illinois. The most popular activity is golf, and the city boasts 12 public and private courses. In fact, Rockford has been called the "Holey City." Other outdoor attractions include five farmers' markets, the Winnebago County Forest Preserve, the 18-mile Pecatonica Prairie Path and Bike Trail, and myriad water sports on the river. At the Riverfront Museum Park, visitors can roam through several museums, including the Discovery Center, or attend a performance by the Rockford Dance Company. Rockford is about 90 minutes from Chicago, Madison, and Milwaukee.

What It's Like

Rockford believes that good students make good citizens. Opportunities for volunteering abound, from going to Thailand with the Humanitarian Action Response Team to constructing homes in Mississippi during spring break to volunteering at Toynbee Hall, a London settlement house.

Each semester, students are required to broaden their horizons by attending at least two events in the College Forum Series, such as the president's Opening Convocation. At the Center for Civic Engagement, students hook up with community agencies in need of volunteers, hold fundraisers, and attend seminars about becoming active citizens.

Good students make good citizens.

Everybody also has to take several core liberal arts classes in such subjects as art, English, and social sciences. As juniors or seniors, students take an upper-level class in public speaking and persuasive writing called Advanced Rhetoric.

Rockford has more than 70 majors, concentrations, and minors, including coaching, journalism, and accounting.

New student orientation lasts approximately one week. During orientation weekend, just about every first-year takes the Plunge and spends a morning volunteering with a community group. The First-Year Experience program guarantees that everybody receives a faculty adviser, learns life and study skills, and takes the same first-year seminar.

As the Regents, students compete on 15 Division athletic teams, including volleyball and tennis. The large Seaver Center for Recreation and Athletics also hosts such intramural teams as dodgeball and basketball. Other activities include the Society of Artsy People, the Association for Political Minds, and the Regent Players, a performing arts troupe.

Popular hangouts on campus include Burpee Commons Lawn and the Lion's Den, which has pool tables and an Xbox. On campus, students choose from eight traditional residence halls, including the big "super singles" of Emerson and the suites of Olson.

Roger Williams University

One Old Ferry Road
Bristol, RI 02809

(401) 253-1040
http://www.rwu.edu/

Why It's Cool

Don't just watch *Law & Order*—live it. RWU's School of Justice Studies gives you everything you need to catch criminals before the commercial break. Choose between two majors: criminal justice and legal studies. Then take classes like Policing in America and Criminalistics. But RWU's got your back, even if you'd rather play a detective than be one. As a theater major, you'll spend a semester in London, learning from established actors, and you'll graduate with a concentration in either acting or design. Can't decide? Do a double major and have the best of both worlds.

BRISTOL, RHODE ISLAND, CALLS ITSELF "AMERICA'S MOST PATRIOTIC TOWN." THE TOWN'S BEEN HOSTING A FOURTH OF JULY CELEBRATION SINCE 1785.

The Details

Campus setting:	small town
Degrees:	bachelor's, master's
Calendar:	semesters
Public/Private:	private nonprofit
Number of full-time faculty:	168
Student-to-teacher ratio:	16:1

Admissions requirements:

- **Options:** common application, deferred entrance, early decision, electronic application
- **Application fee:** $50
- **Required:** essay or personal statement, high school transcript, letter of recommendation, SAT or ACT
- **Application deadlines:** continuous (freshmen), continuous (transfer)
- **Early decision:** 12/1
- **Notification:** continuous (freshmen), continuous (transfer), 12/15 (early decision)

Average high school GPA:	3.06
Average freshman SAT verbal/math score:	537 / 541
Average freshman ACT score:	22
Number of applicants:	5,819
Number of applicants accepted:	4,523
Percentage of students from out of state:	89%
Total freshman enrollment:	1,057
Total enrollment:	5,070
Percentage of students who live in campus housing:	79%
Total tuition fee:	$21,848
Total cost with fees & expenses:	$33,803
Average financial aid package:	$17,796

Where It's At

RWU's 140-acre campus is located on the water in Bristol, Rhode Island. Bordered by Narragansett Bay, RWU offers many opportunities for water sports, sunbathing, and long walks on the beach. The small town of Bristol is home to Colt State Park and the America's Cup Hall of Fame. Several preserved seventeenth-century houses and estates, including Blithewold Mansion and Mount Hope Farm, also attract visitors. Just 30 minutes away, historic Newport has the Tennis Hall of Fame and the Cliff Walk, a path that threads between the Atlantic Ocean and stately mansions. Providence, the state capital, is about half an hour away.

What It's Like

RWU combines academics with practical programs like Reality 101, a crash course in the real world taken by seniors, and the Feinstein Service Learning Program, which lets students apply classroom lessons to community service opportunities. Scholarships for Service gives qualified students who have volunteered for 300 hours a $1,000 grant.

Six schools make up RWU: business; education; justice studies; arts and sciences; architecture, art, and historic preservation; and engineering, computing, and construction management. The 35 majors range from financial services to graphic design communications. Several majors require students to do an internship or participate in a cooperative program.

Seniors take Reality 101.

Regardless of school or major, everybody must take the Core Curriculum. Five interdisciplinary courses are required: Artistic Impulse; Perspectives in Human Behavior; Science: Discoveries in Context; History and the Modern World; and Literature, Philosophy, and the Ascent of Ideas. These classes help students answer fundamental questions about life, such as "How should I behave?" by looking at different aspects of history and culture. There's even a special tutoring center devoted to these specific classes. Students are also required to take five courses, known as the "Core Concentration," in a discipline other than the major.

Approximately 75 student organizations range from the Environmental and Animal Rights Club to the Balls to the Walls Racquetball Club. As the Hawks, students compete on 18 Division III varsity teams, including sailing.

Roughly 80 percent of RWU students live on campus in one of six residential complexes. Four halls have views of the water. Architecture and marine biology majors may elect to live together in living-learning communities. First-years generally live in Cedar Hall, which has singles, doubles, triples, and quads, as well as two basketball courts.

RWU runs study abroad programs throughout the world, including the semester-long program in London for theater majors. Another option is to go abroad during the Winter Intersession (three weeks in January), during Mini-Mester (three weeks in May and June), or during the summer. Short programs are available in Belize and the Czech Republic, among other countries.

Rollins College

1000 Holt Avenue
Winter Park, FL 32789
(407) 646-2000
http://www.rollins.edu/

Why It's Cool

America's favorite vacation destination is also home to a great education at Rollins. Bordering the theme-park metropolis of Orlando, this treasure school gives you a great ride for your admission dollar. But instead of long lines and overpriced snacks, you'll get the Rollins Conference, a seminar for first-years centered around such topics as Activism 101 or How to Get to Carnegie Hall, and the 3/2 Accelerated Management Program, which lets you earn a BA and MBA in one shot. Add to the fact that Rollins has one of the best business schools in the South, and you've got yourself a whole new take on fun in the sun.

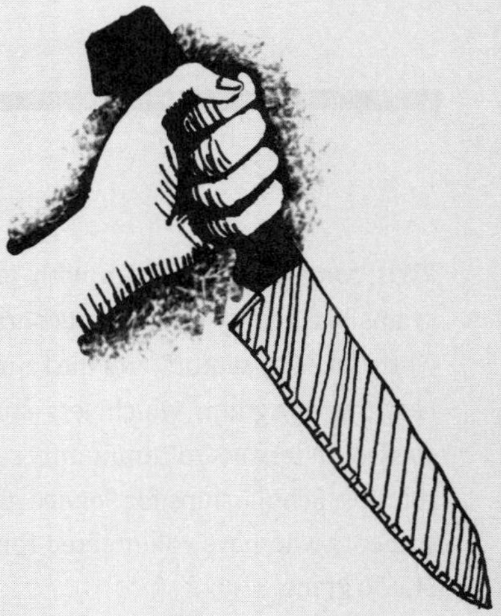

***PSYCHO* STAR ANTHONY PERKINS** IS ROLLINS'S MOST (IN)FAMOUS ALUM.

The Details

Campus setting:	suburban
Degrees:	bachelor's, master's
Calendar:	semesters
Public/Private:	private nonprofit
Number of full-time faculty:	179
Student-to-teacher ratio:	11:1

Admissions requirements:

- **Options:** common application, deferred entrance, early admission, early decision, electronic application
- **Application fee:** $40
- **Required:** essay or personal statement, high school transcript, letter of recommendation, SAT or ACT
- **Application deadlines:** 2/15 (freshmen), 4/15 (transfer)
- **Early decision:** 11/15
- **Notification:** 4/1 (freshmen), continuous (transfer), 12/15 (early decision)

Average high school GPA:	3.40
Average freshman SAT verbal/math score:	594 / 591
Average freshman ACT score:	24
Number of applicants:	2,598
Number of applicants accepted:	1,544
Percentage of students from out of state:	51%
Total freshman enrollment:	486
Total enrollment:	2,571
Percentage of students who live in campus housing:	66%
Total tuition fee:	$26,910
Total cost with fees & expenses:	$36,820
Average financial aid package:	$26,666

Where It's At

Rollins's 67-acre campus is located in the town of Winter Park, Florida. Nicknamed the "City of Culture and Heritage," Winter Park has several museums, including the Morse Museum of American Art and McRae Arts Studios, and performance spaces, including the Winter Park Playhouse and Enzian Theater. Park Avenue features such upscale stores as the Scott Laurent Gallery. Each year, the city hosts the Bach Festival, and the town's Central Park holds frequent jazz concerts. About 15 minutes away, the sprawling metropolis of Orlando has Walt Disney World, SeaWorld, Universal Studios, the Orlando Science Center, Wet 'n Wild (a water park), and Discovery Cove.

What It's Like

Red-roofed buildings, a huge outdoor pool, and the sounds of Lake Virginia lapping the campus on two sides make Rollins one gorgeous place to study the liberal arts or to take a preprofessional program, such as prelaw or prebusiness. Plus, the administration cancels class for a day every spring. Students usually use Fox Day, as this free day is called, to head to the beach. At Rollins, students perfectly balance their drive to succeed with their desire to relax and soak up the sun.

Rollins offers more than 30 majors, ranging from molecular biology to dance. All undergrad students must take classes in several areas, including non-Western cultures and the expressive arts. Everybody must also take three physical education classes and one course that explores ethical values.

One gorgeous place to study the liberal arts

To help orient first-years, Rollins holds Explorations, a series of activities, including a talent show and a popular getaway, during the first weekend of fall semester. First-years also take the interdisciplinary Rollins Conference, seminars like To Hell and Back: Visions of the Apocalypse and Uncalculus (a math course). With views of the lake, McKean Hall houses the first-years participating in living/learning communities. Ward, Holt, and Elizabeth are the other first-year dorms.

Through the 3/2 Accelerated Management Program, students spend three years earning a BA. Then they switch to the Crummer Graduate School to earn a master's in business administration (MBA) over the next two years. Rollins has one of the best business programs in the South, and business administration is a popular major. All told, about 50 percent of Rollins graduates eventually continue on to professional or graduate school.

Off-campus options include getting a minor in Australian studies in Sydney. Field studies, or short classes taught in cool places, run for between two and four weeks. Recent offerings ranged from studying marine biology in Barbados to making art in Scotland.

Among the 75 student organizations are the Outdoor Club and the Film Appreciation Organization. There are 22 Division II athletic teams (the Tars), including excellent waterskiing teams, and ten fraternities and sororities. Most Rollins students go Greek and play on an intramural team.

Red State, Blue State: Most Politically Active Campuses

Think fast: Are you an elephant or a donkey? You'll find plenty of both—and a whole lot more on the political spectrum—at the following colleges and universities.

Antioch College (P. 10)

College of the Ozarks (P. 64)

Earlham College (P. 78)

Eckerd College (P. 80)

Eugene Lang College (P. 90)

The Evergreen State College (P. 92)

Hampshire College (P. 106)

Knox College (P. 122)

Lewis & Clark College (P. 124)

Savannah College of Art and Design

342 Bull Street, PO Box 3146
Savannah, GA 31402

(912) 525-5000
http://www.scad.edu/

Why It's Cool

How would you like to design your own games on super-fast computers, do an internship with Dreamworks, or master travel photography in Lacoste, France? SCAD lets you do all of the above and then some. At the largest art school in the United States, you'll choose from among more than 25 majors, ranging from furniture design to animation. You'll take foundational classes in studio art and the liberal arts, and you'll sell the fruits of your artistic labors each spring during the huge Sidewalk Arts Festival. As if all that wasn't sweet enough, you'll also get every Friday off for "independent study."

AT SCAD, IT'S OK TO PLAY IN THE SAND: THE ANNUAL SAND ARTS FESTIVAL AWARDS PRIZES FOR BEST SAND CASTLE, BEST SAND SCULPTURE, AND BEST WIND SCULPTURE.

The Details

Campus setting:	urban
Degrees:	bachelor's, master's
Calendar:	quarters
Public/Private:	private nonprofit
Number of full-time faculty:	319
Student-to-teacher ratio:	18:1

Admissions requirements:

- **Options:** early admission, electronic application
- **Application fee:** $50
- **Required:** high school transcript, 3 letters of recommendation, SAT or ACT
- **Application deadlines:** continuous (freshmen), continuous (transfer)
- **Early decision:** —
- **Notification:** continuous (freshmen), continuous (transfer)

Average high school GPA:	—
Average freshman SAT verbal/math score:	552 / 538
Average freshman ACT score:	23
Number of applicants:	4,100
Number of applicants accepted:	2,960
Percentage of students from out of state:	85%
Total freshman enrollment:	1,285
Total enrollment:	6,776
Percentage of students who live in campus housing:	33%
Total tuition fee:	$21,600
Total cost with fees & expenses:	$32,300
Average financial aid package:	$8,100

Where It's At

SCAD's 60 buildings stand in the historic district of Savannah, in southeastern Georgia. A free shuttle connects the various facilities. Among Savannah's many attractions are 24 idyllic, tree-lined squares; Bonaventure Cemetery; the Savannah History Museum; and the beach at Tybee Island. Each year, Savannah hosts many events, including the Jazz Festival, the Shakespeare Festival, and a massive St. Patrick's Day celebration. The beaches and resorts of Hilton Head are less than an hour away. Atlanta, about four hours away by car, is home to a second SCAD campus. In addition to the Braves (MLB), the Hawks (NBA), the Falcons (NFL), and the Thrashers (NHL), Atlanta also has the Georgia Aquarium and the World of Coca-Cola museum.

What It's Like

SCAD's got some mega-talented folks, from 50 states and 80 countries. But life at SCAD is about forming artsy communities—not about competition. Students bond in groups like Phusion (which combines photography and fashion), 24 Frames (devoted to film and television), and the Sculpture Club. Think imaginative, inventive, and totally inspired.

The typical SCAD student? Imaginative, inventive, and totally inspired.

Students choose from more than 25 degree programs. Majors include interactive design and game development and cinema studies. All students must take several foundation courses in both the studio arts and the liberal arts, with each department deciding on specific requirements. For instance, a broadcast design and motion graphics major has to take Survey of Western Art, 3-D Design, and Life Drawing, among others.

Housing options range from the apartments at Boundary Village to the doubles and private bathrooms at Turner House. Every on-campus resident gets a dresser, bed, drafting table, and stool. Students also have the option of living in theme houses, in which residents have common interests, including wellness at Turner House (which has its own fitness center). More than 3,000 workstations at SCAD ensure that there's always a computer available.

There are 22 NAIA varsity athletic teams (the Bees), including rowing and cheerleading. The championship equestrian team will benefit from the soon-to-be-completed Waranch Equestrian Center. Everyone gets to work out at SCAD's three fitness centers or take a class in kickboxing or yoga.

Each fall, the Savannah Film Festival screens student and professional films, runs workshops with industry leaders, and hosts talks at SCAD. During the festival, the daily "Coffee Talk" series lets students chat informally with big-name directors and other film professionals about the industry.

Through SCAD-Lacoste, students live and learn in a small village in France, taking such classes as Nineteenth-Century Architecture and Design Semantics. Other programs take students to China, Singapore, Italy, and New York City. SCAD's Job Magnet site helps students find jobs, internships, and information about grad school.

Sierra Nevada College

999 Tahoe Boulevard
Incline Village, NV 89451
(775) 831-1314
http://www.sierranevada.edu/

Why It's Cool

SNC gives you dollars and sense. Here, everybody has to take Entrepreneurship and the Free Enterprise System, regardless of major. You'll not only learn how to research and start your own business, but you'll also see how to apply the "entrepreneurial spirit" to your chosen career. Other optional business classes will show you how to turn inspiration into a corporation and how to raise money for your ventures. The department of management even sponsors international trips so that you can see how everything works globally. Combine all this with cool art classes, and you've got yourself a valuable school.

GET LUCKY. GAMBLING'S LEGAL IN NEVADA, WHICH MEANS YOU CAN TAKE A STUDY BREAK TO SHOOT CRAPS OR HIT THE SLOTS—AND MAYBE WIN SOME CHEESE (CASINO SLANG FOR "MONEY").

The Details

Campus setting:	small town
Degrees:	bachelor's, master's
Calendar:	semesters
Public/Private:	private nonprofit
Number of full-time faculty:	19
Student-to-teacher ratio:	8:1

Admissions requirements:

- **Options:** common application, deferred entrance, early admission, electronic application
- **Application fee:** —
- **Required:** essay or personal statement, high school transcript, letter of recommendation, SAT and SAT Subject Tests, or ACT
- **Application deadlines:** continuous (freshmen), continuous (transfer)
- **Early decision:** —
- **Notification:** continuous (freshmen), continuous (transfer)

Average high school GPA:	3.14
Average freshman SAT verbal/math score:	520 / 514
Average freshman ACT score:	—
Number of applicants:	383
Number of applicants accepted:	262
Percentage of students from out of state:	71%
Total freshman enrollment:	67
Total enrollment:	492
Percentage of students who live in campus housing:	45%
Total tuition fee:	$19,500
Total cost with fees & expenses:	$27,850
Average financial aid package:	$14,000

Where It's At

SNC has two campuses: the Mountain Campus and the all-new Lake Campus, both located in the small town of Incline Village, Nevada. A free shuttle bus makes frequent stops along the 1.5-mile route between campuses. Incline Village relies mostly on tourism, as visitors flock to spectacular Lake Tahoe. In addition to a wide variety of outdoor activities—from sailing to snowboarding to hiking to skiing—the area has the Thunderbird Lodge, a historic mansion; the Emigrant Trail Museum; the Tahoe Maritime Museum; and the Fleischmann Planetarium and Science Center. Since gambling is legal, several local hotels, including Harrah's, have casinos. Reno is about an hour away; San Francisco is about four hours away by car.

What It's Like

Out is in at SNC. Students here *love* the outdoors. Activities revolve around the mountains and Lake Tahoe: skiing, snowboarding, hiking, swimming, parasailing. . . . If you'd rather stay inside, SNC's probably not for you.

SNC has five academic departments: science and technology, humanities and social sciences, international studies, management, and fine arts. Among the varied majors are digital art and ski business and resort management. Just about every classroom is wireless, and everyone is required to have a laptop (students get deep discounts on notebook purchases).

Out is in at SNC.

Art is big on campus too. The entertainment technology minor lets students blend the fine arts and computer science. During the summer, SNC hosts several Visiting Artists Workshops in such areas as jewelry-making and ceramics. All students must take at least one studio art class, such as Guitar Ensemble or Foundations of Digital Design.

At the $24 million Tahoe Center for Environmental Sciences, students conduct research along with faculty from SNC and the University of California–Davis. Projects range from exploring alternative energy sources to continuing SNC's commitment to using green building materials and technologies.

General education requirements include classes like Humans in the Environment and Introduction to Computers. Everybody must also complete Entrepreneurship and Free Enterprise, which covers every aspect of the free-market system, from developing an idea to getting money to starting up a business. Before graduating, seniors must take the Ethics in Life and Work seminar.

The Lake Campus features two brand-new dorms: Prim-Schultz, which features doubles and ski-tuning facilities, and Campbell-Friedman, which has singles with spectacular views of the lake and mountains. Everybody eats at Patterson Hall, which has vegan or vegetarian options at every meal and which will make students' favorite recipes. Three of SNC's most popular events revolve around food: the Thanksgiving Dinner, Valentine's Day Dinner, and Graduation Luau.

Sonoma State University

1801 East Cotati Avenue
Rohnert Park, CA 94928
(707) 664-2880
http://www.sonoma.edu/

Why It's Cool

Bottoms up. The Wine Business Program at Sonoma State University will teach you everything you need to know to start your own winery, from cultivating grapes to designing labels to marketing your product. Spend your summers doing public relations for a local winery or pitching in at the Sonoma Valley Vintners and Growers Alliance. Do a good job, and someday you might get inducted into the school's Wine Business Hall of Fame. But even teetotalers will find a place here: Freshmen Interest Groups connect first-years in living/learning communities, while the soon-to-open Green Music Center promises to attract national and local performers to SSU. We'll toast to that.

NEARBY SAN FRANCISCO HOSTS AN ANNUAL ST. STUPID'S DAY PARADE, IN WHICH PEOPLE DRESS IN COSTUME AND CELEBRATE IDIOCY, LUNACY, AND GENERAL DEBAUCHERY.

The Details

Campus setting:	small town
Degrees:	bachelor's, master's
Calendar:	semesters
Public/Private:	public state
Number of full-time faculty:	262
Student-to-teacher ratio:	24:1

Admissions requirements:

- **Options:** early admission, electronic application
- **Application fee:** $55
- **Required:** high school transcript, SAT or ACT
- **Application deadlines:** 12/31 (freshmen), 1/31 (transfer)
- **Early decision:** —
- **Notification:** continuous (freshmen), continuous (transfer)

Average high school GPA:	3.23
Average freshman SAT verbal/math score:	524 / 529
Average freshman ACT score:	21
Number of applicants:	8,392
Number of applicants accepted:	5,837
Percentage of students from out of state:	1%
Total freshman enrollment:	1,092
Total enrollment:	7,977
Percentage of students who live in campus housing:	35%
Total in-state tuition, fees & expenses:	$13,473
Total out-of-state tuition, fees & expenses:	$23,649
Average financial aid package:	$9,497

Where It's At

SSU's 269-acre campus is located in Rohnert Park, in Sonoma County. California's wine-growing region has more than 200 wineries and vineyards. Other popular activities include golf, hot-air ballooning, visiting spas in nearby Santa Rosa, and gambling. The Pacific Ocean is about 40 minutes away. At the Charles M. Schulz Museum, visitors can learn all about Snoopy and the creator of the *Peanuts* comic strip. About an hour away, the San Francisco Bay area has numerous attractions, including Golden Gate Park; the bohemian shops of Berkeley; the Giants (MLB), 49ers (NFL), Sharks (NHL), and Warriors (NBA); and the San Francisco Museum of Modern Art.

What It's Like

With so much wine around, it's no surprise that SSU students like to have fun. After all, even the five residential villages are named for wine: Verdot, Cabernet, Sauvignon, Zinfandel, and Beaujolais. Both Zinfandel and Beaujolais have pools and hot tubs. Sauvignon has covered balconies, while Verdot has an outdoor basketball court. Everybody loves to socialize.

SSU is part of the California State University system—and SSU is made up of five schools: business and economics, arts and humanities, science and technology, social sciences, and education. Among the more than 40 majors are criminal justice administration, nursing, and Chicano and Latino studies. Interested students can take classes in the Wine Business Program and get a BS in business administration with an emphasis on wine business strategies.

With so much wine around, it's easy to find a party at SSU.

General education requirements include liberal arts courses like The Person in Society and California Ethnic Literature. All students must also take at least one ethnic studies class, such as Mexican American Identity and Society, and at least one class in U.S. history. Some requirements may be met with the seminars offered by the Hutchins Center for Interdisciplinary Learning, including Challenge and Response in the Modern World. Students may design their own majors through Hutchins as well. International Programs helps students sign up to study art in Chile or economics in Zimbabwe.

Some first-years opt to participate in Freshman Interest Groups (FIGs). In addition to living together in the apartments of Cabernet Village, these students take the same two or three classes. Recent FIGs have included K through 12 education and global issues/global careers.

SSU has dozens of student groups, ranging from 12 fraternities and sororities to Project SCHOLARS, which links SSU students to at-risk students in local schools, to sports clubs for ping-pong and fencing. As the Seawolves, SSU sponsors 13 Division II athletic teams, including women's water polo.

Southwestern University

1001 East University Avenue
Georgetown, TX 78626

(512) 863-6511
http://www.southwestern.edu/

Why It's Cool

Paideia . . . it sounds like something you need to see a doctor about, but it's actually the name of the most wicked educational adventure in Texas. As an SU first-year, you can apply to the three-year Paideia Program and become a Paideia Scholar. You'll then explore five "strands" in academic and nonacademic settings: service, leadership, academics, intercultural experiences, and collaborative research and creative works. You'll take seminars with fewer than ten students, and you'll get a personal faculty mentor with whom you'll meet regularly. You'll even get $1,000 to use toward travel or project expenses. Funky name. Awesome program.

JUST SOUTH OF SU, AUSTIN HAS THE LARGEST URBAN BAT COLONY IN NORTH AMERICA. CLOSE TO 1.5 MILLION BATS LIVE UNDER THE CITY'S CONGRESS AVENUE BRIDGE.

The Details

Campus setting:	suburban
Degrees:	bachelor's
Calendar:	semesters
Public/Private:	private religious
Number of full-time faculty:	121
Student-to-teacher ratio:	10:1

Admissions requirements:

- **Options:** common application, deferred entrance, early decision, electronic application
- **Application fee:** $40
- **Required:** essay or personal statement, high school transcript, letter of recommendation, SAT or ACT
- **Application deadlines:** 2/15 (freshmen), 4/1 (transfer)
- **Early decision:** 11/1
- **Notification:** 4/1 (freshmen), continuous (transfer), 12/1 (early decision)

Average high school GPA:	—
Average freshman SAT verbal/math score:	630 / 630
Average freshman ACT score:	25
Number of applicants:	1,888
Number of applicants accepted:	1,238
Percentage of students from out of state:	9%
Total freshman enrollment:	366
Total enrollment:	1,276
Percentage of students who live in campus housing:	83%
Total tuition fee:	$20,220
Total cost with fees & expenses:	$27,279
Average financial aid package:	$16,577

Where It's At

SU's 700-acre campus is located in Georgetown, a town about 30 miles north of Austin, the capital of Texas. The gigantic campus includes a 75-acre, nine-hole golf course, two live-performance theaters, and an aquatic animal research library. Georgetown has several parks along the San Gabriel River, as well as a downtown area composed of historic nineteenth-century buildings. Each April, the town celebrates the arrival of spring with the Red Poppy Festival, which includes live music and a Corvette car show. Austin's numerous attractions range from the Museum of Art to the Austin Zoo to the hip neighborhood of East Sixth Street.

What It's Like

As the saying goes, "Don't mess with Texas." Because most students come from in-state, you'd better have a fondness for Texan culture, which includes horses, cowboy hats, steak, and sweet tea. Students here are polite but fiercely proud of their home state and its treasure school.

SU is divided into the Sarofim School of Fine Arts and the Brown College of Arts and Sciences. Among the approximately 40 majors are feminist studies and kinesiology. The preprofessional program in athletic training lets students begin working as interns their first year.

Polite, proud, and fond of cowboy hats

Choices for the mandatory first-year seminar include You Are What You Eat: Religious Conceptions of Food and The Secret History of the Twentieth Century. Some seminars are designated as learning communities, so students in these courses get to live together in Mabee Hall. Other requirements include courses in the humanities and natural sciences.

As Paideia Scholars, students develop a personalized plan of academic goals with the help of a faculty mentor. Small seminars let scholars discuss readings in newspapers and magazines that they've found meaningful or helpful. Scholars also complete in-class and out-of-class activities in the five core Paideia areas. These students go abroad, volunteer, and work with their mentors on specialized projects. It's like having a special small college within the larger SU community.

Off-campus programs include a semester in New York City or London. SU also runs summer programs in Jamaica, Mexico, and Germany. The department of biology sponsors a well-regarded research program on the SU campus each summer.

About 80 percent of students live on campus in one of eight residence halls and two Greek houses. There are eight fraternities and sororities, 14 Division III athletic teams (the Pirates), and more than 100 other organizations, including the A.S.I.A. Club and SU Independent Filmmakers. The Pirate Bikes program leaves yellow bicycles around campus for anyone to use.

St. John's College

60 College Avenue	**1160 Camino Cruz Blanca**
Annapolis, MD 21401	**Santa Fe, NM 87505**
(410) 263-2371	**(505) 984-6000**
http://www.stjohnscollege.edu/	**http://www.stjohnscollege.edu/**

Why It's Cool

Got books? St. John's sure does. Many, many, many books, in fact. And, over four years, you'll probably read them all. Through the mandatory "Great Books" curriculum, you'll study just about every significant work in the Western literary tradition, chronologically, from Homer to Shakespeare to Freud and beyond. No majors. No departments. Just book after book as you plow through a comprehensive reading list. Sound intense? It is. But it's also one of the most interesting curriculums of any school in the United States. You'll graduate with an extraordinary education. Just don't forget to pack your reading glasses, because you're gonna need them.

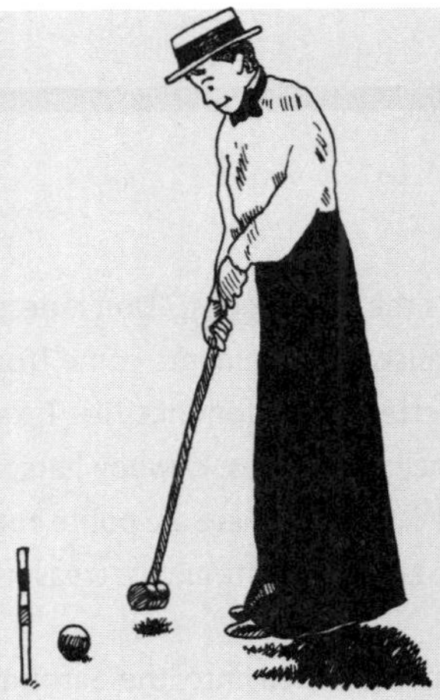

NICELY DONE. ST. JOHN'S HAS WON 18 OF ITS LAST 23 ANNUAL CROQUET MATCHES AGAINST NAVY. STUDENTS GET DRESSED UP TO WATCH.

The Details

Campus setting:	small town
Degrees:	bachelor's, master's
Calendar:	semesters
Public/Private:	private nonprofit
Number of full-time faculty:	73
Student-to-teacher ratio:	8:1

Admissions requirements:

- **Options:** common application, deferred entrance, early admission, electronic application
- **Application fee:** —
- **Required:** essay or personal statement, high school transcript, 2 letters of recommendation, SAT or ACT (recommended)
- **Application deadlines:** continuous (freshmen), continuous (transfer)
- **Early decision:** —
- **Notification:** continuous (freshmen), continuous (transfer)

Average high school GPA:	—
Average freshman SAT verbal/math score:	706 / 650
Average freshman ACT score:	—
Number of applicants:	535
Number of applicants accepted:	360
Percentage of students from out of state:	87%
Total freshman enrollment:	133
Total enrollment:	564
Percentage of students who live in campus housing:	87%
Total tuition fee:	$32,250
Total cost with fees & expenses:	$40,606
Average financial aid package:	$22,262

Where It's At

St. John's has two campuses, and students are allowed to transfer between the two. The entire 32-acre Annapolis, Maryland, campus has been named a National Historic Landmark. Maryland's state capital has many attractions, including the Ballet Theatre of Mary, the Annapolis Maritime Museum, and water sports in Chesapeake Bay.

Santa Fe, the capital of New Mexico, is home to the 250-acre second campus. Residents and tourists alike flock to Santa Fe's art market along Canyon Road, the second largest in the United States. Myriad outdoor activities range from walking the Santa Fe National Historic Trail to climbing the nearby Sangre de Cristo Mountains.

What It's Like

We're not going to lie to you: This school is tough. It's no surprise, then, that students here love a good challenge. Don't expect the conversation to stop once you've left the classroom: Philosophical questions spill over into the dorms, the dining halls, even the athletic fields.

"Johnnies," as students are called, do a preset curriculum known as the "Program": four years of seminars, small groups led by two faculty members called "tutors"; four years of math; four years of language, including ancient Greek and French, as well as instruction in logic and poetry; three years of a laboratory science; and one year of music.

Philosophical questions even spill over into the athletic fields.

Rather than memorize a textbook, students learn from original books. So, in the math tutorials, students read the writings of Newton, while students learning Greek might translate Plato into English and students in freshman laboratory learn biology and chemistry from Aristotle and Pascal. The "Great Books" reading lists move roughly chronologically from ancient Greek works to contemporary classics. Students in the same academic year read the same books.

Both the Annapolis and the Santa Fe campus use the Program as the curriculum. Each also has its own Coffee Shop, a popular hang-out spot. Finally, both campuses get together every Friday night to hear a lecture from a visiting scholar or tutor.

But the two campuses also have different flavors. Annapolis tends to be more reserved: life revolves around McDowell Hall, the eighteenth-century heart of campus. Some of the six dorms were built in the nineteenth century. The colonial past injects some formality into campus life: During the annual spring croquet match against the U.S. Naval Academy, spectators munch on cucumber sandwiches and drink champagne.

The Santa Fe campus is larger and more modern. The dorms are organized around open courtyards. Perhaps the most popular extracurricular activity is the Search and Rescue Team, which provides first aid in the nearby mountains. While Annapolis students release Program stress by frolicking on the bay, Santa Fe students head to the mountains.

Lookin' Good: Most Beautiful Campuses

Like all good parents, we at SparkCollege don't play favorites. We love all our Treasure Schools *equally*. But, when pressed, even we have to admit that the following schools are really, really beautiful.

Agnes Scott College (P. 2)

Allegheny College (P. 6)

Arcadia University (P. 16)

College of Charleston (P. 54)

College of the Atlantic (P. 62)

Cornell College (P. 74)

Elon University (P. 86)

Kalamazoo College (P. 116)

Loyola University Chicago (P. 128)

Miami University (P. 138)

Mount Holyoke College (P. 142)

Stephens College

1200 East Broadway
Columbia, MO 65215

(573) 442-2211
http://www.stephens.edu/

Why It's Cool

Hey, ladies . . . Stephens has got a sweet deal for all you performers out there. With the accelerated degree program in theatre arts, you'll have your name in lights in no time. Star in one of six main stage theatrical productions each year. Get access to a library of 12,000 costumes. Help manage the student-run Seven Star production company, through the digital filmmaking program, or take classes like American Cinema/Culture, Stagecraft/Stage Management, and Theatre Speech. Attend the Indie Filmmaker's Bootcamp, which Stephens hosts each summer, and make a movie in nine days. Bye-bye, performance anxiety. Hello, Hollywood.

EACH SEMESTER, THE CAMPUS-WIDE DOOR SLAM SIGNALS THE START OF ROUND-THE-CLOCK QUIET IN THE DORMS DURING FINALS.

The Details

Campus setting:	urban
Degrees:	bachelor's, master's
Calendar:	semesters
Public/Private:	private nonprofit
Number of full-time faculty:	45
Student-to-teacher ratio:	10:1

Admissions requirements:

- **Options:** common application, deferred entrance, early admission, electronic application
- **Application fee:** $25
- **Required:** essay or personal statement, high school transcript, letter of recommendation, SAT or ACT
- **Application deadlines:** 7/31 (freshmen), — (transfer)
- **Early decision:** —
- **Notification:** 8/15 (freshmen), 8/15 (transfer)

Average high school GPA:	3.50
Average freshman SAT verbal/math score:	546 / 477
Average freshman ACT score:	22
Number of applicants:	408
Number of applicants accepted:	324
Percentage of students from out of state:	55%
Total freshman enrollment:	157
Total enrollment:	705
Percentage of students who live in campus housing:	70%
Total tuition fee:	$19,300
Total cost with fees & expenses:	$26,930
Average financial aid package:	$16,141

Where It's At

Stephens's 86-acre campus is located in Columbia, Missouri. Columbia has been called "Collegetown, USA," because three schools are within walking distance of one another: Stephens, Columbia College, and the University of Missouri–Columbia. The schools border the District, the cultural heart of the city. Each week, the area hosts more than 45 performances at such venues as Cherry Street Artisan and Mojo's. In February, the True/False Festival screens documentaries, while the Twilight Festivals in June and September feature live music, food, and crafts. A popular activity is walking or biking the MKT Trail. St. Louis is about two hours away.

What It's Like

Stephens has been turning girls into women since 1833. Everything at Stephens—from campus life to academics—is organized around the Ten Ideals: leadership, sensitivity, respect, intelligence, support, courage, independence, belief, creativity, and responsibility. But the ladies here don't take themselves too seriously: The bars and nightclubs of the District are great places to meet guys or just hang out.

Spot and Whiskers are welcome in some Stephens dorms.

The more than 30 majors include equestrian science and fashion merchandising. Several joint programs let qualified students earn a BA or BS at Stephens, then transfer to another school for an MA or JD. For instance, after majoring in biology, students can switch to Washington University to earn a master's in occupational therapy.

First-years at Stephens are divided into learning communities, groups of about 40 women. These groups take roughly ten liberal arts courses together throughout their time at Stephens, including classes in writing and women's health. Each community also gets four faculty mentors.

Students automatically get singles in the six residence halls, unless they request to live in doubles. Residential life at Stephens is homey, to say the least: Roblee rooms have hardwood floors and ceiling fans, while Searcy and Prunty Halls allow students to have dogs and cats in their rooms.

Among the student groups on campus are two sororities, six Division III athletic teams, the Martin Luther King Jr. Student Union, and the student-run radio station, Sweet 90.5. Theatre arts majors perform with the student-run Warehouse Theatre and the professional Macklanburg Playhouse.

All students have access to the eight museums on campus, including the Botany Herbarium and the Entomology Museum. The Costume Research Library has more than 12,000 garments, some dating back to 1790, available for study.

Study abroad programs range from a yearlong program in England to summer programs in Japan and Costa Rica. With the Paris Fashion Industry Seminar, students spend four weeks studying museums and designers in France. During the summer, the Indie Filmmakers' Bootcamp comes to campus to teach the fundamentals of moviemaking.

Thomas Aquinas College

10000 North Ojai Road
Santa Paula, CA 93060
(805) 525-4417
http://www.thomasaquinas.edu/

Why It's Cool

Adios, textbooks. So long, lectures. Sayonara, majors. Say hello to the "Great Books" curriculum. At Thomas Aquinas, you'll spend four years reading the most significant works of Western civilization. You'll begin with Homer in your first year and work your way through to Tolstoy and Twain as a senior. In between, you'll use Euclid to master mathematics, Mendel to learn science, Aristotle to probe philosophy, Shakespeare to study psychology. You'll meet for intense discussions with classmates and professors. And, before graduating, you'll complete a big project on the topic of your choice. Over four years, you'll become an expert in the Catholic liberal arts.

THE ANNUAL TRIVIAL AND QUADRIVIAL PURSUIT GAME FEATURES TOUGH QUESTIONS BY PROFESSORS DESIGNED TO TEST STUDENT KNOWLEDGE AND LET BRAINIACS SHOW OFF.

The Details

Campus setting:	rural
Degrees:	bachelor's
Calendar:	semesters
Public/Private:	private religious
Number of full-time faculty:	30
Student-to-teacher ratio:	11:1

Admissions requirements:

- **Options:** deferred entrance, early admission
- **Application fee:** —
- **Required:** essay or personal statement, high school transcript, 3 letters of recommendation, SAT or ACT
- **Application deadlines:** continuous (freshmen)
- **Early decision:** —
- **Notification:** continuous (freshmen)

Average high school GPA:	3.66
Average freshman SAT verbal/math score:	668 / 632
Average freshman ACT score:	27
Number of applicants:	209
Number of applicants accepted:	172
Percentage of students from out of state:	54%
Total freshman enrollment:	104
Total enrollment:	331
Percentage of students who live in campus housing:	99%
Total tuition fee:	$18,600
Total cost with fees & expenses:	$24,850
Average financial aid package:	$15,826

Where It's At

TAC's 131-acre campus is located in Santa Paula, the "Citrus Capital of the World." Sunny southern California has lots of stuff to do, from hiking the Los Padres National Forest (next door to campus) to driving to Los Angeles (about an hour away) to frolicking on Ventura Beach. Murals depicting the town's history cover downtown Santa Paula, which also boasts several historic buildings, including the nineteenth-century Balcom and Hardison Houses. During the spring and summer, Santa Paula hosts such events as Farm Fest, the Citrus Festival, and the Heritage Valley Festival. The beaches, galleries, and vineyards of Santa Barbara are about 45 minutes away by car.

What It's Like

TACers, as students are known, tend to be committed, conservative, and Christian. Classes usually start at 8:30 A.M. and run until 3:30 P.M., with a two-hour break for lunch. Each class begins with a prayer. Meals are served at 7:30, 11:45, and 5:30. The regular schedule frees you up to read, study, think, and read some more.

Read. Study. Think. Read some more.

Thomas Aquinas calls its "Great Books" curriculum the ideal education in Catholic liberal arts. Everybody reads canonical texts in several main subjects: philosophy, literature, laboratory science, theology, mathematics, music, and Latin. The curriculum moves roughly chronologically, beginning with the foundations of Western literature and continuing into the twentieth century.

Each class year reads the same books, so all first-years begin with *The Odyssey,* while all seniors study Darwin and Dostoyevsky. Rather than lectures, students attend small discussion-style seminars led by a professor (known as a "tutor"). Together, they try to answer questions about each work, such as "What's the author saying?" and "What's the truth?" using the Socratic method. Most seminars require papers at the end of the semester.

There are no majors, specializations, minors, electives, or lectures. But unlike other schools with a "Great Books" curriculum, Thomas Aquinas emphasizes truth and reality within the context of Catholicism. Faith matters at this school. As seniors, students do a special thesis on a topic or author of their choice, chosen from the reading they've done.

Students live in the doubles of one of six residence halls: St. Katharine's, St. Therese of Lisieux, and St. Monica for women, and Blessed Junipero Serra, St. Bernard's, and Sts. Peter and Paul for men. Men are not allowed in the women's dorms. Ever.

To relax after class, students hang out informally on the lush, landscaped grounds of campus. Several dances are held each year too. After all, even intellectuals need to let loose once in a while.

Tuskegee University

102 Old Admin Building **(334) 727-8011**
Tuskegee, AL 36088 **http://www.tuskegee.edu/**

Why It's Cool

At Tuskegee, you won't just memorize formulas or stare at slides while taking classes in the really strong science and engineering programs. Instead, you'll help NASA develop technologies to better utilize food in space, or you'll use computers to analyze the secrets of cells, contributing vital information to the new field of bioinformatics. This historically black college is also home to the nation's first Center for Bioethics, devoted to ensuring ethical medical treatments for minorities and to increasing minority participation in scientific research. Put on a lab coat, roll up your sleeves, and jump in.

WHILE AT TUSKEGEE, GEORGE WASHINGTON CARVER DEVELOPED MORE THAN 300 RECIPES AND GOODS USING PEANUTS, INCLUDING MEAT LOAF, HAND LOTION, GOITER TREATMENT, PAPER, AND SOAP.

The Details

Campus setting:	small town
Degrees:	bachelor's, master's, doctoral
Calendar:	semesters
Public/Private:	private nonprofit
Number of full-time faculty:	218
Student-to-teacher ratio:	12:1

Admissions requirements:

- **Options:** early admission, electronic application
- **Application fee:** $25
- **Required:** high school transcript, SAT or ACT
- **Application deadlines:** 4/15 (freshmen), 4/15 (transfer)
- **Early decision:** —
- **Notification:** —

Average high school GPA:	3.20
Average freshman SAT verbal/math score:	455 / 469
Average freshman ACT score:	19
Number of applicants:	1,326
Number of applicants accepted:	1,068
Percentage of students from out of state:	57%
Total freshman enrollment:	697
Total enrollment:	2,870
Percentage of students who live in campus housing:	63%
Total tuition fee:	$11,290
Total cost with fees & expenses:	$18,403
Average financial aid package:	$13,824

Where It's At

Tuskegee is located in the town of Tuskegee, Alabama. The Tuskegee Human and Civil Rights Multicultural Center; The Oaks, the preserved home of Booker T. Washington; the turn-of-the-century Kirk's Old Farm Museum; and the Tuskegee Airmen National Historic Site are some of the area's most famous tourist destinations. Hikers and bird-watchers frequent the Tuskegee National Forest, which includes the Tsinia Wildlife Viewing Area—home to birds, beavers, and other animals. Montgomery, the state capital, is about 40 minutes away by car. Among its attractions are the Montgomery Zoo and the Rosa Parks Museum and Library.

What It's Like

Fabulous parties help fuel the social, friendly atmosphere at Tuskegee. The biggest party is Homecoming, a weeklong celebration that draws upward of 20,000 alumni and visitors to campus. In addition to the football game, activities include a step-show (a synchronized dance performance and competition), a fashion show, concerts, and a block party. In fact, students refer to the school and themselves collectively as the Tuskegee Family, emphasizing the close-knit community. Students here make friends for life.

Fabulous parties with the Tuskegee Family

Tuskegee was founded in 1881 to provide career training to African Americans, and this sense of practical application lives on in the "curriculum for success," as Tuskegee calls its educational philosophy, and its emphasis on "learning by doing." Solid programs in engineering and the sciences are complemented by required classes in the liberal arts. First-years are required to attend Orientation.

Students choose from among the more than 35 majors offered by Tuskegee's five colleges: agricultural, environmental, and natural sciences; liberal arts and education; veterinary medicine, nursing, and allied health; business and information science; and engineering, architecture, and physical science. Majors range from food and nutritional science to social work.

Among the student organizations are two fraternities, four sororities, the renowned Tuskegee Choir, and the award-winning student paper, *Campus Digest*. The Marching Crimson Piper Band has more than 150 members and features performances by drum majors and piperettes. Ten varsity athletic teams, including tennis and basketball, compete as the Golden Tigers in the SIAC.

First-years and sophomores are required to live on campus. Housing options include traditional dorms, including Sammy L. Younge Jr. Hall, and the Commons Apartments. The dorms are not co-ed, though we hear they're pretty cool. Plus, the on-campus snack bar, Grill 155, has good cookies and makes its own ice cream.

Unity College

90 Quaker Hill Road
Unity, ME 04988
(207) 948-3131
http://www.unity.edu/

Why It's Cool

If you're more comfortable in hiking boots than heels or loafers or if you'd rather clear a trail than crunch numbers, meet your treasure school. Here, you'll combine a love of the outdoors with practical career training. So don't worry about not having a job when you graduate. Not only does Unity have more environmental programs than any college in the United States, including the only major in conservation law enforcement, it's got an extensive Career Resource Center, which will hook you up with an internship or job interview, no matter what you major in. Better find a tie to match that North Face jacket.

UNITY OFFERS AN ONLINE SUSTAINABILITY "IN-A-BOX" COURSE, A BRIEF INTRODUCTION TO THE SCIENTIFIC PRINCIPLES BEHIND ENERGY CONSERVATION, WASTE REDUCTION, AND OTHER ENVIRONMENTAL ISSUES.

The Details

Campus setting:	rural
Degrees:	bachelor's
Calendar:	semesters
Public/Private:	private nonprofit
Number of full-time faculty:	32
Student-to-teacher ratio:	13:1

Admissions requirements:

- **Options:** common application, deferred entrance, early admission, early action, electronic application
- **Application fee:** $25
- **Required:** essay or personal statement, high school transcript, 2 letters of recommendation
- **Application deadlines:** continuous (freshmen), continuous (transfer)
- **Early action:** 1/15
- **Notification:** — (freshmen), — (transfer), 2/1 (early action)

Average high school GPA:	3.06
Average freshman SAT verbal/math score:	504 / 499
Average freshman ACT score:	—
Number of applicants:	436
Number of applicants accepted:	382
Percentage of students from out of state:	62%
Total freshman enrollment:	159
Total enrollment:	521
Percentage of students who live in campus housing:	66%
Total tuition fee:	$16,740
Total cost with fees & expenses:	$24,310
Average financial aid package:	$12,979

Where It's At

Unity's 240-acre campus is located in the tiny town of Unity, in central Maine. The Unity Centre hosts musical and theatrical performances, and the Unity Community Center holds a farmers' market from May to November. Every Thursday, stock car racers and fans descend on Unity Raceway, nicknamed "Maine's Toughest Oval." Among the area's other attractions are Fort Halifax and the Perkins Arboretum. Anglers head to Lake Winnecook, while hikers roam around the 42,000-acre Unity Wetlands and skiers trek to Sunday River and Lost Valley. Augusta, the state capital, is about an hour away, and Portland is about 90 minutes away.

What It's Like

Unity attracts largely left-leaning, outdoorsy students looking for an intimate campus community. The environmental focus begins immediately, during the required new student orientation wilderness trip (NOVA). Groups of first-years spend a week bonding while hiking through Acadia National Park, kayaking at Moosehead Lake, learning to rock climb, or having some other type of adventure. If you're not into being outside, then Unity's probably not right for you.

Among the majors are ecology and environmental humanities. With the conservation law enforcement major, students can train to become park rangers or border patrollers. The Career Resource Center not only helps students find internships and jobs but also hands out information about funding for graduate school. And it gives advice about how to apply a major to a particular career. For instance, the center recommends that wildlife majors learn to identify birds and to drive farm equipment.

Wildlife majors are encouraged to learn to drive farm equipment.

Popular student clubs include the Wildlife Club, Ice Hockey, and Constructive Activists. The Vibrant Community Project links Unity students to the Unity community through volunteering opportunities, such as working with the Big Brothers/Big Sisters of Midcoast Maine. Several Unity classes have a service-learning component, which combines classroom instruction with community service. About 70 percent of students do an internship, such as clearing trails with the Unity Historical Society.

First-years at Unitylive in one of the three traditional dorms—Wood, Westview, and Eastview—all of which offer doubles. Upperclass students live in Cianchette Hall or the Cottages, coed apartments for small groups. With a few exceptions, students are required to live on campus until they've taken 60 course credits (about two years' worth of classes).

Unity's Dining Hall offers vegetarian options at every meal, and there's even a make-your-own waffle station. Plus, the hall uses produce grown in the Unity Community Garden. At this school, the meals are good for you—and good for the environment.

University of Alaska Southeast

11120 Glacier Highway **(907) 465-6457**
Juneau, AK 99801 **http://www.uas.alaska.edu/**

Why It's Cool

Crystal-clear streams will be your textbooks, and glaciers will be your teachers. At UAS, the outdoors will be your campus. Literally. You'll attend class on mountaintops and at the Juneau Icefield, 1,500 miles of frozen water. You'll do research in the Arctic, backpack through southeastern Alaska, learn how to survive in the deep snow, and maybe train to be a wilderness first-responder (a person who provides first aid and basic life support). You might even study native Alaskan languages and cultures. UAS calls all this the "Unfair Advantage": a liberal arts education that draws on the magnificent natural resources of Alaska. We call it "unbelievable."

JUNEAU'S HOME TO 30,000 PEOPLE—AND 20,000 BALD EAGLES.

The Details

Campus setting:	small town
Degrees:	bachelor's, master's
Calendar:	semesters
Public/Private:	public state
Number of full-time faculty:	96
Student-to-teacher ratio:	12:1

Admissions requirements:

- **Options:** deferred entrance, early admission
- **Application fee:** $40
- **Required:** high school transcript, SAT or ACT
- **Application deadlines:** continuous (freshmen), continuous (transfer)
- **Early decision:** —
- **Notification:** —

Average high school GPA:	2.93
Average freshman SAT verbal/math score:	511 / 499
Average freshman ACT score:	20
Number of applicants:	396
Number of applicants accepted:	248
Percentage of students from out of state:	15%
Total freshman enrollment:	139
Total enrollment:	3,379
Percentage of students who live in campus housing:	—
Total in-state tuition, fees & expenses:	$9,212
Total out-of-state tuition, fees & expenses:	$15,308
Average financial aid package:	$6,655

Where It's At

UAS's main campus is located in Juneau, the capital of Alaska. Generally, the weather is mild in both winter and summer, although Juneau gets a lot of rain. Outdoor activities abound, especially snowboarding and skiing at Eaglecrest, a local destination for winter sports; hiking at Mendenhall Glacier; and sea kayaking and whale watching in Glacier Bay National Park. The Mount Roberts Tramway connects the wildlife, trails, and great views of Mount Roberts to the shops and restaurants of the downtown waterfront, which includes the infamous Red Dog Saloon. An international airport links Juneau to the rest of the world.

What It's Like

As a regional state school, UAS naturally attracts a lot of students from within Alaska. And as a school with access to a tremendous outdoor laboratory, UAS attracts a lot of budding scientists and earthy types.

The Unfair Advantage gives students incredible opportunities. Anthropology majors can learn indigenous Alaskan languages from native speakers, while marine biology majors can gather samples in Glacier Bay. Any student can become certified through the Outdoor Studies and Leadership Program by taking nine months of such classes as Perspectives on the Natural World; Fly Tying, Casting, and Fishing; and Northwest Coast Cultures.

Banfield Hall has tremendous views and its very own dorm dog.

All students must fulfill general education requirements in writing, speaking, and math, among other liberal arts fields. To give students a broad education and to help them develop multiple interests, UAS requires that students take classes from several different departments: To satisfy the two-course social science requirement, for instance, students might decide to take anthropology and government, or history and psychology.

Housing options include on-campus apartments and the co-ed Banfield Hall, with views of a nearby forest and the Juneau Ice Field. Banfield also comes with a "lodge dog," a dog that lives in the hall and that residents are allowed to walk and play with.

Through UAS exchange programs, students can earn academic credit while studying at other institutions in the United States, Canada, and 35 other countries. On campus, students can write for the *Whalesong*, the UAS paper; make crafts with the FiberArts/Batik Club; or scale the climbing wall at the Student Recreation Center.

Each year, the Day of Caring lets students give back to the community by spending a day volunteering. Each fall, around Halloween, the campus gets together for Scary Stories on a Dark Night. In the spring, the Humanities Department sponsors the Humanities Conference, in which students present original writing or artwork on a particular theme, such as identity.

Welcome to the Monkey House: Most Unusual Dorms

At these colleges and universities, dorms are so much more than a cement shoebox—they're renovated mansions (**Augustana** [p. 20]), they're full-service hotels (**The University of Tampa** [p. 212]), they have their own pools and hot tubs (**The University of Tampa** and **Sonoma State** [p. 186]), they allow dogs and cats (**Eckerd** [p. 80] and **Stephens** [p. 194]).

Here are some other schools with totally rad housing options:

Arcadia University (P. 16)

Live like a king or queen in the suites at the Grey Towers Castle, a nineteenth-century castle.

Bates College (P. 26)

After your first year, you can move into renovated Victorian houses just a block away from campus.

Berea College (P. 32)

Berea students designed the Ecovillage, 32 houses built with recycled materials.

Binghamton University (P. 34)

Modeled on England's Oxford University, BU's seven residential complexes are groups of dorms, each with its own dining hall and academic center.

College of Charleston (P. 54)

The college owns 22 residential houses, renovated carriage houses that often feature narrow staircases, fireplaces, hardwood floors, and porches.

The College of Wooster (P. 66)

Seniors can live in special senior-only housing so that they can concentrate on their final projects and prepare for life after graduation.

Loyola University Chicago (P. 128)

The brand-new Water Tower residential facility is a 25-floor dorm smack in the center of downtown Chicago.

Macalester College (P. 130)

Six language houses give residents the chance to immerse themselves in another language, including French, Chinese, Spanish, Russian, Japanese, and German. No English allowed.

Sierra Nevada College (P. 184)

The all-new Prim-Schulz Hall features views of the mountains or the water, as well as a place to tune and store your skis.

University of Alaska Southeast (P. 202)

Co-ed Banfield Hall comes with its very own lodge dog, a four-legged friend that gets fed and taken care of by residents.

University of Mary Washington

1301 College Avenue **Fredericksburg, VA 22401**

(540) 654-1000 **http://www.umw.edu/**

Why It's Cool

An education at this public school will give you all the advantages of a private liberal arts college (small classes, devoted faculty, research opportunities galore) without breaking your bank. Across-the-Curriculum courses will give you expertise in five key areas: speaking, writing, global consciousness, race and gender issues, and environmental awareness. After mastering those areas, you'll then tackle eight learning goals, including developing an appreciation for science and understanding the philosophical bases for Western civilization. It ain't easy. But, in return, you'll score a mind bulging with facts and a well-rounded personality.

THE CIVIL WAR BATTLE OF FREDERICKSBURG WAS FOUGHT NEAR UMW IN 1862.

The Details

Campus setting:	small town
Degrees:	bachelor's, master's
Calendar:	semesters
Public/Private:	public state
Number of full-time faculty:	206
Student-to-teacher ratio:	17:1

Admissions requirements:

- **Options:** common application, deferred entrance, electronic application
- **Application fee:** $35
- **Required:** essay or personal statement, high school transcript, SAT or ACT, SAT Subject Tests (recommended)
- **Application deadlines:** 2/1 (freshmen), 3/1 (transfer)
- **Early decision:** —
- **Notification:** 4/1 (freshmen), 5/1 (transfer)

Average high school GPA:	3.63
Average freshman SAT verbal/math score:	620 / 611
Average freshman ACT score:	—
Number of applicants:	4,472
Number of applicants accepted:	2,676
Percentage of students from out of state:	35%
Total freshman enrollment:	866
Total enrollment:	4,792
Percentage of students who live in campus housing:	70%
Total in-state tuition, fees & expenses:	$11,872
Total out-of-state tuition, fees & expenses:	$20,278
Average financial aid package:	$5,300

Where It's At

UMW's 176-acre campus is located in Fredericksburg, a small town in northwest Virginia. A free bus shuttles students to Fredericksburg's four-block historic antique row, which features more than 100 shops and restaurants. The Battle of Fredericksburg was fought here in 1862, and the area's many preserved Civil War–era plantations draw historians and tourists alike. At the Hugh Mercer Apothecary Shop, visitors can learn about colonial medicine, while Mary Washington's will is on display at the town courthouse. Outdoor activities include tubing down the Rappahannock River and camping and picnicking in the 1,300-acre Westmoreland State Park. Both Richmond, the state capital, and Washington, D.C., are about an hour away.

What It's Like

Academics matter at UMW. The various requirements are designed to give students breadth and depth in the liberal arts. In addition to Across-the-Curriculum and the major, students also have to take classes that fulfill eight general education goals. These goals range from taking a foreign language to solving problems with math to understanding human culture through artistic expression. Finally, students need to demonstrate their ability to use technology to manage information before graduating. To fulfill this requirement, students take online tutorials in such subjects as searching the library catalog and creating spreadsheets, or they simply take regular classes with a technological component.

Students can create a self-designed major through upper-level coursework in two or more departments. Recent special majors have included human resources management and nonfiction writing. UMW also offers more than 30 majors, including geography and historic preservation.

The International Academic Services office helps students find internships, jobs, and academic programs on six continents. Through the UMW exchange program, students can study in Australia, Ireland, and Wales, among other locations. On campus, students take classes or work at UMW's Art Galleries, which display work by local and national artists, as well as students and faculty. The department of history and American studies sponsors free lectures throughout the spring semester on various historical figure and themes.

Think *and* play hard.

UMW has more than 80 student clubs and organizations, ranging from academic societies (Mathematics Association of America) to intramural and sports teams (Mad Mary, the Ultimate Frisbee club) to shared interests (Anarchist Social Theory Club). There are 21 Division III athletic teams (the Eagles), including field hockey, equestrian, and rowing. On Fridays, different campus groups host parties, such as the annual Drag Show and the Hip-Hop Festival. Students at Mary Washington think *and* play hard.

University of Montevallo

Palmer Hall, Station 6030
Montevallo, AL 35115

(205) 665-6000
http://www.montevallo.edu/

Why It's Cool

What's great about UM? Well, for starters, the grounds are so beautiful that the core section has been named a National Historic District. Then there's the prestigious Undergraduate Research program, which will not only let you do graduate-level research in the sciences but will also give you a couple hundred ducats as a grant. Four liberal studies classes combine lectures and seminars to examine cultures from ancient times to the twentieth century. And lest we forget: You can spend your spring break in Costa Rica having adventures with Outward Bound, and UM has the oldest homecoming celebration in the country, *four* full nights of fun.

COLLEGE NIGHT IS UM'S BIGGEST CELEBRATION: A FRIENDLY FIGHT BETWEEN THE PURPLE COWS AND THE GOLDEN LIONS TO SEE WHICH TEAM OF STUDENTS HAS THE BEST DANCE MOVES, JOKES, COSTUMES, AND SONGS.

The Details

Campus setting:	small town
Degrees:	bachelor's, master's
Calendar:	semesters
Public/Private:	public state
Number of full-time faculty:	136
Student-to-teacher ratio:	17:1

Admissions requirements:

- **Options:** common application, deferred entrance, early admission, electronic application
- **Application fee:** $25
- **Required:** high school transcript, SAT or ACT, ACT (recommended)
- **Application deadlines:** 8/1 (freshmen), continuous (transfer)
- **Early decision:** —
- **Notification:** —

Average high school GPA:	3.29
Average freshman SAT verbal/math score:	—/—
Average freshman ACT score:	22
Number of applicants:	1,245
Number of applicants accepted:	999
Percentage of students from out of state:	4%
Total freshman enrollment:	488
Total enrollment:	3,061
Percentage of students who live in campus housing:	35%
Total in-state tuition, fees & expenses:	$9,924
Total out-of-state tuition, fees & expenses:	$15,114
Average financial aid package:	$7,150

Where It's At

UM's 160-acre campus is located in the small town of Montevallo, smack-dab in the center of Alabama. Hikers, campers, hunters, and picnickers flock to Montevallo's many parks, including Oak Mountain State Park and Orr Park. Other local attractions range from the Aldrich Coal Mine Museum to the Montevallo Golf Club to the Eclipse Coffee and Book Shop. Every year in May, the Brierfield Bluegrass Festival brings local and national musical acts to town. About 45 minutes away, Birmingham has the Visionland theme park, the Birmingham Zoo, the Museum of Art, an annual festival of the arts, and the Civil Rights Institute.

What It's Like

Spirited, *enthusiastic*, and *passionate*. Students adore UM so much they come back even after they've graduated to participate in College Night, the longest-running homecoming celebration in the United States. For four nights, students and alums alike watch as two teams, the purple and the gold, compete in a series of performances and athletic contests.

Showing the UM love happens 24-7. Students head to the arena at the all-new, 90,000-square-foot Student Activity Center to cheer the championship men's basketball team or one of the other nine Division II teams. In addition, students rush one of 14 fraternities and sororities, run groups like the Model Arab League/Model UN, compete on the Falconettes Dance Team, and publish the *Alabamian* (the student newspaper) and the *Montage* (the yearbook). Plus, they play sand volleyball, bowl in the on-campus bowling alley, and sunbathe around the campus lake.

Showing the UM love happens 24-7.

UM wants its students to have as broad a knowledge base as possible, so courses in such liberal arts as science, math, humanities, and communications are required. Everybody must pass a computer applications class so that all graduates can handle twenty-first-century technology. Students seeking a BA must also take two years of French, German, or Spanish (students going for a BS take more math and science).

Four colleges make up UM: education, fine arts, business, and arts and sciences. All told, the colleges offer around 75 majors, including social work and speech-language pathology. Through the family and consumer sciences department, students can take courses in retail merchandising and dietetics.

On campus, UM students gather to hang out and watch TV at Farmer Hall (the student union), hold meetings at the Stewart Student Retreat, and grab a bite at Jazzman's. Most students live in one of nine residence halls, including the singles at Main and Fuller. Residents can even repaint their room walls in whatever colors they like.

University of Redlands

1200 East Colton Avenue
Redlands, CA 92373

(909) 793-2121
http://www.redlands.edu/

Why It's Cool

Live what you learn, learn what you live. This could be the mantra at the Johnston Center for Interdisciplinary Studies, a unique program within the university. Enroll here, and you won't get grades, nor will you take any required classes. Instead, you'll design your own major and receive written feedback from your profs. Each semester, you and your faculty adviser will draw up a specialized learning contract that lists activities and study plans. If you're looking for something more traditional, don't worry: Redlands has got you covered with such majors as accounting and managerial studies and such preprofessional programs as premed and prelaw.

AT 415 FEET TALL AND 275 FEET WIDE, THE *R* LOOMING OVER CAMPUS IS HUMONGOUS.

The Details

Campus setting:	small town
Degrees:	bachelor's, master's
Calendar:	4-4-1
Public/Private:	private nonprofit
Number of full-time faculty:	163
Student-to-teacher ratio:	11:1

Admissions requirements:

- **Options:** common application, deferred entrance, electronic application
- **Application fee:** $45
- **Required:** essay or personal statement, high school transcript, 2 letters of recommendation, SAT or ACT
- **Application deadlines:** 12/15 (freshmen), 3/1 (transfer)
- **Early decision:** —
- **Notification:** continuous (freshmen), continuous (transfer)

Average high school GPA:	3.54
Average freshman SAT verbal/math score:	587 / 586
Average freshman ACT score:	23
Number of applicants:	2,934
Number of applicants accepted:	2,211
Percentage of students from out of state:	28%
Total freshman enrollment:	604
Total enrollment:	2,451
Percentage of students who live in campus housing:	73%
Total tuition fee:	$25,224
Total cost with fees & expenses:	$35,220
Average financial aid package:	$23,475

Where It's At

Redlands is located in the tiny city of Redlands, in southern California. A trolley links the university to the city's downtown, home to locally owned shops; notable restaurants, such as the Farm and Caprice Café; and stately nineteenth-century Victorian houses. Every Thursday, downtown Redlands hosts Market Night, with entertainment, food, and a farmers' market, along historic State Street. But the city also has several festivals throughout the spring and summer, ranging from the Cinco de Mayo Celebration to the Shakespeare Festival Series to the annual Flower Show. The beaches, nightclubs, museums, and malls of Los Angeles are about an hour away.

What It's Like

This campus community stays connected by eating together at the Hunsaker University Center's dining halls. Slurp a smoothie at the Plaza Café, or have a special sit-down meal at the University Club (so popular that you need a reservation). If you're lucky, everyone might break out into the nonsensical Redlands chant, which includes lines like "Skizzle Wazzle / Wang Tang / Orky Porky Dominorky."

"Skizzle Wazzle / Wang Tang / Orky Porky Dominorky"

Singing is more organized at the Feast of Lights, an annual candlelit liturgical celebration in December. But this sense of community extends far beyond campus. Students take several liberal arts courses, including at least one Community Service Activity Course. Into the Streets, for example, pairs students with agencies around southern California. Other courses take students to China for two weeks to teach English or to Utah to intern at an animal shelter.

Study abroad options include a yearlong program in Hong Kong and a music-intensive program in Germany, among others. Some students choose to go abroad during the monthlong May Term. On campus, the shorter term gives students a chance to focus on one fun subject, such as Chinese/Japanese Calligraphy or Popular Culture, without worrying about other classes. Among the more than 40 majors are global business and the Johnston Center's design-your-own specialization.

About 75 percent of students live on campus in one of 12 residence halls. Bekins and Holt house students in a co-ed complex that also includes faculty offices and a coffeehouse. First-years live off of Frosh Quad, in the doubles and triples of Williams and the carpeted East Halls.

As the Bulldogs, students compete across 19 Division III varsity teams, and they're particularly strong in men's and women's water polo. There are five fraternities and five sororities; about 30 percent of students go Greek. Other Redlands student groups include the a cappella group Those Guys, Wilderness Connections, and the Car Club.

The University of Tampa

401 West Kennedy Boulevard
Tampa, FL 33606
(813) 253-3333
http://www.utampa.edu/

Why It's Cool

Get experienced at UT. The First-Year Experience will take you from nervous newbie to seasoned sophomore. You'll take Gateways, a yearlong class in everything you've ever wanted to know about college (but were afraid to ask). Study tips, cool hangouts, rad extracurriculars, the best spots to sunbathe—anything goes. But the experiences don't stop after the first year: As part of the Baccalaureate Experience, you'll take core courses in the liberal arts designed to transform you into a been-there, know-how-to-do-that kind of individual—you know, the kind of person who gets hired *fast*.

UT HAS SOME OF THE FINEST EXAMPLES OF MOORISH ARCHITECTURE IN THE UNITED STATES.

The Details

Campus setting:	urban
Degrees:	bachelor's, master's
Calendar:	semesters
Public/Private:	private nonprofit
Number of full-time faculty:	201
Student-to-teacher ratio:	17:1

Admissions requirements:

- **Options:** common application, deferred entrance, early admission, electronic application
- **Application fee:** $35
- **Required:** essay or personal statement, high school transcript, letter of recommendation, SAT or ACT
- **Application deadlines:** continuous (freshmen), continuous (transfer)
- **Early decision:** —
- **Notification:** — (freshmen), continuous (transfer)

Average high school GPA:	3.28
Average freshman SAT verbal/math score:	546 / 546
Average freshman ACT score:	23
Number of applicants:	5,306
Number of applicants accepted:	2,821
Percentage of students from out of state:	53%
Total freshman enrollment:	956
Total enrollment:	4,879
Percentage of students who live in campus housing:	65%
Total tuition fee:	$17,250
Total cost with fees & expenses:	$25,681
Average financial aid package:	$14,398

Where It's At

UT's 100 acres lie along the Hillsborough River in downtown Tampa, Florida. In addition to the historic Ybor City entertainment district, Tampa has several museums, including the Gallery of Photographic Arts and the Museum of Science and Industry. The world's largest feline sanctuary, Big Cat Rescue, offers tours of its animals and grounds, as do Busch Gardens Theme Park and the Lowry Park Zoo. Sports fans root for the Devil Rays (MLB), Lightning (NHL), and Buccaneers (NFL). Each year, Tampa hosts the Gasparilla Pirate Festival, a Mardi Gras–like parade, and the Bonk Festival of New Music, a gathering of cutting-edge performers and composers.

What It's Like

UT's location in the Sunshine State doesn't mean that students here slack off. Quite the contrary: Students here study *while* they sunbathe. The rigorous Baccalaureate Experience features core courses in the liberal arts, specifically writing, the humanities, and the natural sciences. This curriculum is designed to help students appreciate art, communicate effectively, understand other cultures, and solve problems creatively.

As part of the First-Year Experience, newbies take Global Issues, in which every class studies a different country. The course culminates in the Global Village Simulation, which features food and entertainment from each country. In World Affairs, students study on campus for seven weeks and then head off to either Italy or China. Another option is the Semester at Sea, in which students study on a cruise-ship-turned-university.

Dorm amenities include air conditioning, maid service, pool access . . .

On campus, UT's College of Liberal Arts offers more than 40 majors and preprofessional programs. Close to 25 percent of students major in science. Other popular majors include criminology, performing arts, and education. Students can also earn certificates in gerontology, Latin American studies, and European studies to complement their majors.

Before graduation, all students prepare a co-curricular transcript, in which they list all the activities they've done while at UT. Students can choose from more than 100 on-campus groups, including eight fraternities, ten sororities, the P.E.A.C.E. Volunteer Center, and *Respondez!*, a student nonfiction journal. Among the 13 Division II varsity athletic teams (the Spartans) are crew and volleyball.

About 65 percent of students live on campus. The nine residence halls range from traditional dorms to apartments to the Ashley Plaza Hotel, a functioning hotel that also houses students. Amenities include maid service, air conditioning, and unlimited use of the pool.

The University of the South

735 University Avenue	**(931) 598-1000**
Sewanee, TN 37383	**http://www.sewanee.edu/**

Why It's Cool

Become master of Sewanee's domain. Here, you'll have free reign over the campus's 10,000 acres, nicknamed the "Domain." As the second-largest campus in the United States, this bad boy's just begging to be tamed. A walk along the 22-mile perimeter trail takes you through four different types of forests. There's also a living herbarium and the interdisciplinary Landscape Analysis Laboratory, which uses the surrounding land for case studies. OK, so you might come here for the incredible natural resources, but you'll stay for the terrific academics, which include almost 40 majors. We know we would.

EVERY YEAR, MEDIEVALISTS FROM ACROSS THE NATION MEET AT SEWANEE FOR THE MEDIEVAL COLLOQUIUM.

The Details

Campus setting:	small town
Degrees:	bachelor's, master's, doctoral
Calendar:	semesters
Public/Private:	private religious
Number of full-time faculty:	137
Student-to-teacher ratio:	10:1

Admissions requirements:

- **Options:** common application, deferred entrance, early admission, early decision, electronic application
- **Application fee:** $45
- **Required:** essay or personal statement, high school transcript, 2 letters of recommendation, SAT or ACT, SAT Subject Tests (recommended)
- **Application deadlines:** 2/1 (freshmen), 4/1 (transfer)
- **Early decision:** 11/15
- **Notification:** 4/1 (freshmen), continuous (transfer), 12/15 (early decision)

Average high school GPA:	3.45
Average freshman SAT verbal/math score:	627 / 619
Average freshman ACT score:	25
Number of applicants:	2,070
Number of applicants accepted:	1,328
Percentage of students from out of state:	78%
Total freshman enrollment:	398
Total enrollment:	1,492
Percentage of students who live in campus housing:	92%
Total tuition fee:	$25,374
Total cost with fees & expenses:	$33,300
Average financial aid package:	$19,864

Where It's At

Sewanee's gigantic campus is located in the tiny town of Sewanee, Tennessee. Area attractions include High Point and Pearl's, two popular restaurants; the Bear Trace, five 18-hole golf courses designed by Jack Nicklaus; the Jack Daniels Distillery; and the Monteagle Winery. Chattanooga, a city about an hour away, is home to the Tennessee Aquarium, the Hunter Museum of American Art, the Bluff View Art District, and a ten-mile River Walk. At the South Cumberland State Park, visitors can hike along waterfalls, play badminton, tour a museum filled with local artifacts, and have picnics. Nashville, the state capital, is about two hours away by car.

What It's Like

Community counts at Sewanee. About 90 percent of students live on campus, and about 70 percent rush a fraternity or sorority. Students also constitute an important part of the surrounding Sewanee community. They volunteer at the local soup kitchen and homeless shelter through the Community Service Council, act as companions to the elderly through the Senior Citizens Program, and do other good things for their neighbors. And with the All Saints' Chapel Outreach Program, students may spend their spring breaks building houses in Honduras or feeding the homeless in New York City.

As part of an old tradition, some students dress up for class.

More than 130 organizations offer 700 leadership opportunities. Students run the Bike Shop, as well as the Outing Club, which sponsors adventures in the outdoors. Every night, the Sewanee Union shows movies. At the Fowler Center, students can learn to rock climb at the 12-foot-high Bouldering Wall. There are 22 varsity sports, including equestrian and baseball.

Popular majors include political science and biology. All students must fulfill general education requirements, including courses in math, literature, and philosophy and religion. Students also complete two writing-intensive courses and two physical education courses.

First-years and sophomores complete four courses in the Interdisciplinary Humanities Program, which explore Western history and ideas. New students also participate in the First-Year Program (FYP), featuring small seminars that combine in-class and out-of-class experiences. Each FYP focuses on a topic, like Philosophy Through Film: Socrates, Jesus, and Cowboys or The Struggle Between Good and Evil: Fairy Tales in Literature and Music.

The outdoorsy students of Sewanee don't mind getting gussied up once in a while for class to honor an old tradition. And at least once a year, students put on even fancier duds for the formal Mountain Top Ball.

Smarties, Brainiacs, and Eggheads: Highest Percentage in Graduate Programs

These schools specialize in preparing their students for . . . more school. OK, so not everyone who graduates from these schools goes on to get a master's or doctorate, but a lot definitely do.

University of Tulsa

600 South College Avenue
Tulsa, OK 74104
(918) 631-2000
http://www.utulsa.edu/

Why It's Cool

Do you dream in HTML or XML? Do you spend your days—or nights—trolling the web? Do you long to use your keyboard to fight the bad guys? If so, TU's got the program for you: Cyber Corps. Through the Center for Information Security, TU will train you to become an expert in cyberterrorism. You'll take classes in computer science, and you'll graduate with high-level security certification. For at least one summer, you'll intern with the Feds at a government agency. But that's not all: You'll also get a two-year scholarship *and* $1,000 per month. TU helps you log on and do good.

BURN, BABY, BURN. THE HUGE HOMECOMING BONFIRE IS JUST ONE OF THE MANY TRADITIONS AT TU THAT HELP STUDENTS LET LOOSE AND BOND.

The Details

Campus setting:	urban
Degrees:	bachelor's, master's, doctoral
Calendar:	semesters
Public/Private:	private religious
Number of full-time faculty:	308
Student-to-teacher ratio:	11:1

Admissions requirements:

- **Options:** common application, deferred entrance, early admission, electronic application
- **Application fee:** $35
- **Required:** high school transcript, letter of recommendation, SAT or ACT
- **Application deadlines:** continuous (freshmen), continuous (transfer)
- **Early decision:** —
- **Notification:** continuous (freshmen), continuous (transfer)

Average high school GPA:	3.70
Average freshman SAT verbal/math score:	612 / 616
Average freshman ACT score:	24
Number of applicants:	2,621
Number of applicants accepted:	1,944
Percentage of students from out of state:	28%
Total freshman enrollment:	677
Total enrollment:	4,174
Percentage of students who live in campus housing:	64%
Total tuition fee:	$17,550
Total cost with fees & expenses:	$24,756
Average financial aid package:	$19,097

Where It's At

TU is located in Tulsa, the second-largest city in Oklahoma. Nearby Cherry Street offers shops, galleries, and such restaurants as Atomic Burrito and Panera Bread Co. At night, students head to the Brookside entertainment district to play pool at Sharky's or grab a bite at Garlic Rose. Among Tulsa's other attractions are the Oklahoma Jazz Hall of Fame, the Brady Arts District, the Tulsa Zoo, and River Parks, more than 20 miles of shoreline alongside the Arkansas River. Each May, the Oklahoma Blues Festival brings local and national musical acts to town. Home to the Myriad Botanical Gardens and the Frontier City Theme Park, Oklahoma City is about 90 minutes away.

What It's Like

Students of all stripes hang out on the U, the grassy area at the center of campus, and at the Allen Chapman Activity Center (known as "Ack Ack"). Roughly 27 percent of students are international or belong to a minority group, making for an extremely diverse population. But the campus bonds over Greek life and sports: Just about everyone turns out to cheer on the Golden Hurricanes, particularly the football and basketball teams. There are 18 Division I athletic teams in all.

Springfest and Oozefest, Mabee and the Toilet Bowl

Three colleges make up TU: arts and sciences, business administration, and engineering and natural sciences. Among the strongest majors are English; computer science, including the Cyber Corps Program; and petroleum engineering. All students have the chance to participate in the Tulsa Undergraduate Research Challenge Program, which gives students money to do independent projects in any field, from working in a laboratory to writing an original musical score.

The many study abroad opportunities include language classes in Spain and Russia, law programs in Ireland and Argentina, and a nursing program in France. On campus, TU recognizes more than 300 student organizations, ranging from the Angolan Student Association to the TU Ballroom Dancers to Trio Tulsa, a chamber music group.

TU has five dorms. Each year, residents of the all-male John Mabee Hall host the Toilet Bowl, an intense flag-football game. Some first-years live in Twin South Hall, which features a huge indoor atrium. Another residential option is to live in Greek housing, run by each of the 12 fraternities and sororities.

Traditions are big at TU. Each April, bands play on campus as part of Springfest. Perhaps the most popular annual event is Oozefest, which features mud volleyball games. TU certainly maintains an excellent balance of academics and fun, as well as traditions and innovations.

Warren Wilson College

PO Box 9000
Asheville, NC 28815
(828) 298-3325
http://www.warren-wilson.edu/

Why It's Cool

This school's slogan says it all: "We're not for everyone . . . but then maybe you're not everyone." WWC offers unique, hearty souls the Triad: a curriculum that combines labor, learning, and volunteering. You'll toil 15 hours per week at an on-campus job, take a combination of requirements and electives, and perform 100 hours of community service over four years, including 25 hours devoted to one cause. There's no doubt about it: The Triad will put your hands, heart, and head to work. We're getting tired just thinking about it.

THROUGH THE WORK PROGRAM, STUDENTS DO EVERYTHING FROM WORKING AS ADMINISTRATIVE ASSISTANTS TO WELDING AS APPRENTICE BLACKSMITHS AND COOKING AT THE COWPIE CAFÉ.

The Details

Campus setting:	small town
Degrees:	bachelor's, master's
Calendar:	semesters
Public/Private:	private religious
Number of full-time faculty:	60
Student-to-teacher ratio:	11:1

Admissions requirements:

- **Options:** common application, deferred entrance, early admission, early decision, electronic application
- **Application fee:** —
- **Required:** essay or personal statement, high school transcript, 2 letters of recommendation, SAT or ACT
- **Application deadlines:** 3/15 (freshmen), 3/15 (transfer)
- **Early decision:** 11/15
- **Notification:** continuous (freshmen), 4/1 (transfer), 12/1 (early decision)

Average high school GPA:	3.31
Average freshman SAT verbal/math score:	614 / 572
Average freshman ACT score:	26
Number of applicants:	737
Number of applicants accepted:	588
Percentage of students from out of state:	78%
Total freshman enrollment:	210
Total enrollment:	865
Percentage of students who live in campus housing:	88%
Total tuition fee:	$18,910
Total cost with fees & expenses:	$25,370
Average financial aid package:	$12,906

Where It's At

Located just 10 minutes from Asheville, North Carolina, WWC's 1,100 acres are in the rural Swannanoa Valley. The campus is divided into a 300-acre farm and 735-acre forest. Students can take a free bus into Asheville, a small, vibrant community filled with artisans, food co-ops, and art-deco architecture. The Appalachian Crafts Center and 16 Patton are among the town's many art galleries. Every summer, a local troupe performs Shakespeare in the city's amphitheater. Hikers, rock climbers, and skiers head to the Great Smokey Mountains National Park and the Blue Ridge Mountains. Atlanta is about four hours away, and Nashville is about five hours away.

What It's Like

Students sometimes joke that WWC stands for "We Work Constantly." To offset the cost of tuition, all students must work on campus, regardless of financial need. Every student joins one of more than 110 work crews, ranging from Auto Shop to Admissions Office. You'll definitely be busy at this treasure school.

During their community service, students devote about a quarter of their time to an Extended Project, which focuses on one particular issue. Students then write a narrative essay analyzing their experiences. Service and Extended Project opportunities include coaching youth teams in Asheville and maintaining the 25 miles of hiking trails that cross the campus.

Students aren't afraid to come to class covered in dirt.

Through the WorldWide program, students study and serve abroad on six continents. Most courses combine several weeks of on-campus study with a few weeks of travel during the winter or on summer break. Participants have studied ecology in Alaska, ecosystems in Costa Rica, and international development in Sri Lanka. Students can also study abroad through traditional exchange programs in China, Germany, and France, among other countries.

WWC offers more than 45 majors and concentrations, as well as close to 30 minors. In addition to completing the requirements of the Triad and major, students must take courses in eight liberal arts subjects, including artistic expression and natural science. First-years take two required courses: a small interdisciplinary seminar, on such topics as the Biology of Identity and Appalachian Music and Dance, and a composition class.

Roughly 90 percent of WWC students live on campus in one of 13 residence halls, including the new EcoDorm, which features an energy-efficient design. Among the 12 varsity athletic and adventure sports teams are mountain biking and soccer.

The hard workers here love the outdoors—and they they aren't afraid to come to class covered in dirt. Each spring on Work Day, students, faculty, and staff put aside their regular duties and help beautify the campus. At WWC, work is a beautiful thing.

Washington College

300 Washington Avenue
Chestertown, MD 21620
(410) 778-2800
http://www.washcoll.edu/

Why It's Cool

If you long to lie by the shores of a river, scribbling your heart out, this might be the school for you. George Washington helped found Washington College in 1782, and it's been innovating ever since. The campus is situated along the Chester River, so teachers from every department often hold classes outdoors. But the real draw is the Sophie Kerr Prize, an annual monetary award (recently totaling $61,000—no lie!) given to the senior who shows the most literary promise. That's major moolah for any young scribe.

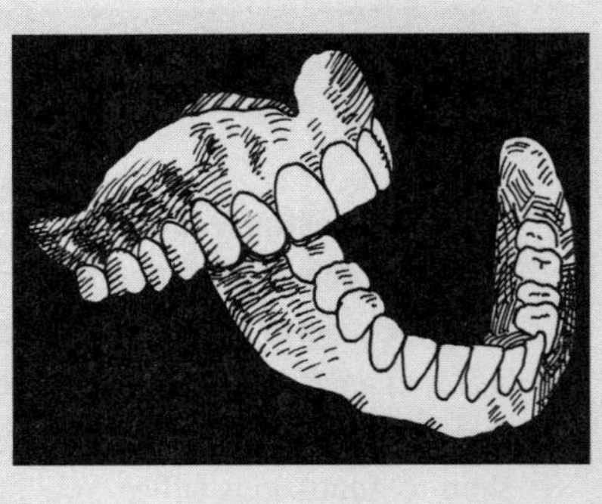

CONTRARY TO POPULAR BELIEF, GEORGE WASHINGTON'S WOODEN TEETH WERE ACTUALLY MADE FROM HIPPOPOTAMUS IVORY TUSKS.

The Details

Campus setting:	small town
Degrees:	bachelor's, master's
Calendar:	semesters
Public/Private:	private nonprofit
Number of full-time faculty:	90
Student-to-teacher ratio:	12:1

Admissions requirements:

- **Options:** common application, deferred entrance, early decision, early action, electronic application
- **Application fee:** $40
- **Required:** essay or personal statement, high school transcript, letter of recommendation, SAT or ACT
- **Application deadlines:** 3/1 (freshmen), 6/1 (transfer), 12/1 (early action)
- **Early decision:** 11/15
- **Notification:** continuous (freshmen), continuous (transfer), 12/15 (early decision), 12/20 (early action)

Average high school GPA:	3.43
Average freshman SAT verbal/math score:	586 / 572
Average freshman ACT score:	24
Number of applicants:	2,031
Number of applicants accepted:	1,207
Percentage of students from out of state:	45%
Total freshman enrollment:	302
Total enrollment:	1,426
Percentage of students who live in campus housing:	80%
Total tuition fee:	$25,990
Total cost with fees & expenses:	$33,050
Average financial aid package:	$17,107

Where It's At

Washington College's 112-acre campus is located in Chestertown, on Maryland's eastern shore. Founded in 1706, the town boasts several historic buildings, in addition to the happening restaurants Andy's and Black-Eyed Susan—within walking distance from campus. The college also owns two acres of waterfront along the Chester River, and canoeing and sailing are among the most popular activities in the area. Every year, the Chestertown Wildlife Exhibition and Sale brings artisans and craftspeople to town, and notable homes host visitors during the annual Candlelight Walking Tour. Baltimore, Washington, D.C., and Philadelphia are each near by.

What It's Like

WC describes its academics as providing "an intensely personalized education." And with an average class size of 17, academic life is definitely intimate. Most classes require between 10 and 12 hours of studying each week—not including time spent in the classroom. With such small classes, there's no place to hide if you haven't completed the homework. Hello, hard work. Good-bye, laziness and procrastination.

First-years take either a community seminar, which deals with issues in the Chesapeake Bay, or a nation seminar, which explores such themes as images of America on film and the effects of global warming on the environment. The required world seminar deals with an international issue; past seminars have included Myth and Magic in Latin America and The History of Dance.

"An intensely personalized education . . ."

Other requirements include ten liberal arts courses. Washington offers roughly 25 undergraduate programs of study, including creative writing, human development, and drama. All seniors complete a Senior Obligation, a final project, paper, performance, or comprehensive examination within the major that is evaluated by faculty members.

Academic all-stars (students with a GPA of 3.6 or above) are eligible for the Douglass Cater Society of Junior Fellows, the most prestigious group of scholars on campus. Members apply for monetary grants for independent, off-campus research. Past projects have ranged from an internship at the British Museum to studying globalization in Ecuador.

Among the more than 50 student organizations are the Musicians' Union and the Skeet and Trap Shooting Club. About 20 to 25 percent of students join the three fraternities and three sororities. Through the Recreational Sports program, students can take classes in yoga or participate in club sports, including volleyball. There are 16 Division III varsity athletic teams, including the championship co-ed sailing team (about a quarter of all students belong to a varsity team).

Westminster College

1840 South 1300 East
Salt Lake City, UT 84105
(801) 484-7651
http://www.westminstercollege.edu

Why It's Cool

What do Tom Cruise, Tom Petty, and Westminster have in common? *Planes*. Tom Cruise has *Top Gun*, Tom Petty has "Learning to Fly," and Westminster has a major in aviation. Picture yourself piloting your very own Piper plane. First, you'll practice flying the friendly skies in a state-of-the-art cockpit at the on-campus Aviation Simulation Center. Then, you'll head to the Flight Operations Center, part of the Salt Lake City International Airport, for real runs in the air. You can even earn certified flight instructor credentials. Westminster gives you wings—and a whole lot more.

SALT LAKE CITY'S GOT A LAW THAT FORBIDS PEOPLE FROM WALKING DOWN THE STREET CARRYING A VIOLIN IN A PAPER BAG. POLYGAMY'S QUASI-LEGAL THERE TOO, BUT THAT'S ANOTHER STORY.

The Details

Campus setting:	suburban
Degrees:	bachelor's, master's
Calendar:	4-4-1
Public/Private:	private nonprofit
Number of full-time faculty:	117
Student-to-teacher ratio:	10:1

Admissions requirements:

- **Options:** common application, deferred entrance, electronic application
- **Application fee:** $40
- **Required:** essay or personal statement, high school transcript, letter of recommendation, SAT or ACT
- **Application deadlines:** 4/15 (freshmen), continuous (transfer)
- **Early decision:** —
- **Notification:** 10/1 (freshmen), continuous (transfer)

Average high school GPA:	3.58
Average freshman SAT verbal/math score:	575 / 552
Average freshman ACT score:	23
Number of applicants:	867
Number of applicants accepted:	756
Percentage of students from out of state:	9%
Total freshman enrollment:	314
Total enrollment:	2,417
Percentage of students who live in campus housing:	26%
Total tuition fee:	$18,192
Total cost with fees & expenses:	$25,112
Average financial aid package:	$15,651

Where It's At

Westminster is just 15 minutes from downtown Salt Lake City, the capital of Utah. "Sugarhouse," as the neighborhood around Westminster is known, offers several coffeehouses and eclectic restaurants, including Bluekats Coffee and Junk Food. There's also the large Sugarhouse Park. Major city attractions include the Great Salt Lake, the temple of the Church of Jesus Christ of Latter-day Saints, Clark Planetarium, Lagoon amusement park, and the Utah Museum of Fine Arts. About 30 minutes away from campus are world-renowned ski resorts, including Alta and Snowbird, in the Rocky Mountains. Dinosaur National Monument, Arches National Park, and Canyonlands National Park are all about a day's drive away.

What It's Like

Westminster attracts bright, extroverted students able to balance academics with socializing. The Winter at Westminster program brings students from other schools to Westminster for the semester. During the morning, students take classes and then spend the afternoon skiing, snowboarding, or doing some other winter activity. The popular program is available to Westminster students too.

In addition to aviation, Westminster offers about 25 majors, including financial services, art administration, and nursing. Notable minors include gender studies and paleontology. At the high-tech Gore Center for Business, Aviation, and Entrepreneurship, students can crunch numbers at the Center for Financial Analysis or get ready to fly at the Westminster hangar.

Bouldering, foosballing, snowboarding, studying . . .

All students must demonstrate proficiency in writing, using a computer, math, and public speaking. Other requirements range from taking a social science course to taking classes in beginning drawing, stagecraft, or physical education.

First-years live together in the doubles of either Carelson or Hogle Halls. Upperclass students live in singles in the apartment-style Behnkenl, Stock, and Olwell Halls.

The new Health, Wellness, and Athletic Center features state-of-the-art equipment and workout rooms. Westminster sponsors eight NAIA Division I athletic teams, known as the Griffins, including cross-country. Intramural clubs range from bouldering (a type of rock climbing) to foosball to sand volleyball.

Among the 40 student organizations are the service group Circle K, the Geek Club, and Students for a Free Tibet. The Volunteer Center hooks up students with community service groups, such as America Reads, which pairs Westminster reading tutors with students in local schools.

Each year, the KeyBank Cultural Diversity Lecture Series brings distinguished speakers to campus, and the Weeks Poetry Series sponsors visiting writers. While we adore Westminster for encouraging students to get out and ski, we also admire its commitment to multiculturalism.

Willamette University

900 State Street
Salem, OR 97301

(503) 370-6300
http://www.willamette.edu/

Why It's Cool

There's more to Willamette than just a gorgeous campus. Sure, you'll stroll to class alongside the flowing waters of the Mill Race stream and you'll pass by the Star Trees, a grotto of five giant sequoias (the largest redwoods on any college campus). But you'll also be right across the street from the Oregon State Capitol. Learn about government in class or read about civics in your textbook, then head over and see how everything *really* works by volunteering for or doing an internship with Oregon's lawmakers and legislators. It's no surprise that the politics department here is hot, hot, hot.

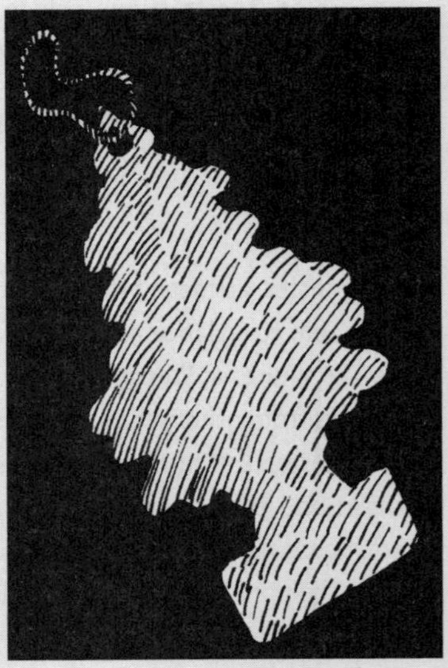

WILLAMETTE'S MOTTO IS "PURE EDUCATION WITH A FRESH PINE SCENT."

The Details

Campus setting:	urban
Degrees:	bachelor's, master's
Calendar:	semesters
Public/Private:	private religious
Number of full-time faculty:	193
Student-to-teacher ratio:	11:1

Admissions requirements:

- **Options:** common application, deferred entrance, early action, electronic application
- **Application fee:** $50
- **Required:** essay or personal statement, high school transcript, letter of recommendation, SAT or ACT
- **Application deadlines:** 2/1 (freshmen), 2/1 (transfer)
- **Early action:** 12/1
- **Notification:** 4/1 (freshmen), 4/1 (transfer), 1/15 (early action)

Average high school GPA:	3.75
Average freshman SAT verbal/math score:	632 / 627
Average freshman ACT score:	25
Number of applicants:	2,291
Number of applicants accepted:	1,896
Percentage of students from out of state:	58%
Total freshman enrollment:	510
Total enrollment:	2,663
Percentage of students who live in campus housing:	69%
Total tuition fee:	$26,690
Total cost with fees & expenses:	$35,452
Average financial aid package:	$21,027

Where It's At

Willamette's 61-acre campus is within walking distance from Waldo Park, the world's smallest park at 0.005 acre, and the banks of the Willamette River in Salem, Oregon. For nine months out of each year, the city hosts First Wednesdays, in which artisans and musicians display their wares and perform in the hip downtown area.

Outdoor activities are numerous, naturally: Surfers head out to the Oregon Coast, skiers travel to the Hoodoo Mountain Resort, and hikers travel to Crater Lake National Park and to Mount St. Helens National Park. Portland is less than an hour away by car, and Seattle is just four hours away.

What It's Like

Willamette's got it all: a beautiful campus in the capital of Oregon, great academics, awesome athletic facilities, and truly excellent parties. Each spring, the campus comes together for Wulapalooza, a huge celebration of spring, complete with bands, foods, arts and crafts, speakers, and dancing.

Currently, all first-years and sophomores are required to live in one of the 21 residential buildings, but Willamette has begun moving toward a residential commons system in which small groups of upperclass students will live alongside a faculty mentor in on-campus suites and apartments. These groups will eat, learn, and socialize together in the $14 million Kaneko Commons.

Think Eden, smack-dab in the middle of Salem.

Students choose from around 30 departments offering such majors as geography, comparative literature and the history of ideas, and environmental science. More than 50 percent of students study abroad in Chile, China, and South Africa, among other locations.

First-years at Willamette get a taste of college life before the official orientation with the five-day Jump Start, an optional program in which small groups do community service. During their first year, students take a special class as part of Willamette's general education requirements called the World Views seminar. In 2005, the theme of the seminar was War and Its Alternatives.

Other requirements at Willamette include three writing-centered classes; two analytical reasoning and quantitative classes, such as chemistry or economics; and six so-called Modes of Inquiry courses, which introduce students to the different types of exploration involved in such disciplines as science and history.

The Willamette Bearcats compete on 20 Division III varsity teams and many intramural clubs. All told, students can have close to 100 campus organizations to choose from. Everybody hangs out at the Bistro, a student-run café.

Willamette's first graduate was a woman in 1859. Today's graduates receive a bachelor of arts or bachelor of music degree and a fresh-smelling, first-rate education.

Eat, Drink, and Be Merry: Most Popular Town/City Festivals

No matter how great your campus is, sometimes you just need to get away. Here's a list of the coolest things to do off campus.

Alma College (P. 8) HIGHLAND FESTIVAL

Appalachian State University (P. 14) APPALACHIAN SUMMER FESTIVAL

College of Charleston (P. 54) SPOLETO FESTIVAL

Elon University (P. 86) GREENSBORO'S EASTERN MUSIC FESTIVAL

The Evergreen State College (P. 92) DIXIELAND JAZZ FESTIVAL

Goucher College (P. 100) TOWSON'S SPRING FESTIVAL

Grinnell College (P. 104) HAPPY DAYS FESTIVAL

Hendrix College (P. 112) TOAD SUCK DAZE FESTIVAL

Kalamazoo College (P. 116) GILMORE INTERNATIONAL KEYBOARD FESTIVAL

Marlboro College (P. 136) MARLBORO MUSIC FESTIVAL

Miami University (P. 138) OUTDOOR SUMMER MUSIC FESTIVAL

Millsaps College (P. 140) CHIMNEYVILLE CRAFTS FESTIVAL

New College of Florida (P. 148) SARASOTA FILM FESTIVAL

North Central College (P. 150) OKTOBERFEST

Presbyterian College (P. 158) CLINTON FALL FESTIVAL

Rollins College (P. 178) BACH FESTIVAL

Savannah College of Art and Design (P. 182)
SIDEWALK ARTS FESTIVAL; SAVANNAH FILM FESTIVAL

Stephens College (P. 194) TRUE/FALSE FESTIVAL

University of Alaska Southeast (P. 202) BRIERFIELD BLUEGRASS FESTIVAL

University of Redlands (P. 210) CINCO DE MAYO CELEBRATION

The University of Tampa (P. 212)
GASPARILLA PIRATE FESTIVAL; BONK FESTIVAL OF NEW MUSIC

Appendices

Appendix I:
Geographical Locations by Region

Northeast

Allegheny College (MEADVILLE, PA)

Arcadia University (GLENSIDE, PA)

Bates College (LEWISTON, ME)

Binghamton University (BINGHAMTON, NY)

Centenary College (HACKETTSTOWN, NJ)

The College of New Jersey (EWING, NJ)

College of the Atlantic (BAR HARBOR, ME)

The Cooper Union for the Advancement of Science and Art (NEW YORK, NY)

Elmira College (ELMIRA, NY)

Emerson College (BOSTON, MA)

Eugene Lang College (NEW YORK, NY)

Goucher College (BALTIMORE, MD)

Green Mountain College (POULTNEY, VT)

Hampshire College (AMHERST, MA)

Keene State College (KEENE, NH)

Manhattanville College (PURCHASE, NY)

Marlboro College (MARLBORO, VT)

Mount Holyoke College (SOUTH HADLEY, MA)

Muhlenberg College (ALLENTOWN, PA)

Purchase College (PURCHASE, NY)

Roger Williams University (BRISTOL, RI)

St. John's College (ANNAPOLIS, MD)

Unity College (UNITY, ME)

Washington College (CHESTERTOWN, MD)

Southeast

Agnes Scott College (DECATUR, GA)

Appalachian State University (BOONE, NC)

Belhaven College (JACKSON, MS)

Berea College (BEREA, KY)

Birmingham-Southern College (BIRMINGHAM, AL)

Centre College (DANVILLE, KY)

College of Charleston (CHARLESTON, SC)

Eckerd College (ST. PETERSBURG, FL)

Elon University (ELON, NC)

Hendrix College (CONWAY, AR)

Millsaps College (JACKSON, MS)

New College of Florida (SARASOTA, FL)

Presbyterian College (CLINTON, SC)

Randolph-Macon College (ASHLAND, VA)

Rhodes College (MEMPHIS, TN)

Rollins College (WINTER PARK, FL)

Savannah College of Art and Design (SAVANNAH, GA)

Tuskegee University (TUSKEGEE, AL)

University of Mary Washington (FREDERICKSBURG, VA)

University of Montevallo (MONTEVALLO, AL)

The University of Tampa (TAMPA, FL)

The University of the South (SEWANEE, TN)

Warren Wilson College (ASHEVILLE, NC)

Midwest

Alma College (ALMA, MI)

Antioch College (YELLOW SPRINGS, OH)

Augsburg College (MINNEAPOLIS, MN)

Augustana College (ROCK ISLAND, IL)

Beloit College (BELOIT, WI)

Coe College (CEDAR RAPIDS, IA)

College for Creative Studies (DETROIT, MI)

College of the Ozarks (POINT LOOKOUT, MO)

The College of Wooster (WOOSTER, OH)

Cornell College (MOUNT VERNON, IA)

Earlham College (RICHMOND, IN)

Goshen College (GOSHEN, IN)

Grinnell College (GRINNELL, IA)

Hanover College (HANOVER, IN)

Hiram College (HIRAM, OH)

Kalamazoo College (KALAMAZOO, MI)

Knox College (GALESBURG, IL)

Loyola University Chicago (CHICAGO, IL)

Macalester College (ST. PAUL, MN)

Miami University (OXFORD, OH)

North Central College (NAPERVILLE, IL)

Ohio Northern University (ADA, OH)

Ripon College (RIPON, WI)

University of Tulsa (TULSA, OK)

Rockford College (ROCKFORD, IL)

Stephens College (COLUMBIA, MO)

Northwest

Albertson College of Idaho (CALDWELL, ID)

Carroll College (HELENA, MT)

Chaminade University of Honolulu (HONOLULU, HI)

The Evergreen State College (OLYMPIA, WA)

Fairhaven College (BELLINGHAM, WA)

Lewis & Clark College (PORTLAND, OR)

Linfield College (MCMINNVILLE, OR)

Reed College (PORTLAND, OR)

University of Alaska Southeast (JUNEAU, AK)

Willamette University (SALEM, OR)

West Coast and Southwest

Austin College (SHERMAN, TX)

College of Santa Fe (SANTA FE, NM)

Colorado School of Mines (GOLDEN, CO)

Deep Springs College (DEEP SPRINGS, CA)

Occidental College (LOS ANGELES, CA)

Prescott College (PRESCOTT, AZ)

Sierra Nevada College (INCLINE VILLAGE, NV)

Sonoma State University (ROHNERT PARK, CA)

Southwestern University (GEORGETOWN, TX)

St. John's College (SANTA FE, NM)

Thomas Aquinas College (SANTA PAULA, CA)

University of Redlands (REDLANDS, CA)

Westminster College (SALT LAKE CITY, UT)

Appendix II:
List of Majors, Departments, and Programs of Study

Agnes Scott College

- Anthropology
- Art/Art Studies, General
- Astrophysics
- Biochemistry
- Biology/Biological Sciences, General
- Chemistry, General
- Classics and Languages, Literatures and Linguistics, General
- Creative Writing
- Drama and Dramatics/Theatre Arts, General
- Economics, General
- English Language and Literature, General
- French Language and Literature
- German Language and Literature
- History, General
- Interdisciplinary Studies
- International Relations and Affairs
- Literature
- Mathematics, General
- Music, General
- Philosophy
- Physics, General
- Political Science and Government, General
- Psychology, General
- Religion/Religious Studies
- Sociology
- Spanish Language and Literature
- Women's Studies

Albertson College of Idaho

- Accounting
- Anthropology
- Art/Art Studies, General
- Biology/Biological Sciences, General
- Business Administration and Management, General
- Chemistry, General
- Computer Science
- Creative Writing
- Drama and Dramatics/Theatre Arts, General
- Economics, General
- English Language and Literature, General
- History, General
- International Business/Trade/Commerce
- International Economics
- Kinesiology and Exercise Science
- Mathematics, General
- Music, General
- Philosophy
- Physical Education Teaching and Coaching
- Physics, General
- Political Science and Government, General
- Pre-Medicine/Pre-Medical Studies
- Psychology, General
- Religion/Religious Studies
- Sociology
- Spanish Language and Literature
- Sport and Fitness Administration/Management

Allegheny College

- Applied Economics
- Art/Art Studies, General
- Art History, Criticism and Conservation
- Biochemistry
- Biology/Biological Sciences, General
- Business/Managerial Economics
- Chemistry, General
- Communication Studies/Speech Communication and Rhetoric
- Computer Science
- Computer Software Engineering
- Creative Writing
- Drama and Dramatics/Theatre Arts, General
- Economics, General
- Education, General
- English Language and Literature, General
- Environmental Science
- Environmental Studies
- Fine/Studio Arts, General
- Fine Arts and Art Studies, Other
- French Language and Literature
- Geology/Earth Science, General
- German Language and Literature
- Health/Medical Preparatory Programs, Other
- History, General
- International/Global Studies
- International Relations and Affairs
- Journalism
- Mass Communication/Media Studies
- Mathematics, General
- Multi-/Interdisciplinary Studies, Other
- Music, General
- Music Performance, General
- Neuroscience
- Philosophy
- Physics, General
- Political Science and Government, General
- Pre-Dentistry Studies
- Pre-Law Studies
- Pre-Medicine/Pre-Medical Studies
- Pre-Nursing Studies
- Pre-Pharmacy Studies
- Pre-Veterinary Studies
- Psychology, General
- Religion/Religious Studies
- Spanish Language and Literature
- Technical and Business Writing
- Women's Studies

Alma College

- Accounting
- Anthropology
- Art/Art Studies, General

- Art Teacher Education
- Biochemistry
- Biological and Physical Sciences
- Biology/Biological Sciences, General
- Biology Teacher Education
- Business Administration and Management, General
- Chemistry, General
- Chemistry Teacher Education
- Communication and Media Studies, Other
- Computer Science
- Computer Teacher Education
- Dance, General
- Design and Visual Communications, General
- Drama and Dramatics/Theatre Arts, General
- Early Childhood Education and Teaching
- Economics, General
- Education, General
- Elementary Education and Teaching
- English/Language Arts Teacher Education
- English Language and Literature, General
- Fine/Studio Arts, General
- French Language and Literature
- French Language Teacher Education
- German Language and Literature
- German Language Teacher Education
- Gerontology
- Graphic Design
- Health Science
- Health Teacher Education
- History, General
- History Teacher Education
- Humanities/Humanistic Studies
- International Business/Trade/Commerce
- Kindergarten/Preschool Education and Teaching
- Kinesiology and Exercise Science
- Liberal Arts and Sciences/Liberal Studies
- Marketing/Marketing Management, General
- Mathematics, General
- Mathematics Teacher Education
- Medical Illustration/Medical Illustrator
- Modern Languages
- Music, General
- Music Performance, General
- Music Teacher Education
- Philosophy
- Physical Education Teaching and Coaching
- Physics, General
- Physics Teacher Education
- Political Science and Government, General
- Pre-Dentistry Studies
- Pre-Law Studies
- Pre-Medicine/Pre-Medical Studies
- Pre-Theology/Pre-Ministerial Studies
- Pre-Veterinary Studies
- Psychology, General
- Psychology Teacher Education
- Public Health, General (MPH, DPH)
- Religion/Religious Studies
- Science Teacher Education/General Science Teacher Education
- Secondary Education and Teaching
- Social Sciences, General
- Social Science Teacher Education
- Social Studies Teacher Education
- Sociology
- Spanish Language and Literature
- Spanish Language Teacher Education

Antioch College

- African American/Black Studies
- African Studies
- Anthropology
- Behavioral Sciences
- Biological and Physical Sciences
- Biology/Biological Sciences, General
- Biomedical Sciences, General
- Business Administration and Management, General
- Chemistry, General
- Cinematography and Film/Video Production
- Communication Studies/Speech Communication and Rhetoric
- Comparative Literature
- Computer Science
- Creative Writing
- Dance, General
- Drama and Dramatics/Theatre Arts, General
- Drawing
- Economics, General
- Education, General
- English Language and Literature, General
- Environmental Biology
- Environmental Studies
- European Studies/Civilization
- French Language and Literature
- Geology/Earth Science, General
- German Language and Literature
- History, General
- Human Development and Family Studies, General
- Humanities/Humanistic Studies
- Interdisciplinary Studies
- International Relations and Affairs
- Japanese Language and Literature
- Junior High/Intermediate/Middle School Education and Teaching
- Literature
- Mass Communication/Media Studies
- Mathematics, General
- Music, General
- Natural Sciences
- Peace Studies and Conflict Resolution
- Philosophy
- Physical Sciences
- Physics, General
- Political Science and Government, General
- Pre-Law Studies
- Pre-Medicine/Pre-Medical Studies
- Pre-Veterinary Studies
- Psychology, General
- Religion/Religious Studies
- Science Teacher Education/General Science Teacher Education
- Sculpture
- Secondary Education and Teaching
- Social Sciences, General
- Sociology
- Spanish Language and Literature
- Visual and Performing Arts, General
- Women's Studies

Appalachian State University

- Accounting
- Advertising
- Anthropology
- Apparel and Textiles, General
- Art/Art Studies, General
- Arts Management
- Art Teacher Education
- Athletic Training/Trainer
- Audiology/Audiologist and Speech-Language Pathology/Pathologist
- Biology/Biological Sciences, General
- Biology Teacher Education
- Business Administration and Management, General
- Business Teacher Education
- Chemistry, General
- Chemistry Teacher Education
- Child Development
- City/Urban, Community and Regional Planning

- Clinical Laboratory Science/Medical Technology/Technologist
- Communication Disorders, General
- Computer Science
- Criminal Justice/Safety Studies
- Drama and Dance Teacher Education
- Drama and Dramatics/Theatre Arts, General
- Ecology
- Economics, General
- Education/Teaching of Individuals with Specific Learning Disabilities
- Electrical, Electronic and Communications Engineering Technology/Technician
- Elementary Education and Teaching
- English/Language Arts Teacher Education
- English Language and Literature, General
- Family and Consumer Sciences/Home Economics Teacher Education
- Finance, General
- Fine/Studio Arts, General
- Foods, Nutrition, and Wellness Studies, General
- French Language and Literature
- French Language Teacher Education
- Geography
- Geology/Earth Science, General
- Gerontology
- Graphic and Printing Equipment Operator, General Production
- Graphic Design
- Health/Health Care Administration/Management
- Health Teacher Education
- History, General
- History Teacher Education
- Hospitality Administration/Management, General
- Industrial Design
- Industrial Production Technologies/Technicians, Other
- Industrial Technology/Technician
- Insurance
- International Business/Trade/Commerce
- Journalism
- Junior High/Intermediate/Middle School Education and Teaching
- Kindergarten/Preschool Education and Teaching
- Kinesiology and Exercise Science
- Liberal Arts and Sciences/Liberal Studies
- Library Science/Librarianship
- Management Information Systems, General
- Marketing/Marketing Management, General
- Mathematics, General
- Mathematics Teacher Education
- Music Management and Merchandising
- Music Performance, General
- Music Teacher Education
- Music Therapy/Therapist
- Parks, Recreation, and Leisure Facilities Management
- Philosophy and Religious Studies, Other
- Physical Education Teaching and Coaching
- Physics, General
- Physics Teacher Education
- Political Science and Government, General
- Psychology, General
- Public Health Education and Promotion
- Public Relations/Image Management
- Radio and Television
- Social Studies Teacher Education
- Social Work
- Sociology
- Spanish Language and Literature
- Spanish Language Teacher Education
- Speech and Rhetorical Studies
- Statistics, General
- Teacher Education and Professional Development, Specific Subject Areas, Other
- Technology Teacher Education/Industrial Arts Teacher Education

Arcadia University

- Accounting
- Acting
- Art/Art Studies, General
- Art History, Criticism and Conservation
- Art Teacher Education
- Biology/Biological Sciences, General
- Business Administration and Management, General
- Ceramic Arts and Ceramics
- Chemistry, General
- Commercial and Advertising Art
- Computer and Information Sciences, General
- Computer Programming/Programmer, General
- Computer Science
- Drama and Dramatics/Theatre Arts, General
- Drawing
- Early Childhood Education and Teaching
- Education, General
- Elementary Education and Teaching
- English Language and Literature, General
- Environmental Biology
- Finance, General
- Fine/Studio Arts, General
- Health/Health Care Administration/Management
- History, General
- Human Resources Management/Personnel Administration, General
- Human Services, General
- Interior Design
- International Business/Trade/Commerce
- Kindergarten/Preschool Education and Teaching
- Liberal Arts and Sciences/Liberal Studies
- Literature
- Management Information Systems, General
- Marketing/Marketing Management, General
- Mass Communication/Media Studies
- Mathematics, General
- Medical Illustration/Medical Illustrator
- Metal and Jewelry Arts
- Natural Sciences
- Philosophy
- Photography
- Physiological Psychology/Psychobiology
- Political Science and Government, General
- Pre-Dentistry Studies
- Pre-Law Studies
- Pre-Medicine/Pre-Medical Studies
- Pre-Veterinary Studies
- Psychology, General
- Secondary Education and Teaching
- Sociology
- Spanish Language and Literature

Augsburg College

- Accounting
- Aeronautics/Aviation/Aerospace Science and Technology, General
- Art/Art Studies, General
- Art History, Criticism and Conservation
- Art Teacher Education
- Astrophysics
- Athletic Training/Trainer
- Behavioral Sciences

- Biological and Physical Sciences
- Biology/Biological Sciences, General
- Business/Managerial Economics
- Business Administration and Management, General
- Chemistry, General
- Computer Science
- Criminal Justice/Safety Studies
- Drama and Dramatics/Theatre Arts, General
- East Asian Studies
- Economics, General
- Education, General
- Education/Teaching of Individuals with Emotional Disturbances
- Elementary Education and Teaching
- English Language and Literature, General
- Finance, General
- Fine/Studio Arts, General
- French Language and Literature
- German Language and Literature
- Health Teacher Education
- History, General
- Humanities/Humanistic Studies
- Interdisciplinary Studies
- International Business/Trade/Commerce
- International Relations and Affairs
- Kindergarten/Preschool Education and Teaching
- Liberal Arts and Sciences/Liberal Studies
- Management Information Systems, General
- Marketing/Marketing Management, General
- Mass Communication/Media Studies
- Mathematics, General
- Music, General
- Music Teacher Education
- Music Therapy/Therapist
- Natural Sciences
- Nursing/Registered Nurse Training
- Philosophy
- Physical Education Teaching and Coaching
- Physician Assistant
- Physics, General
- Political Science and Government, General
- Pre-Dentistry Studies
- Pre-Law Studies
- Pre-Medicine/Pre-Medical Studies
- Pre-Veterinary Studies
- Psychology, General
- Religion/Religious Studies
- Scandinavian Languages, Literatures, and Linguistics
- Secondary Education and Teaching
- Social Sciences, General
- Social Work
- Sociology
- Spanish Language and Literature
- Speech and Rhetorical Studies
- Theology/Theological Studies
- Urban Studies/Affairs
- Women's Studies

Augustana College

- Accounting
- Anthropology
- Art/Art Studies, General
- Art History, Criticism and Conservation
- Art Teacher Education
- Asian Studies/Civilization
- Biology/Biological Sciences, General
- Business Administration and Management, General
- Chemistry, General
- Chinese Language and Literature
- Classics and Languages, Literatures and Linguistics, General
- Computer Science
- Creative Writing
- Drama and Dramatics/Theatre Arts, General
- Economics, General
- Education, General
- Elementary Education and Teaching
- Engineering, Other
- Engineering Physics
- English Language and Literature, General
- Environmental Studies
- Finance, General
- Fine/Studio Arts, General
- French Language and Literature
- Geography
- Geology/Earth Science, General
- German Language and Literature
- History, General
- Japanese Language and Literature
- Jazz/Jazz Studies
- Latin Language and Literature
- Liberal Arts and Sciences/Liberal Studies
- Literature
- Marketing/Marketing Management, General
- Mass Communication/Media Studies
- Mathematics, General
- Mathematics and Computer Science
- Music, General
- Music Performance, General
- Music Teacher Education
- Occupational Therapy/Therapist
- Philosophy
- Physical Education Teaching and Coaching
- Physics, General
- Piano and Organ
- Political Science and Government, General
- Predentistry Studies
- Pre-Law Studies
- Pre-Medicine/Pre-Medical Studies
- Pre-Veterinary Studies
- Psychology, General
- Public Administration
- Religion/Religious Studies
- Religious/Sacred Music
- Scandinavian Languages, Literatures, and Linguistics
- Science Teacher Education/General Science Teacher Education
- Secondary Education and Teaching
- Sociology
- Spanish Language and Literature
- Speech and Rhetorical Studies
- Speech-Language Pathology/Pathologist
- Speech Therapy
- Swedish Language and Literature
- Violin, Viola, Guitar and Other Stringed Instruments
- Voice and Opera
- Wind and Percussion Instruments
- Women's Studies

Austin College

- American/United States Studies/Civilization
- Art/Art Studies, General
- Biology/Biological Sciences, General
- Business Administration and Management, General
- Chemistry, General
- Classics and Classical Languages, Literatures, and Linguistics, Other
- Classics and Languages, Literatures and Linguistics, General
- Communication Studies/Speech Communication and Rhetoric
- Computer Science
- Economics, General
- English Language and Literature, General
- Environmental Studies
- French Language and Literature
- German Language and Literature

- History, General
- International Economics
- International Relations and Affairs
- Latin American Studies
- Latin Language and Literature
- Mathematics, General
- Multi-/Interdisciplinary Studies, Other
- Music, General
- Philosophy
- Physical Education Teaching and Coaching
- Physics, General
- Political Science and Government, General
- Psychology, General
- Religion/Religious Studies
- Sociology
- Spanish Language and Literature

Bates College

- African-American/Black Studies
- American/United States Studies/Civilization
- Anthropology
- Art/Art Studies, General
- Biochemistry
- Biology/Biological Sciences, General
- Chemistry, General
- Chinese Language and Literature
- Classical, Ancient Mediterranean and Near Eastern Studies and Archaeology
- Drama and Dramatics/Theatre Arts, General
- East Asian Studies
- Economics, General
- Engineering, General
- English Language and Literature, General
- Environmental Studies
- French Language and Literature
- Geology/Earth Science, General
- German Language and Literature
- History, General
- Japanese Language and Literature
- Mathematics, General
- Multi-/Interdisciplinary Studies, Other
- Music, General
- Neuroscience
- Philosophy
- Physics, General
- Political Science and Government, General
- Psychology, General
- Religion/Religious Studies
- Russian Language and Literature
- Sociology
- Spanish Language and Literature
- Speech and Rhetorical Studies
- Women's Studies

Belhaven College

- Accounting
- Art/Art Studies, General
- Athletic Training/Trainer
- Bible/Biblical Studies
- Biology/Biological Sciences, General
- Business Administration and Management, General
- Chemistry, General
- Communication Studies/Speech Communication and Rhetoric
- Computer Science
- Creative Writing
- Dance, General
- Drama and Dramatics/Theatre Arts, General
- Elementary Education and Teaching
- English Language and Literature, General
- History, General
- Humanities/Humanistic Studies
- Information Science/Studies
- Mathematics, General
- Music, General
- Pastoral Studies/Counseling
- Philosophy
- Psychology, General
- Sport and Fitness Administration/Management
- Theatre

Beloit College

- Anthropology
- Art History, Criticism and Conservation
- Art Teacher Education
- Asian Studies/Civilization
- Biochemistry
- Biology/Biological Sciences, General
- Business/Managerial Economics
- Business Administration and Management, General
- Cell/Cellular Biology and Histology
- Chemistry, General
- Classics and Languages, Literatures and Linguistics, General
- Comparative Literature
- Computer Science
- Creative Writing
- Drama and Dramatics/Theatre Arts, General
- Economics, General
- Education, General
- Elementary Education and Teaching
- Engineering, General
- English Language and Literature, General
- Environmental Biology
- Environmental Studies
- European Studies/Civilization
- Fine/Studio Arts, General
- French Language and Literature
- Geology/Earth Science, General
- German Language and Literature
- History, General
- Interdisciplinary Studies
- International Relations and Affairs
- Latin American Studies
- Literature
- Mass Communication/Media Studies
- Mathematics, General
- Modern Languages
- Molecular Biology
- Museology/Museum Studies
- Music, General
- Music Teacher Education
- Philosophy
- Physics, General
- Political Science and Government, General
- Pre-Dentistry Studies
- Pre-Law Studies
- Pre-Medicine/Pre-Medical Studies
- Psychology, General
- Religion/Religious Studies
- Romance Languages, Literatures, and Linguistics, General
- Russian Language and Literature
- Russian Studies
- Science Teacher Education/General Science Teacher Education
- Secondary Education and Teaching
- Sociobiology
- Sociology
- Spanish Language and Literature
- Women's Studies

Berea College

- Agricultural Business and Management, General
- Agriculture, General
- Art/Art Studies, General
- Art History, Criticism and Conservation
- Art Teacher Education
- Biology/Biological Sciences, General
- Biology Teacher Education

- Business Administration and Management, General
- Chemistry, General
- Child Development
- Classics and Languages, Literatures and Linguistics, General
- Developmental and Child Psychology
- Dietetics/Dietitians
- Drama and Dramatics/Theatre Arts, General
- Economics, General
- Education, General
- Elementary Education and Teaching
- English/Language Arts Teacher Education
- English Language and Literature, General
- Family and Consumer Economics and Related Services, Other
- Family and Consumer Sciences/Home Economics Teacher Education
- Fine/Studio Arts, General
- Foreign Language Teacher Education
- French Language and Literature
- French Language Teacher Education
- German Language and Literature
- German Language Teacher Education
- History, General
- Industrial Technology/Technician
- Junior High/Intermediate/Middle School Education and Teaching
- Kindergarten/Preschool Education and Teaching
- Mass Communication/Media Studies
- Mathematics, General
- Mathematics Teacher Education
- Music, General
- Music Teacher Education
- Nursing/Registered Nurse Training
- Philosophy
- Physical Education Teaching and Coaching
- Physics, General
- Political Science and Government, General
- Pre-Dentistry Studies
- Pre-Medicine/Pre-Medical Studies
- Pre-Veterinary Studies
- Psychology, General
- Religion/Religious Studies
- Secondary Education and Teaching
- Sociology
- Spanish Language and Literature
- Spanish Language Teacher Education
- Technology Education/Industrial Arts
- Women's Studies

Binghamton University

- Accounting
- African American/Black Studies
- African Studies
- Anthropology
- Arabic Language and Literature
- Art/Art Studies, General
- Art History, Criticism and Conservation
- Asian-American Studies
- Biochemistry
- Biology/Biological Sciences, General
- Biomedical/Medical Engineering
- Chemistry, General
- Classics and Languages, Literatures and Linguistics, General
- Comparative Literature
- Computer Engineering, General
- Computer Science
- Drama and Dramatics/Theatre Arts, General
- Drawing
- Economics, General
- Electrical, Electronics and Communications Engineering
- English Language and Literature, General
- Environmental Studies
- Film/Cinema Studies
- Fine/Studio Arts, General
- French Language and Literature
- Geography
- Geology/Earth Science, General
- German Language and Literature
- Hebrew Language and Literature
- History, General
- Industrial Engineering
- Information Science/Studies
- Interdisciplinary Studies
- Italian Language and Literature
- Jewish/Judaic Studies
- Latin American Studies
- Linguistics
- Literature
- Management Science, General
- Mathematics, General
- Mechanical Engineering
- Medieval and Renaissance Studies
- Music, General
- Music Performance, General
- Nursing/Registered Nurse Training
- Philosophy
- Physics, General
- Physiological Psychology/Psychobiology
- Political Science and Government, General
- Pre-Law Studies
- Psychology, General
- Sociology
- Spanish Language and Literature

Birmingham-Southern College

- Accounting
- Art/Art Studies, General
- Art History, Criticism and Conservation
- Art Teacher Education
- Asian Studies/Civilization
- Biology/Biological Sciences, General
- Business Administration and Management, General
- Chemistry, General
- Computer Science
- Dance, General
- Drama and Dramatics/Theatre Arts, General
- Drawing
- Economics, General
- Education, General
- Elementary Education and Teaching
- English Language and Literature, General
- Fine/Studio Arts, General
- French Language and Literature
- German Language and Literature
- History, General
- Human Resources Management/Personnel Administration, General
- Interdisciplinary Studies
- International Business/Trade/Commerce
- Kindergarten/Preschool Education and Teaching
- Mathematics, General
- Music, General
- Music History, Literature, and Theory
- Music Teacher Education
- Painting
- Philosophy
- Physics, General
- Piano and Organ
- Political Science and Government, General
- Pre-Dentistry Studies
- Pre-Law Studies
- Pre-Medicine/Pre-Medical Studies
- Printmaking
- Psychology, General
- Religion/Religious Studies

- Sculpture
- Secondary Education and Teaching
- Sociology
- Spanish Language and Literature
- Voice and Opera

Carroll College

- Accounting
- Acting
- Biology/Biological Sciences, General
- Biology Teacher Education
- Business/Managerial Economics
- Business Administration and Management, General
- Chemistry, General
- Civil Engineering, General
- Clinical Laboratory Science/Medical Technology/Technologist
- Communication Studies/Speech Communication and Rhetoric
- Computer Science
- Drama and Dramatics/Theatre Arts, General
- Education, General
- Elementary Education and Teaching
- Engineering, General
- English/Language Arts Teacher Education
- English Language and Literature, General
- Environmental Studies
- Finance, General
- French Language and Literature
- General Studies
- Health Information/Medical Records Administration/Administrator
- History, General
- History Teacher Education
- International Relations and Affairs
- Latin Language and Literature
- Mathematics, General
- Mathematics Teacher Education
- Nursing/Registered Nurse Training
- Philosophy
- Physical Education Teaching and Coaching
- Political Science and Government, General
- Pre-Dentistry Studies
- Pre-Law Studies
- Pre-Medicine/Pre-Medical Studies
- Pre-Pharmacy Studies
- Pre-Veterinary Studies
- Psychology, General
- Public Administration
- Public Relations/Image Management
- Religion/Religious Studies
- Religious Education
- Secondary Education and Teaching
- Social Sciences, General
- Social Science Teacher Education
- Social Work
- Sociology
- Spanish Language and Literature
- Spanish Language Teacher Education
- Sport and Fitness Administration/Management
- Teaching English as a Second or Foreign Language/ESL Language Instructor
- Technical and Business Writing
- Technical Theatre/Theatre Design and Technology
- Theology/Theological Studies
- Visual and Performing Arts, General

Centenary College

- Accounting
- Biology/Biological Sciences, General
- Business Administration and Management, General
- Commercial and Advertising Art
- Criminology
- Education, General
- Elementary Education and Teaching
- English Language and Literature, General
- Equestrian/Equine Studies
- Fashion/Apparel Design
- History, General
- Information Science/Studies
- International Relations and Affairs
- Marketing/Marketing Management, General
- Mass Communication/Media Studies
- Mathematics, General
- Political Science and Government, General
- Psychology, General
- Secondary Education and Teaching
- Sociology
- Special Education and Teaching, General
- Sport and Fitness Administration/Management
- Technical Theatre/Theatre Design and Technology

Centre College

- Anthropology
- Art/Art Studies, General
- Art History, Criticism and Conservation
- Biochemistry
- Biology/Biological Sciences, General
- Chemistry, General
- Classics and Languages, Literatures and Linguistics, General
- Computer Science
- Drama and Dramatics/Theatre Arts, General
- Economics, General
- Elementary Education and Teaching
- English Language and Literature, General
- French Language and Literature
- German Language and Literature
- History, General
- International Relations and Affairs
- Mathematics, General
- Molecular Biology
- Music, General
- Philosophy
- Physics, General
- Physiological Psychology/Psychobiology
- Political Science and Government, General
- Psychology, General
- Religion/Religious Studies
- Secondary Education and Teaching
- Sociology
- Spanish Language and Literature

Chaminade University of Honolulu

- Anthropology
- Art
- Behavioral Sciences
- Biology
- Business
- Chemistry
- Communications
- Computer Science
- Criminology & Criminal Science
- Education
- English
- Environmental Studies
- Fine Arts
- Foreign Languages
- Forensic Sciences
- Geography
- Hawaiian & Pacific Studies
- Historical & Policital Studies
- History
- Humanities
- Interior Design

- International Studies
- Mathematics
- Performing Arts Minor
- Philosophy
- Physics
- Political Science
- Psychology
- Religious Studies
- Social Studies
- Sociology

Coe College

- Accounting
- Acting
- African-American/Black Studies
- American/United States Studies/Civilization
- Architecture
- Area, Ethnic, Cultural, and Gender Studies, Other
- Art/Art Studies, General
- Art Teacher Education
- Asian Studies/Civilization
- Athletic Training/Trainer
- Biochemistry
- Biological and Physical Sciences
- Biology/Biological Sciences, General
- Business Administration and Management, General
- Ceramic Arts and Ceramics
- Chemistry, General
- Classics and Languages, Literatures and Linguistics, General
- Computer Science
- Creative Writing
- Directing and Theatrical Production
- Drama and Dramatics/Theatre Arts, General
- Economics, General
- Education, General
- Elementary Education and Teaching
- English Language and Literature, General
- Environmental Studies
- Fine/Studio Arts, General
- French Language and Literature
- French Studies
- Gender Studies
- German Language and Literature
- German Studies
- Health and Physical Education/Fitness, Other
- History, General
- Interdisciplinary Studies
- Liberal Arts and Sciences/Liberal Studies
- Literature
- Mathematics, General
- Molecular Biology
- Music, General
- Music Performance, General
- Music Teacher Education
- Music Theory and Composition
- Nursing/Registered Nurse Training
- Painting
- Philosophy
- Photography
- Physical Education Teaching and Coaching
- Physical Sciences
- Physics, General
- Political Science and Government, General
- Pre-Dentistry Studies
- Pre-Law Studies
- Pre-Medicine/Pre-Medical Studies
- Pre-Veterinary Studies
- Psychology, General
- Public Relations/Image Management
- Religion/Religious Studies
- Science Teacher Education/General Science Teacher Education
- Secondary Education and Teaching
- Sociology
- Spanish and Iberian Studies
- Spanish Language and Literature
- Speech and Rhetorical Studies
- Technical Theatre/Theatre Design and Technology
- Writing

College for Creative Studies

- Advertising Design
- Animation and Digital Media
- Art Education
- Crafts
- Fine Arts
- Graphic Design
- Illustration
- Interior Design
- Photography
- Product Design
- Transportation Design

College of Charleston

- Accounting
- Anthropology
- Art History, Criticism and Conservation
- Arts Management
- Biochemistry
- Biology/Biological Sciences, General
- Business Administration and Management, General
- Chemistry, General
- Classics and Languages, Literatures and Linguistics, General
- Communication Studies/Speech Communication and Rhetoric
- Computer and Information Sciences, General
- Drama and Dramatics/Theatre Arts, General
- Early Childhood Education and Teaching
- Economics, General
- Elementary Education and Teaching
- English Language and Literature, General
- Fine/Studio Arts, General
- French Language and Literature
- Geology/Earth Science, General
- German Language and Literature
- Historic Preservation and Community Planning
- History, General
- Information Science/Studies
- International Business/Trade/Commerce
- Junior High/Intermediate/Middle School Education and Teaching
- Marine Biology and Biological Oceanography
- Mathematics, General
- Music, General
- Philosophy
- Physical Education Teaching and Coaching
- Physics, General
- Political Science and Government, General
- Pre-Dentistry Studies
- Pre-Medicine/Pre-Medical Studies
- Psychology, General
- Religion/Religious Studies
- Secondary Education and Teaching
- Sociology
- Spanish Language and Literature
- Special Education and Teaching, General
- Urban Studies/Affairs

The College of New Jersey

- Accounting
- Art/Art Studies, General
- Art History, Criticism and Conservation
- Art Teacher Education
- Biology/Biological Sciences, General
- Biology Teacher Education
- Biomedical/Medical Engineering
- Business/Managerial Economics
- Business Administration and Management, General
- Chemistry, General
- Chemistry Teacher Education
- Commercial and Advertising Art
- Computer and Information Sciences, General
- Computer Engineering, General
- Criminal Justice/Law Enforcement Administration
- Economics, General
- Education, General
- Education/Teaching of Individuals with Hearing Impairments, Including Deafness
- Electrical, Electronics, and Communications Engineering
- Elementary Education and Teaching
- Engineering Science
- Documentary Studies
- English/Language Arts Teacher Education
- English Language and Literature, General
- Finance, General
- Fine/Studio Arts, General
- History, General
- History Teacher Education
- Intermedia/Multimedia
- International Business/Trade/Commerce
- International Relations and Affairs
- Kindergarten/Preschool Education and Teaching
- Mathematics, General
- Mathematics Teacher Education
- Mechanical Engineering
- Music, General
- Music Teacher Education
- Nursing/Registered Nurse Training
- Philosophy
- Physical Education Teaching and Coaching
- Physics, General
- Physics Teacher Education
- Political Science and Government, General
- Pre-Law Studies
- Pre-Medicine/Pre-Medical Studies
- Psychology, General
- Secondary Education and Teaching
- Sociology
- Spanish Language and Literature
- Spanish Language Teacher Education
- Special Education and Teaching, General
- Speech and Rhetorical Studies
- Statistics, General
- Technology Teacher Education/Industrial Arts Teacher Education
- Women's Studies

College of Santa Fe

- Accounting
- Acting
- Art History, Criticism, and Conservation
- Arts Management
- Art Therapy/Therapist
- Business Administration and Management, General
- Business Teacher Education
- Computer Science
- Counseling Psychology
- Creative Writing
- Criminal Justice/Law Enforcement Administration
- Drama and Dramatics/Theatre Arts, General
- Dramatic/Theatre Arts and Stagecraft, Other
- Early Childhood Education and Teaching
- Elementary Education and Teaching
- English/Language Arts Teacher Education
- English Language and Literature, General
- Environmental Science
- Film/Cinema Studies
- Fine/Studio Arts, General
- Humanities/Humanistic Studies
- Industrial and Organizational Psychology
- Intermedia/Multimedia
- International Business/Trade/Commerce
- Management Information Systems, General
- Moving Image Arts
- Multi-/Interdisciplinary Studies, Other
- Music, Other
- Natural Resources/Conservation, General
- Natural Resources Management and Policy
- Painting
- Pastoral Studies/Counseling
- Photography
- Political Science and Government, General
- Printmaking
- Psychology, General
- Public Administration
- Regional Studies (U.S., Canadian, Foreign)
- Religion/Religious Studies
- Science Teacher Education/General Science Teacher Education
- Sculpture
- Secondary Education and Teaching
- Social Science Teacher Education
- Technical Communication
- Technical Theatre/Theatre Design and Technology
- Theatre/Theatre Arts Management

College of the Atlantic

- Human Ecology

College of the Ozarks

- Accounting
- Acting
- Agribusiness/Agricultural Business Operations
- Agricultural Mechanization, General
- Agricultural Mechanization, Other
- Agricultural Teacher Education
- Agronomy and Crop Science
- Animal Sciences, General
- Apparel and Textiles, General
- Applied Horticulture/Horticultural Operations, General
- Art/Art Studies, General
- Art Teacher Education
- Avionics Maintenance Technology/Technician
- Biology/Biological Sciences, General
- Biology Teacher Education
- Broadcast Journalism
- Business/Managerial Economics
- Business Administration and Management, General
- Business Teacher Education
- Chemistry, General
- Chemistry Teacher Education

- Child Care and Support Services Management
- Child Development
- Child Development, Care and Guidance
- Clinical Laboratory Science/Medical Technology/Technologist
- Communication, Journalism and Related Programs, Other
- Computer and Information Sciences, General
- Computer Science
- Consumer Services and Advocacy
- Corrections
- Criminal Justice/Law Enforcement Administration
- Criminal Justice/Police Science
- Criminology
- Dietetics/Dietitians
- Drama and Dramatics/Theatre Arts, General
- Education, General
- Elementary Education and Teaching
- Engineering, General
- English/Language Arts Teacher Education
- English Language and Literature, General
- Family and Community Services
- Family and Consumer Sciences/Home Economics Teacher Education
- Family and Consumer Sciences/Human Sciences, General
- Fine/Studio Arts, General
- Foods, Nutrition, and Wellness Studies, General
- Forensic Science and Technology
- French Language and Literature
- French Language Teacher Education
- German Language and Literature
- Gerontology
- Graphic and Printing Equipment Operator, General Production
- Health/Medical Preparatory Programs, Other
- Health and Physical Education, General
- Health Science
- History, General
- History, Other
- History Teacher Education
- Horticultural Science
- Hotel/Motel Administration/Management
- Information Technology
- Interdisciplinary Studies
- International Business/Trade/Commerce
- Journalism
- Junior High/Intermediate/Middle School Education and Teaching
- Marketing/Marketing Management, General
- Mass Communication/Media Studies
- Mathematics, General
- Mathematics Teacher Education
- Multi-/Interdisciplinary Studies, Other
- Music, General
- Music, Other
- Music Management and Merchandising
- Music Teacher Education
- Parks, Recreation and Leisure Facilities Management
- Philosophy
- Philosophy and Religious Studies, Other
- Physical Education Teaching and Coaching
- Political Science and Government, General
- Poultry Science
- Pre-Law Studies
- Pre-Medicine/Pre-Medical Studies
- Pre-Pharmacy Studies
- Pre-Veterinary Studies
- Psychology, General
- Public Relations/Image Management
- Religion/Religious Studies
- Religious/Sacred Music
- Science, Technology and Society
- Science Teacher Education/General Science Teacher Education
- Secondary Education and Teaching
- Social Work
- Sociology
- Spanish Language and Literature
- Speech and Rhetorical Studies
- Technology Education/Industrial Arts
- Technology Teacher Education/Industrial Arts Teacher Education
- Wildlife and Wildlands Science and Management

The College of Wooster

- African-American/Black Studies
- Archeology
- Area, Ethnic, Cultural, and Gender Studies, Other
- Art History, Criticism and Conservation
- Biochemistry
- Biology/Biological Sciences, General
- Business/Managerial Economics
- Chemistry, General
- Classics and Languages, Literatures and Linguistics, General
- Communication Studies/Speech Communication and Rhetoric
- Comparative Literature
- Computer Science
- Drama and Dramatics/Theatre Arts, General
- Economics, General
- English Language and Literature, General
- Fine/Studio Arts, General
- French Language and Literature
- Geology/Earth Science, General
- German Language and Literature
- German Studies
- History, General
- Interdisciplinary Studies
- International Relations and Affairs
- Latin Language and Literature
- Mass Communication/Media Studies
- Mathematics, General
- Molecular Biology
- Multi-/Interdisciplinary Studies, Other
- Music, General
- Music History, Literature, and Theory
- Music Performance, General
- Music Teacher Education
- Music Theory and Composition
- Music Therapy/Therapist
- Philosophy
- Physics, General
- Physics, Other
- Political Science and Government, General
- Psychology, General
- Religion/Religious Studies
- Russian Studies
- Sociology
- Spanish Language and Literature
- Urban Studies/Affairs
- Women's Studies

Colorado School of Mines

- Chemical Engineering
- Chemistry and Geochemistry
- Economics and Business
- Electrical Engineering
- Engineering, General
- Engineering Physics
- Geological/Geophysical Engineering
- Mathematics and Computer Science
- Metallurgica and Materials Engineering
- Mining Engineering
- Petroleum Engineering

The Cooper Union for the Advancement of Science and Art

- Architecture
- Chemical Engineering
- Civil Engineering, General
- Electrical, Electronics and Communications Engineering
- Engineering, General
- Fine/Studio Arts, General
- Mechanical Engineering
- Visual and Performing Arts, General

Cornell College

- Architecture
- Art/Art Studies, General
- Art History, Criticism and Conservation
- Biochemistry
- Biology/Biological Sciences, General
- Chemistry, General
- Classics and Languages, Literatures and Linguistics, General
- Computer Science
- Drama and Dramatics/Theatre Arts, General
- Economics, General
- Elementary Education and Teaching
- English Language and Literature, General
- Environmental Studies
- Ethnic, Cultural Minority, and Gender Studies, Other
- Ethnic and Cultural Studies
- French Language and Literature
- Geology/Earth Science, General
- German Language and Literature
- Health and Physical Education/Fitness, Other
- History, General
- Interdisciplinary Studies
- International Business/Trade/Commerce
- International Relations and Affairs
- Latin American Studies
- Latin Language and Literature
- Liberal Arts and Sciences/Liberal Studies
- Mathematics, General
- Medieval and Renaissance Studies
- Modern Greek Language and Literature
- Modern Languages
- Multi-/Interdisciplinary Studies, Other
- Music, General
- Music Teacher Education
- Philosophy
- Physical Education Teaching and Coaching
- Physics, General
- Political Science and Government, General
- Psychology, General
- Religion/Religious Studies
- Russian Language and Literature
- Secondary Education and Teaching
- Sociology
- Spanish Language and Literature
- Speech and Rhetorical Studies
- Women's Studies

Deep Springs College

- Not applicable

Earlham College

- African-American/Black Studies
- Art/Art Studies, General
- Biology/Biological Sciences, General
- Business Administration and Nonprofit Management, General
- Chemistry, General
- Classics and Languages, Literatures, and Linguistics, General
- Computer Science
- Drama and Dramatics/Theatre Arts, General
- Economics, General
- Education, General
- English Language and Literature, General
- Environmental Studies
- French Language and Literature
- Geology/Earth Science, General
- Geosciences
- German Language and Literature
- History, General
- Interdisciplinary Studies
- International Relations and Affairs
- Japanese Studies
- Latin American Studies
- Mathematics, General
- Music, General
- Peace Studies and Conflict Resolution
- Philosophy
- Physics, General
- Political Science and Government, General
- Pre-Law Studies
- Pre-Medicine/Pre-Medical Studies
- Psychology, General
- Religion/Religious Studies
- Sociology
- Spanish Language and Literature
- Women's Studies

Eckerd College

- American/United States Studies/Civilization
- Anthropology
- Art/Art Studies, General
- Biology/Biological Sciences, General
- Business Administration and Management, General
- Chemistry, General
- Chinese Language and Literature
- Clinical Laboratory Science/Medical Technology/Technologist
- Communication Studies/Speech Communication and Rhetoric
- Comparative Literature
- Computer Science
- Creative Writing
- Drama and Dramatics/Theatre Arts, General
- East Asian Languages, Literatures, and Linguistics, General
- Economics, General
- English Language and Literature, General
- Environmental Studies
- Foreign Languages and Literatures, General
- French Language and Literature
- German Language and Literature
- History, General
- Human Development and Family Studies, General
- Humanities/Humanistic Studies
- Human Resources Management/Personnel Administration, General
- Interdisciplinary Studies
- International Business/Trade/Commerce
- International Relations and Affairs
- Literature
- Marine Biology and Biological Oceanography
- Mathematics, General
- Modern Languages
- Music, General
- Philosophy
- Physics, General
- Political Science and Government, General

- Psychology, General
- Religion/Religious Studies
- Russian Language and Literature
- Sociology
- Spanish Language and Literature
- Women's Studies

Elmira College

- Accounting
- American/United States Studies/Civilization
- Anthropology
- Art/Art Studies, General
- Art Teacher Education
- Audiology/Audiologist and Speech-Language Pathology/Pathologist
- Biochemistry
- Biology/Biological Sciences, General
- Biology Teacher Education
- Business/Managerial Economics
- Business Administration and Management, General
- Chemistry, General
- Chemistry Teacher Education
- Classics and Languages, Literatures, and Linguistics, General
- Clinical Laboratory Science/Medical Technology/Technologist
- Criminal Justice/Law Enforcement Administration
- Drama and Dramatics/Theatre Arts, General
- Economics, General
- Education, General
- Elementary Education and Teaching
- English/Language Arts Teacher Education
- English Language and Literature, General
- Environmental Studies
- European Studies/Civilization
- Fine/Studio Arts, General
- Foreign Languages and Literatures, General
- Foreign Language Teacher Education
- French Language and Literature
- French Language Teacher Education
- History, General
- History Teacher Education
- Humanities/Humanistic Studies
- Human Services, General
- Information Science/Studies
- Interdisciplinary Studies
- International Business/Trade/Commerce
- International Relations and Affairs
- Junior High/Intermediate/Middle School Education and Teaching
- Liberal Arts and Sciences/Liberal Studies
- Literature
- Marketing/Marketing Management, General
- Mathematics, General
- Mathematics Teacher Education
- Mental Health/Rehabilitation
- Modern Languages
- Music, General
- Nursing/Registered Nurse Training
- Nursing Science (MS, PhD)
- Philosophy
- Political Science and Government, General
- Pre-Dentistry Studies
- Pre-Law Studies
- Pre-Medicine/Pre-Medical Studies
- Pre-Veterinary Studies
- Psychology, General
- Religion/Religious Studies
- Romance Languages, Literatures, and Linguistics, General
- Science Teacher Education/General Science Teacher Education
- Secondary Education and Teaching
- Social Sciences, General
- Social Science Teacher Education
- Social Studies Teacher Education
- Social Work
- Sociology
- Spanish Language and Literature
- Spanish Language Teacher Education
- Speech Teacher Education

Elon University

- Accounting
- Art/Art Studies, General
- Athletic Training/Trainer
- Biology/Biological Sciences, General
- Broadcast Journalism
- Business/Corporate Communications
- Business Administration and Management, General
- Chemistry, General
- Clinical Laboratory Science/Medical Technology/Technologist
- Communication Studies/Speech Communication and Rhetoric
- Computer Science
- Drama and Dramatics/Theatre Arts, General
- Economics, General
- Education, General
- Elementary Education and Teaching
- Engineering, General
- English Language and Literature, General
- Environmental Studies
- Foreign Languages and Literatures, General
- French Language and Literature
- Health Teacher Education
- History, General
- Human Services, General
- International Studies
- Journalism
- Junior High/Intermediate/Middle School Education and Teaching
- Mathematics, General
- Music, General
- Music Performance, General
- Music Teacher Education
- Parks, Recreation, and Leisure Studies
- Philosophy
- Physical Education Teaching and Coaching
- Physics, General
- Political Science and Government, General
- Pre-Dentistry Studies
- Pre-Law Studies
- Pre-Medicine/Pre-Medical Studies
- Pre-Veterinary Studies
- Psychology, General
- Public Administration
- Religion/Religious Studies
- Science Teacher Education/General Science Teacher Education
- Secondary Education and Teaching
- Social Science Teacher Education
- Social Studies Teacher Education
- Sociology
- Spanish Language and Literature
- Special Education and Teaching, General
- Sport and Fitness Administration/Management

Emerson College

- Acting
- Advertising
- Audiology/Audiologist and Speech-Language Pathology/Pathologist
- Broadcast Journalism
- Cinematography and Film/Video Production
- Communication Disorders, General
- Communication Studies/Speech Communication and Rhetoric
- Creative Writing
- Drama and Dance Teacher Education
- Drama and Dramatics/Theatre Arts, General
- Education/Teaching of Individuals with Speech or Language Impairments

- Film/Cinema Studies
- Interdisciplinary Studies
- Intermedia/Multimedia
- Journalism
- Marketing/Marketing Management, General
- Mass Communication/Media Studies
- Playwriting and Screenwriting
- Political Communication
- Public Relations/Image Management
- Publishing
- Radio, Television, and Digital Communication, Other
- Radio and Television
- Radio and Television Broadcasting Technology/Technician
- Speech and Rhetorical Studies
- Speech-Language Pathology/Pathologist
- Speech Therapy
- Technical Theatre/Theatre Design and Technology
- Visual and Performing Arts, General

Eugene Lang College

- The Arts
- Cultural Studies and Media
- Education Studies
- Literature
- Philosophy
- Psychology
- Religious Studies
- Science, Technology & Society/ Quantitative Reason
- Social and Historical Inquiry
- Urban Studies
- Writing

The Evergreen State College

- American Indian/Native American Studies
- Area, Ethnic, Cultural, and Gender Studies, Other
- Art/Art Studies, General
- Biological and Physical Sciences
- Biology/Biological Sciences, General
- Business Administration and Management, General
- Cinematography and Film/Video Production
- Classics and Languages, Literatures and Linguistics, General
- Computer and Information Sciences, General
- Drama and Dramatics/Theatre Arts, General
- Environmental Studies
- Ethnic and Cultural Studies
- Fine/Studio Arts, General
- Humanities/Humanistic Studies
- Intermedia/Multimedia
- International/Global Studies
- Liberal Arts and Sciences/Liberal Studies
- Multi-/Interdisciplinary Studies, Other
- Natural Sciences
- Physical Sciences
- Political Science and Government, General
- Social Sciences, General
- Visual and Performing Arts, General

Fairhaven College

- Self-designed

Goshen College

- Accounting
- Art/Art Studies, General
- Art Teacher Education
- Art Therapy/Therapist
- Bible/Biblical Studies
- Bilingual and Multilingual Education
- Biology/Biological Sciences, General
- Broadcast Journalism
- Business Administration and Management, General
- Business Teacher Education
- Chemistry, General
- Child Development
- Computer Science
- Drama and Dramatics/Theatre Arts, General
- Economics, General
- Education, General
- Elementary Education and Teaching
- English Language and Literature, General
- Environmental Studies
- Family and Community Services
- German Language and Literature
- Hispanic-American, Puerto Rican, and Mexican-American/Chicano Studies
- History, General
- Information Science/Studies
- Journalism
- Kindergarten/Preschool Education and Teaching
- Liberal Arts and Sciences/Liberal Studies
- Mass Communication/Media Studies
- Mathematics, General
- Music, General
- Music Teacher Education
- Natural Sciences
- Nursing/Registered Nurse Training
- Peace, Justice, and Conflict Sudies
- Physical Education Teaching and Coaching
- Physical Sciences
- Physics, General
- Political Science and Government, General
- Pre-Dentistry Studies
- Pre-Law Studies
- Pre-Medicine/Pre-Medical Studies
- Pre-Veterinary Studies
- Psychology, General
- Religion/Religious Studies
- Science Teacher Education/General Science Teacher Education
- Secondary Education and Teaching
- Sign Language Interpretation and Translation
- Social Work
- Sociology
- Spanish Language and Literature
- Teaching English as a Second or Foreign Language/ESL Language Instructor

Goucher College

- American/United States Studies/Civilization
- Art/Art Studies, General
- Biology/Biological Sciences, General
- Chemistry, General
- Computer Science
- Dance, General
- Drama and Dramatics/Theatre Arts, General
- Economics, General
- Education, General
- Elementary Education and Teaching
- English Language and Literature, General
- French Language and Literature
- Historic Preservation and Conservation
- History, General
- Interdisciplinary Studies
- International Relations and Affairs
- Management Science, General
- Mass Communication/Media Studies
- Mathematics, General

- Music, General
- Philosophy
- Physics, General
- Political Science and Government, General
- Psychology, General
- Religion/Religious Studies
- Russian Language and Literature
- Sociology
- Spanish Language and Literature
- Special Education and Teaching, General
- Women's Studies

Green Mountain College

- Adventure Recreation
- Art
- Arts Management
- Art w/ K–12 Certificate in Education
- Biology
- Business
- Commercial Recreation
- Communications & Journalism
- Elementary Education
- Elementary Ed w/ Special Education Endorsement
- English
- English w/ Secondary Education Certificate
- Environmental Studies
- Environmental Management
- Fine Arts
- History
- History with Secondary Education Certificate
- Hospitality Management
- Liberal Studies
- Natural Resources Management
- Philosophy
- Psychology
- Recreation
- Resort Management
- Self-designed Major
- Sociology/Anthropology
- Visual/Performing Arts
- Writing

Grinnell College

- African-American/Black Studies
- American/United States Studies/Civilization
- Anthropology
- Archeology
- Art/Art Studies, General
- Biochemistry
- Biological and Physical Sciences
- Biology/Biological Sciences, General
- Central/Middle and Eastern European Studies
- Chemistry, General
- Chinese Language and Literature
- Classics and Languages, Literatures and Linguistics, General
- Computer Science
- Drama and Dramatics/Theatre Arts, General
- East Asian Studies
- Economics, General
- Education, General
- Elementary Education and Teaching
- English Language and Literature, General
- Environmental Biology
- Environmental Studies
- French Language and Literature
- German Language and Literature
- History, General
- Interdisciplinary Studies
- International/Global Studies
- Latin American Studies
- Linguistics
- Mathematics, General
- Music, General
- Philosophy
- Physics, General
- Political Science and Government, General
- Pre-Medicine/Pre-Medical Studies
- Psychology, General
- Religion/Religious Studies
- Russian Language and Literature
- Science, Technology and Society
- Secondary Education and Teaching
- Sociology
- Spanish Language and Literature
- Western European Studies
- Women's Studies

Hampshire College

- Self-designed

Hanover College

- Anthropology
- Art/Art Studies, General
- Art History, Criticism and Conservation
- Biology/Biological Sciences, General
- Business Administration and Management, General
- Chemistry, General
- Classics and Languages, Literatures and Linguistics, General
- Computer Science
- Drama and Dramatics/Theatre Arts, General
- Economics, General
- English Language and Literature, General
- French Language and Literature
- Geology/Earth Science, General
- German Language and Literature
- History, General
- International/Global Studies
- Latin American Studies
- Mass Communication/Media Studies
- Mathematics, General
- Medieval and Renaissance Studies
- Music, General
- Philosophy
- Physical Education Teaching and Coaching
- Physics, General
- Political Science and Government, General
- Psychology, General
- Sociology
- Spanish Language and Literature
- Theology/Theological Studies

Hendrix College

- Accounting
- American Studies
- Art
- Biochemistry/Molecular Biology
- Biology
- Chemistry
- Computer Science
- Early Childhood Education
- Economics
- Economics & Business
- English
- Environmental Studies
- French
- German
- History
- Interdisciplinary Studies
- International Relations and Global Studies
- Kinesiology
- Mathematics
- Music
- Philosophy

- Philosophy & Religion
- Physics
- Politics
- Psychology
- Religion
- Sociology/Anthropology
- Spanish
- Theatre Arts

Hiram College

- Accounting and Financial Management
- Art
- Biochemistry
- Biology
- Biomedical Humanities
- Biomedical Humanities (accelerated 3-year program)
- Chemistry
- Classical Studies
- Communications
- Computer Science
- Creative Writing
- Economics
- Education
- English
- Environmental Studies
- French
- History
- Management
- Mathematics
- Music
- Neuroscience
- Philosophy
- Physics
- Political Science
- Psychology
- Religious Studies
- Sociology
- Spanish
- Studio Art
- Theatre Arts

Kalamazoo College

- Anthropology and Sociology
- Art
- Art and Art History
- Art History
- Biology
- Chemistry
- Classical Studies
- Computer Science
- Economics and Business
- English
- French Language and Literature
- German Language and Literature
- Health Sciences
- History
- Human Development and Social Relations
- Interdepartmental Major
- International and Area Studies
- Mathematics
- Music
- Philosophy
- Physics
- Political Science
- Psychology
- Religion
- Spanish Language and Literature
- Theatre Arts

Keene State College

- American Studies
- Applied Computer Science
- Art
- Biology
- Chemistry
- Chemistry & Physics
- Communication
- Computer Mathematics
- Economics
- Education
- Engineering (transfer programs)
- English
- Environmental Studies
- Film Studies
- French
- General Science
- Geography
- Geology
- Health Science
- History
- Individualized Major
- Journalism
- Management
- Mathematics
- Mathematics & Physics
- Music
- Music Education
- Music Performance
- Physical Education
- Safety Studies
- Social Science
- Sociology
- Spanish
- Technology Studies
- Theatre & Dance

Knox College

- American Studies
- Anthropology and Sociology
- Art
- Art History
- Biochemistry
- Biology
- Black Studies
- Chemistry
- Computer Science
- Creative Writing
- Economics
- Elementary Education
- English Literature
- Environmental Studies
- Financial Mathematics
- French
- Gender and Women's Studies
- German
- Greek
- Greek and Roman Culture
- History
- Independent Studies
- Integrated International Studies
- International Relations
- Latin
- Mathematics
- Modern Languages
- Modern Languages and Classics
- Music
- Neuroscience
- Philosophy
- Physics
- Political Science
- Psychology
- Secondary Education
- Social Studies Education
- Spanish
- Theatre

Lewis & Clark College

- Art/Art Studies, General
- Biochemistry
- Biology
- Chemistry
- Communication Studies/Speech Communication and Rhetoric
- Computer Science

- Drama and Dramatics/Theatre Arts, General
- East Asian Studies
- Economics, General
- English Language and Literature, General
- Environmental Studies
- Foreign Languages and Literatures, General
- French Language and Literature
- German Language and Literature
- Hispanic Studies
- History, General
- International Affairs
- Mathematics, General
- Modern Languages
- Music, General
- Philosophy
- Physics, General
- Political Science and Government, General
- Pre-Engineering
- Psychology, General
- Religious Studies
- Sociology & Anthropology
- Spanish Language and Literature

Linfield College

- Accounting
- Anthropology
- Area, Ethnic, Cultural, and Gender Studies, Other
- Art/Art Studies, General
- Athletic Training/Trainer
- Biology/Biological Sciences, General
- Business/Commerce, General
- Chemistry, General
- Communication Studies/Speech Communication and Rhetoric
- Computer Science
- Creative Writing
- Drama and Dramatics/Theatre Arts, General
- Economics, General
- Elementary Education and Teaching
- English Language and Literature, General
- Environmental Studies
- Finance, General
- French Language and Literature
- German Language and Literature
- Health and Physical Education, General
- History, General
- International Business/Trade/Commerce
- Japanese Language and Literature
- Kinesiology and Exercise Science
- Mathematics, General
- Music, General
- Philosophy
- Physical Sciences
- Physics, General
- Political Science and Government, General
- Psychology, General
- Religion/Religious Studies
- Sociology
- Spanish Language and Literature

Loyola University Chicago

- Accounting
- Ancient/Classical Greek Language and Literature
- Anthropology
- Art/Art Studies, General
- Art History, Criticism and Conservation
- Biochemistry
- Biology/Biological Sciences, General
- Business/Managerial Economics
- Business Administration and Management, General
- Ceramic Arts and Ceramics
- Chemistry, General
- Classics and Languages, Literatures and Linguistics, General
- Communication, Journalism and Related Programs, Other
- Communication Studies/Speech Communication and Rhetoric
- Computer Science
- Criminal Justice/Safety Studies
- Drama and Dramatics/Theatre Arts, General
- Economics, General
- Elementary Education and Teaching
- English Language and Literature, General
- Environmental Studies
- Finance, General
- Fine Arts and Art Studies, Other
- Foods, Nutrition, and Wellness Studies, General
- French Language and Literature
- German Language and Literature
- History, General
- Humanities/Humanistic Studies
- Human Resources Management/ Personnel Administration, General
- Information Science/Studies
- International Relations and Affairs
- Italian Language and Literature
- Journalism
- Kindergarten/Preschool Education and Teaching
- Latin Language and Literature
- Management Information Systems, General
- Marketing/Marketing Management, General
- Mathematics, General
- Mathematics and Computer Science
- Metal and Jewelry Arts
- Music, General
- Natural Sciences
- Nursing/Registered Nurse Training
- Operations Management and Supervision
- Philosophy
- Photography
- Physics, General
- Political Science and Government, General
- Pre-Dentistry Studies
- Pre-Law Studies
- Pre-Medicine/Pre-Medical Studies
- Pre-Theology/Pre-Ministerial Studies
- Pre-Veterinary Studies
- Psychology, General
- Psychology, Other
- Social Psychology
- Social Work
- Sociology
- Spanish Language and Literature
- Special Education and Teaching, General
- Statistics, General
- Theology/Theological Studies

Macalester College

- Anthropology
- Art History, Criticism and Conservation
- Asian Studies/Civilization
- Biology/Biological Sciences, General
- Chemistry, General
- Classics and Languages, Literatures and Linguistics, General
- Communication Studies/Speech Communication and Rhetoric
- Computer Science
- Drama and Dramatics/Theatre Arts, General
- Economics, General
- English Language and Literature, General
- Environmental Studies
- Fine/Studio Arts, General

- French Language and Literature
- Geography
- Geology/Earth Science, General
- History, General
- Humanities/Humanistic Studies
- Interdisciplinary Studies
- International Relations and Affairs
- Latin American Studies
- Latin Language and Literature
- Linguistics
- Mathematics, General
- Modern Greek Language and Literature
- Music, General
- Neuroscience
- Philosophy
- Physics, General
- Political Science and Government, General
- Psychology, General
- Religion/Religious Studies
- Russian Language and Literature
- Russian Studies
- Sociology
- Spanish Language and Literature
- Urban Studies/Affairs
- Women's Studies

Manhattanville College

- American/United States Studies/Civilization
- Art History, Criticism and Conservation
- Art Teacher Education
- Asian Studies/Civilization
- Biochemistry
- Biology/Biological Sciences, General
- Biology Teacher Education
- Business Administration and Management, General
- Chemistry, General
- Chemistry Teacher Education
- Classics and Languages, Literatures and Linguistics, General
- Computer Science
- Dance, General
- Economics, General
- Education, General
- Elementary Education and Teaching
- English/Language Arts Teacher Education
- English Language and Literature, General
- Finance, General
- Fine/Studio Arts, General
- French Language and Literature
- French Language Teacher Education
- German Studies
- History, General
- International Relations and Affairs
- Legal Studies, General
- Mathematics, General
- Mathematics Teacher Education
- Music, General
- Music Teacher Education
- Philosophy
- Physics, General
- Political Science and Government, General
- Pre-Medicine/Pre-Medical Studies
- Psychology, General
- Religion/Religious Studies
- Romance Languages, Literatures, and Linguistics, General
- Secondary Education and Teaching
- Social Studies Teacher Education
- Sociology
- Spanish Language and Literature
- Spanish Language Teacher Education

Marlboro College

- African Studies
- American/United States Studies/Civilization
- Anthropology
- Applied Mathematics
- Art/Art Studies, General
- Art History, Criticism and Conservation
- Asian Studies/Civilization
- Astronomy
- Astrophysics
- Behavioral Sciences
- Bible/Biblical Studies
- Biochemistry
- Biology/Biological Sciences, General
- Botany/Plant Biology
- Cell/Cellular Biology and Histology
- Central/Middle and Eastern European Studies
- Ceramic Arts and Ceramics
- Chemistry, General
- Classics and Languages, Literatures and Linguistics, General
- Comparative Literature
- Computer Science
- Creative Writing
- Dance, General
- Developmental and Child Psychology
- Drama and Dramatics/Theatre Arts, General
- Drawing
- East Asian Studies
- Ecology
- Economics, General
- English Language and Literature, General
- Environmental Biology
- Environmental Studies
- Ethnic and Cultural Studies
- European Studies/Civilization
- Experimental Psychology
- Film/Cinema Studies
- Fine/Studio Arts, General
- Folklore
- French Language and Literature
- German Language and Literature
- History, General
- History Of Philosophy
- Humanities/Humanistic Studies
- Interdisciplinary Studies
- International Economics
- International Relations and Affairs
- Italian Language and Literature
- Latin American Studies
- Latin Language and Literature
- Linguistics
- Literature
- Mathematics, General
- Medieval and Renaissance Studies
- Modern Greek Language and Literature
- Modern Languages
- Molecular Biology
- Music, General
- Music History, Literature, and Theory
- Natural Resources/Conservation, General
- Natural Sciences
- Philosophy
- Photography
- Physics, General
- Political Science and Government, General
- Portuguese Language and Literature
- Pre-Law Studies
- Pre-Medicine/Pre-Medical Studies
- Pre-Veterinary Studies
- Psychology, General
- Religion/Religious Studies
- Romance Languages, Literatures, and Linguistics, General
- Russian Studies
- Sculpture
- Social Sciences, General
- Sociology
- Spanish Language and Literature
- Women's Studies

Miami University

- Accounting
- Aerospace, Aeronautical and Astronautical Engineering
- African-American/Black Studies
- American/United States Studies/Civilization
- Ancient/Classical Greek Language and Literature
- Anthropology
- Architecture
- Art/Art Studies, General
- Art History, Criticism and Conservation
- Art Teacher Education
- Athletic Training/Trainer
- Audiology/Audiologist and Speech-Language Pathology/Pathologist
- Biochemistry
- Biology/Biological Sciences, General
- Biology Teacher Education
- Botany/Plant Biology
- Business/Commerce, General
- Business/Managerial Economics
- Business Administration and Management, General
- Chemistry, General
- Child Development
- City/Urban, Community and Regional Planning
- Classics and Languages, Literatures and Linguistics, General
- Clinical Laboratory Science/Medical Technology/Technologist
- Computer and Information Sciences, General
- Computer Systems Analysis/Analyst
- Creative Writing
- Dietetics/Dietitians
- Drama and Dramatics/Theatre Arts, General
- Economics, General
- Electrical, Electronics and Communications Engineering
- Elementary Education and Teaching
- Engineering/Industrial Management
- Engineering Physics
- Engineering Technology, General
- English/Language Arts Teacher Education
- English Language and Literature, General
- Environmental Design/Architecture
- Family and Consumer Economics and Related Services, Other
- Family and Consumer Sciences/Home Economics Teacher Education
- Family and Consumer Sciences/Human Sciences, General
- Finance, General
- Fine/Studio Arts, General
- French Language and Literature
- Geography
- Geology/Earth Science, General
- German Language and Literature
- Health and Physical Education, General
- Health Teacher Education
- History, General
- Human Development and Family Studies, General
- Human Resources Management/Personnel Administration, General
- Industrial Engineering
- Interdisciplinary Studies
- Interior Design
- International Relations and Affairs
- Journalism
- Junior High/Intermediate/Middle School Education and Teaching
- Kindergarten/Preschool Education and Teaching
- Kinesiology and Exercise Science
- Latin Language and Literature
- Linguistics
- Management Information Systems, General
- Management Science, General
- Marketing/Marketing Management, General
- Mass Communication/Media Studies
- Mathematics, General
- Mechanical Engineering
- Medical Microbiology and Bacteriology
- Multi-/Interdisciplinary Studies, Other
- Music, General
- Music Performance, General
- Music Teacher Education
- Nursing/Registered Nurse Training
- Operations Management and Supervision
- Operations Research
- Organizational Behavior Studies
- Philosophy
- Physical Education Teaching and Coaching
- Physics, General
- Political Science and Government, General
- Pre-Dentistry Studies
- Pre-Law Studies
- Pre-Medicine/Pre-Medical Studies
- Pre-Veterinary Studies
- Psychology, General
- Public Administration
- Purchasing, Procurement/Acquisitions and Contracts Management
- Religion/Religious Studies
- Russian Language and Literature
- Science Teacher Education/General Science Teacher Education
- Secondary Education and Teaching
- Social Studies Teacher Education
- Social Work
- Sociology
- Spanish Language and Literature
- Special Education and Teaching, General
- Speech and Rhetorical Studies
- Speech-Language Pathology/Pathologist
- Sport and Fitness Administration/Management
- Statistics, General
- Systems Science and Theory
- Technical and Business Writing
- Wood Science and Wood Products/Pulp and Paper Technology
- Zoology/Animal Biology

Millsaps College

- Accounting
- American Studies
- Art
- Biology
- Business Administration
- Chemistry
- Christian Education
- Classical Studies
- Computer Science
- Economics
- Education
- English
- Environmental Studies
- European Studies
- French
- Geology
- German
- History
- Human Services
- International Studies
- Management
- Mathematics
- Music
- Philosophy
- Physics
- Political Science
- Psychology
- Religious Studies
- Self-designed Majors

- Sociology/Anthropology
- Spanish
- Theatre
- Women's Studies
- Writing

Mount Holyoke College

- African American & African Studies
- American Studies
- Ancient Studies
- Anthropology
- Architectural Studies
- Art History
- Art Studio
- Asian Studies
- Astronomy
- Biochemistry
- Biological Sciences
- Chemistry
- Classics
- Complex Organizations
- Program
- Computer Science
- Critical Social Thought
- Dance
- Economics
- Education
- Engineering
- English
- Environmental Studies
- European Studies
- Film Studies
- French
- Geography
- Geology
- German Studies
- History
- Interdepartmental Courses
- Interdisciplinary Minors
- International Relations
- Italian
- Jewish Studies
- Latin American Studies
- Mathematics
- Medieval Studies
- Music
- Neuroscience & Behavior
- Philosophy
- Physical Education & Athletics
- Physics
- Politics
- Premedical Studies
- Psychology & Education
- Religion
- Romance Languages & Literatures
- Russian & Eurasian Studies
- Sociology
- Spanish
- Statistics
- Theatre Arts
- Women's Studies

Muhlenberg College

- Accounting
- American/United States Studies/Civilization
- Anthropology
- Art/Art Studies, General
- Art History, Criticism and Conservation
- Biochemistry
- Biology/Biological Sciences, General
- Business Administration and Management, General
- Chemistry, General
- Computer Science
- Dance, General
- Drama and Dramatics/Theatre Arts, General
- Economics, General
- Elementary Education and Teaching
- English Language and Literature, General
- Environmental Science
- Fine/Studio Arts, General
- French Language and Literature
- German Language and Literature
- History, General
- Human Resources Management/Personnel Administration, General
- International Economics
- International Relations and Affairs
- Mathematics, General
- Music, General
- Natural Sciences
- Philosophy
- Physical Sciences
- Physics, General
- Political Science and Government, General
- Pre-Dentistry Studies
- Pre-Law Studies
- Pre-Medicine/Pre-Medical Studies
- Pre-Veterinary Studies
- Psychology, General
- Religion/Religious Studies
- Russian Studies
- Secondary Education and Teaching
- Social Sciences, General
- Sociology
- Spanish Language and Literature

New College of Florida

- Anthropology
- Art History, Criticism and Conservation
- Biology/Biological Sciences, General
- Chemistry, General
- Classics and Classical Languages, Literatures, and Linguistics, Other
- Comparative Literature
- Economics, General
- English Language and Literature, General
- Environmental Studies
- Fine/Studio Arts, General
- Foreign Languages and Literatures, General
- French Language and Literature
- French Studies
- General Studies
- Germanic Languages, Literatures, and Linguistics, General
- German Language and Literature
- History, General
- Humanities/Humanistic Studies
- International/Global Studies
- Liberal Arts and Sciences/Liberal Studies
- Literature
- Marine Biology and Biological Oceanography
- Mathematics, General
- Medieval and Renaissance Studies
- Music, General
- Music History, Literature, and Theory
- Natural Sciences
- Neurobiology and Neurophysiology
- Philosophy
- Physics, General
- Political Science and Government, General
- Psychology, General
- Public Policy Analysis
- Religion/Religious Studies
- Russian Language and Literature
- Social Sciences, General
- Sociology
- Spanish Language and Literature
- Urban Studies/Affairs

North Central College

- Accounting
- Actuarial Science
- Anthropology
- Applied Mathematics
- Art
- Arts & Letters
- Athletic Training
- Biochemistry
- Biology
- Broadcast Communication
- Business Administration
- Chemistry
- Classical Civilizations & Latin
- Computer Science
- East Asian Studies
- Economics
- Education
- Engineering
- English
- Entrepreneurship & Small Business Management
- Exercise Science
- Finance
- French
- German
- Global Studies
- Health Sciences
- History
- Humanities
- Human Resource Management
- Individualized major
- Information Systems
- Interactive Media
- International Business
- International Studies
- Japanese
- Jazz Studies
- Journalism
- Liberal Studies
- Management
- Management Information Systems
- Marketing
- Mathematics
- Medical Physics
- Modern & Classical Languages
- Music
- Nuclear Medicine
- Nursing
- Organizational Communication
- Philosophy
- Physical Education
- Physics
- Political Science
- Psychology
- Radiation Therapy
- Religious Studies
- Science
- Social Science/History
- Sociology & Anthropology
- Spanish
- Speech Communication
- Sport Management
- Theatre

Occidental College

- American/United States Studies/Civilization
- Anthropology
- Art History, Criticism and Conservation
- Asian Studies/Civilization
- Biochemistry
- Biology/Biological Sciences, General
- Business/Managerial Economics
- Chemistry, General
- Cognitive Psychology and Psycholinguistics
- Comparative Literature
- Diplomacy and World Affairs
- Drama and Dramatics/Theatre Arts, General
- Economics, General
- Environmental Studies
- Fine/Studio Arts, General
- French Language and Literature
- Geology/Earth Science, General
- Geophysics and Seismology
- History, General
- International Relations and Affairs
- Kinesiology and Exercise Science
- Mathematics, General
- Music, General
- Philosophy
- Physics, General
- Psychobiology
- Political Science and Government, General
- Psychology, General
- Public Policy Analysis
- Religion/Religious Studies
- Sociology
- Spanish Literacy Studies
- Women's Studies

Ohio Northern University

- Accounting
- Art/Art Studies, General
- Art Teacher Education
- Athletic Training/Trainer
- Biochemistry
- Biology/Biological Sciences, General
- Biology Teacher Education
- Business/Commerce, General
- Business Administration and Management, General
- Ceramic Arts and Ceramics
- Chemistry, General
- Chemistry, Other
- Chemistry Teacher Education
- Civil Engineering, General
- Civil Engineering, Other
- Clinical Laboratory Science/Medical Technology/Technologist
- Commercial and Advertising Art
- Communication, Journalism and Related Programs, Other
- Communication Studies/Speech Communication and Rhetoric
- Computer Engineering, General
- Computer Engineering, Other
- Computer Science
- Creative Writing
- Criminal Justice/Law Enforcement Administration
- Criminal Justice/Police Science
- Criminal Justice/Safety Studies
- Design and Visual Communications, General
- Drama and Dramatics/Theatre Arts, General
- Early Childhood Education and Teaching
- Education, General
- Education, Other
- Electrical, Electronics and Communications Engineering
- Elementary Education and Teaching
- Engineering, General
- Engineering, Other
- English/Language Arts Teacher Education
- English Language and Literature, General
- Environmental Studies
- Fine/Studio Arts, General
- Foreign Language Teacher Education
- French Language and Literature
- French Language Teacher Education
- General Studies
- Germanic Languages, Literatures, and Linguistics, Other

- German Language Teacher Education
- Graphic Design
- Health and Physical Education, General
- Health and Physical Education/Fitness, Other
- Health Teacher Education
- History, General
- History Teacher Education
- Industrial Technology/Technician
- International Business/Trade/Commerce
- International Relations and Affairs
- Journalism
- Junior High/Intermediate/Middle School Education and Teaching
- Kindergarten/Preschool Education and Teaching
- Kinesiology and Exercise Science
- Management Science, General
- Management Sciences and Quantitative Methods, Other
- Mass Communication/Media Studies
- Mathematics, General
- Mathematics, Other
- Mathematics Teacher Education
- Mechanical Engineering
- Medicinal and Pharmaceutical Chemistry
- Molecular Biology
- Music, General
- Music, Other
- Music Management and Merchandising
- Music Performance, General
- Music Teacher Education
- Organizational Communication, General
- Painting
- Pharmacy, Pharmaceutical Sciences, and Administration, Other
- Pharmacy
- Philosophy
- Philosophy, Other
- Physical Education Teaching and Coaching
- Physics, General
- Physics, Other
- Physics Teacher Education
- Political Science and Government, General
- Pre-Dentistry Studies
- Pre-Law Studies
- Pre-Medicine/Pre-Medical Studies
- Pre-Theology/Pre-Ministerial Studies
- Pre-Veterinary Studies
- Printmaking
- Psychology, General
- Psychology, Other
- Public Relations/Image Management
- Radio and Television
- Religion/Religious Studies
- Religion/Religious Studies, Other
- Science Teacher Education/General Science Teacher Education
- Sculpture
- Secondary Education and Teaching
- Social Studies Teacher Education
- Sociology
- Spanish Language and Literature
- Spanish Language Teacher Education
- Sport and Fitness Administration/Management
- Statistics, General
- Statistics, Other
- Teacher Education, Multiple Levels
- Technical and Business Writing
- Technology Education/Industrial Arts
- Theatre/Theatre Arts Management
- Visual and Performing Arts, General
- Visual and Performing Arts, Other

Presbyterian College

- Accounting
- Art
- Biology
- Business Administration
- Chemistry
- Computer Science
- Economics
- Early Childhood Education, General
- English
- French
- German
- History
- Mathematics
- Modern Foreign Languages
- Music, General
- Music Education
- Physics
- Political Science
- Psychology
- Religion-Christian Education
- Religion/Philosophy
- Sacred Music
- Social Sciences
- Sociology
- Spanish
- Special Education
- Theatre

Prescott College

- Adventure Education
- Agroecology
- Bilingual Education
- Conservation Biology
- Counseling Psychology
- Cultural and Regional Studies
- Ecopsychology
- Earth Science
- Ecological Design
- Elementary Education
- English as a Second Language
- Environmental Education
- Environmental Policy
- Human Development
- Human Ecology
- Interdisciplinary Arts & Letters
- Marine Studies
- Natural History and Ecology
- Peace Studies
- Performing Arts
- Psychology
- Religion and Philosophy
- Secondary Education
- Self-designed Competence
- Spanish Language & Literature and Latin American Studies
- Special Education
- Therapeutic Use of Adventure Education
- Visual Arts
- Writing and Literature

Purchase College

- Anthropology
- Art/Art Studies, General
- Art History, Criticism and Conservation
- Biology/Biological Sciences, General
- Chemistry, General
- Cinematography and Film/Video Production
- Communication Studies/Speech Communication and Rhetoric
- Creative Writing
- Dance, General
- Drama and Dramatics/Theatre Arts, General
- Economics, General
- Environmental Studies
- Film/Cinema Studies
- French Language and Literature
- History, General
- Journalism
- Liberal Arts and Sciences/Liberal Studies

- Literature
- Mathematics, General
- Modern Languages
- Music, General
- Philosophy
- Playwriting and Screenwriting
- Political Science and Government, General
- Psychology, General
- Sociology
- Spanish Language and Literature
- Technical Theatre/Theatre Design and Technology
- Women's Studies

Randolph-Macon College

- Accounting
- Art History
- Arts Management
- Biology
- Chemistry
- Classical Studies
- Computer Science
- Drama
- Economics
- Economics/Business
- English
- Environmental Studies
- French
- German
- Greek
- History
- International Studies
- Latin
- Mathematics
- Music
- Philosophy
- Physics
- Political Science
- Psychology
- Religious Studies
- Sociology
- Spanish
- Studio Art
- Women's Studies

Reed College

- American Studies
- Anthropology
- Art
- Biochemistry and Molecular Biology
- Biology
- Chemistry
- Chemistry-Physics
- Chinese
- Classics
- Classics-Religion
- Creative Writing
- Dance
- Dance-Theatre
- Economics
- English
- French
- General Literature
- German
- History
- History-Literature
- Humanities
- International and Comparative Policy Studies
- Linguistics
- Literature-Theatre
- Mathematics
- Mathematics-Economics
- Mathematics-Physics
- Music
- Philosophy
- Physics
- Political Science
- Psychology
- Religion
- Russian
- Sociology
- Spanish
- Theatre

Rhodes College

- Anthropology
- Art/Art Studies, General
- Art History, Criticism and Conservation
- Biochemistry
- Biology/Biological Sciences, General
- Business Administration and Management, General
- Chemistry, General
- Classics and Languages, Literatures and Linguistics, General
- Computer Science
- Drama and Dramatics/Theatre Arts, General
- Economics, General
- English Language and Literature, General
- Fine/Studio Arts, General
- French Language and Literature
- German Language and Literature
- History, General
- Interdisciplinary Studies
- International Business/Trade/Commerce
- International Economics
- International Relations and Affairs
- Latin Language and Literature
- Mathematics, General
- Modern Greek Language and Literature
- Music, General
- Philosophy
- Physics, General
- Political Science and Government, General
- Psychology, General
- Religion/Religious Studies
- Russian Studies
- Sociology
- Spanish Language and Literature
- Urban Studies/Affairs

Ripon College

- Anthropology
- Art/Art Studies, General
- Biochemistry
- Biology/Biological Sciences, General
- Business Administration and Management, General
- Chemistry, General
- Communication Studies/Speech Communication and Rhetoric
- Computer Science
- Drama and Dramatics/Theatre Arts, General
- Early Childhood Education and Teaching
- Economics, General
- Education, General
- Elementary Education and Teaching
- English Language and Literature, General
- Environmental Studies
- French Language and Literature
- German Language and Literature
- Global Studies
- History, General
- Interdisciplinary Studies
- Latin American Studies
- Mathematics, General
- Music, General
- Music Teacher Education
- Philosophy
- Physical Education Teaching and Coaching
- Physical Sciences
- Physiological Psychology/Psychobiology

- Political Science and Government, General
- Pre-Dentistry Studies
- Pre-Law Studies
- Pre-Medicine/Pre-Medical Studies
- Pre-Veterinary Studies
- Psychology, General
- Religion/Religious Studies
- Romance Languages, Literatures, and Linguistics, General
- Secondary Education and Teaching
- Sociology
- Spanish Language and Literature

Rockford College

- Accounting
- Anthropology
- Art/Art Studies, General
- Art History, Criticism and Conservation
- Art Teacher Education
- Biochemistry
- Biological and Physical Sciences
- Biology/Biological Sciences, General
- Business/Managerial Economics
- Business Administration and Management, General
- Chemistry, General
- Classics and Languages, Literatures and Linguistics, General
- Computer Science
- Criminal Justice/Law Enforcement Administration
- Developmental and Child Psychology
- Drama and Dramatics/Theatre Arts, General
- Economics, General
- Education, General
- Elementary Education and Teaching
- English Language and Literature, General
- Finance, General
- Fine/Studio Arts, General
- French Language and Literature
- German Language and Literature
- History, General
- Humanities/Humanistic Studies
- International Economics
- International Relations and Affairs
- Journalism
- Latin Language and Literature
- Literature
- Management Information Systems, General
- Marketing/Marketing Management, General
- Mathematics, General
- Modern Greek Language and Literature
- Music History, Literature, and Theory
- Nursing/Registered Nurse Training
- Philosophy
- Physical Education Teaching and Coaching
- Political Science and Government, General
- Pre-Dentistry Studies
- Pre-Law Studies
- Pre-Medicine/Pre-Medical Studies
- Pre-Veterinary Studies
- Psychology, General
- Science Teacher Education/General Science Teacher Education
- Social Sciences, General
- Social Work
- Sociology
- Spanish Language and Literature
- Urban Studies/Affairs

Roger Williams University

- Accounting
- American/United States Studies/Civilization
- Anthropology
- Architecture
- Art/Art Studies, General
- Art History, Criticism and Conservation
- Biology/Biological Sciences, General
- Business Administration and Management, General
- Chemistry, General
- Chemistry, Other
- Communication and Media Studies, Other
- Computer Science
- Construction Management
- Creative Writing
- Criminal Justice/Law Enforcement Administration
- Dance, General
- Drama and Dramatics/Theatre Arts, General
- Elementary Education and Teaching
- English Language and Literature, General
- Environmental/Environmental Health Engineering
- Environmental Science
- Finance, General
- Financial Planning and Services
- Foreign Languages and Literatures, General
- Health/Health Care Administration/Management
- Historic Preservation and Conservation
- History, General
- International Business/Trade/Commerce
- Legal Assistant/Paralegal
- Legal Professions and Studies, Other
- Liberal Arts and Sciences/Liberal Studies
- Management Information Systems, General
- Manufacturing Technology/Technician
- Marine Biology and Biological Oceanography
- Marketing/Marketing Management, General
- Mathematics, General
- Multi-/Interdisciplinary Studies, Other
- Philosophy
- Political Science and Government, General
- Pre-Dentistry Studies
- Pre-Medicine/Pre-Medical Studies
- Pre-Veterinary Studies
- Psychology, General
- Public Administration
- Secondary Education and Teaching
- Social Sciences, General
- Sociology
- Visual and Performing Arts, General

Rollins College

- African/African American Studies
- Anthropology
- Archaeology
- Art
- Biology
- Chemistry
- Classical Studies
- Communication
- Computer Science
- Economics
- Education
- English
- Environmental Studies
- European Studies
- Hispanic Studies
- History
- Honors Program
- International Business
- International Relations
- Jewish Studies
- Latin American and Caribbean Affairs

- Mathematics
- Modern Languages and Literatures
- Music
- Philosophy
- Physics
- Political Science
- Psychology
- Religious Studies
- Sociology
- Sustainable Development and the Environment
- Theatre Arts & Dance
- Women's Studies

Savannah College of Art and Design

- Advertising Design
- Animation
- Architectural History
- Architecture
- Art History
- Broadcast Design and Motion Graphics
- Cinema Studies
- Commercial Photography
- Digital Photography
- Documentary Photography
- Fashion
- Fibers
- Film and Television
- Furniture Design
- Graphic Design
- Historic Preservation
- Illustration
- Illustration Design
- Industrial Design
- Interactive Design and Game Development
- Interior Design
- Media and Performing Arts
- Metals and Jewelry
- Painting
- Photography
- Production Design
- Sequential Art
- Sound Design
- Urban Design and Development
- Visual Effects
- Videos on Demand

Sierra Nevada College

- Biology
- Computer Science
- English
- Entrepreneurship
- Environmental Policy
- Environmental Science and Ecology
- Fine Arts
- Hospitality and Tourism Management
- Humanities
- International Studies
- Management
- Psychology
- Ski Business and Resort Management

Sonoma State University

- African-American/Black Studies
- American/United States Studies/Civilization
- American Indian/Native American Studies
- Animal Physiology
- Anthropology
- Applied Mathematics
- Art/Art Studies, General
- Art History, Criticism and Conservation
- Biology/Biological Sciences, General
- Botany/Plant Biology
- Business/Managerial Economics
- Business Administration and Management, General
- Cell/Cellular Biology and Histology
- Chemistry, General
- Clinical/Medical Laboratory Technician
- Computer Science
- Criminal Justice/Law Enforcement Administration
- Developmental and Child Psychology
- Drama and Dramatics/Theatre Arts, General
- Drawing
- Ecology
- Economics, General
- English Language and Literature, General
- Environmental Education
- Environmental Studies
- Ethnic and Cultural Studies
- Fine/Studio Arts, General
- French Language and Literature
- Geography
- Geology/Earth Science, General
- Health Science
- Hispanic-American, Puerto Rican, and Mexican-American/Chicano Studies
- History, General
- Interdisciplinary Studies
- International Relations and Affairs
- Liberal Arts and Sciences/Liberal Studies
- Literature
- Marine Biology and Biological Oceanography
- Mass Communication/Media Studies
- Mathematics, General
- Medical Microbiology and Bacteriology
- Multi-/Interdisciplinary Studies, Other
- Music, General
- Music Teacher Education
- Nursing/Registered Nurse Training
- Philosophy
- Physical Education Teaching and Coaching
- Physics, General
- Political Science and Government, General
- Pre-Dentistry Studies
- Pre-Law Studies
- Pre-Medicine/Pre-Medical Studies
- Pre-Veterinary Studies
- Printmaking
- Psychology, General
- Sculpture
- Sociology
- Spanish Language and Literature
- Statistics, General
- Women's Studies
- Zoology/Animal Biology

Southwestern University

- Accounting
- American/United States Studies/Civilization
- Animal Sciences, General
- Art/Art Studies, General
- Art History, Criticism and Conservation
- Art Teacher Education
- Biology/Biological Sciences, General
- Business Administration and Management, General
- Chemistry, General
- Computer Science
- Drama and Dramatics/Theatre Arts, General
- Economics, General
- English Language and Literature, General
- Experimental Psychology

- Fine/Studio Arts, General
- French Language and Literature
- German Language and Literature
- History, General
- International Relations and Affairs
- Literature
- Mass Communication/Media Studies
- Mathematics, General
- Modern Languages
- Music, General
- Music History, Literature, and Theory
- Music Teacher Education
- Philosophy
- Physical Education Teaching and Coaching
- Physics, General
- Piano and Organ
- Political Science and Government, General
- Psychology, General
- Religion/Religious Studies
- Religious/Sacred Music
- Social Sciences, General
- Sociology
- Spanish Language and Literature
- Women's Studies

St. John's College

- Not applicable

Stephens College

- Accounting
- Advertising
- Biology/Biological Sciences, General
- Biomedical Sciences, General
- Broadcast Journalism
- Business Administration and Management, General
- Child Development
- Creative Writing
- Dance, General
- Drama and Dramatics/Theatre Arts, General
- Early Childhood Education and Teaching
- Elementary Education and Teaching
- English Language and Literature, General
- Environmental Studies
- Equestrian/Equine Studies
- Fashion Merchandising
- Fashion/Apparel Design
- Horse Husbandry/Equine Science and Management
- Interdisciplinary Studies
- International Relations and Affairs
- Kindergarten/Preschool Education and Teaching
- Liberal Arts and Sciences/Liberal Studies
- Marketing/Marketing Management, General
- Mass Communication/Media Studies
- Modern Languages
- Natural Sciences
- Occupational Therapy/Therapist
- Philosophy
- Political Science and Government, General
- Pre-Law Studies
- Pre-Medicine/Pre-Medical Studies
- Pre-Veterinary Studies
- Psychology, General
- Public Relations/Image Management
- Radio and Television

Thomas Aquinas College

- Not applicable

Tuskegee University

- Accounting
- Aerospace, Aeronautical and Astronautical Engineering
- Agricultural Business and Management, General
- Agriculture, General
- Agronomy and Crop Science
- Animal Sciences, General
- Architecture
- Biology/Biological Sciences, General
- Building/Home/Construction Inspection/Inspector
- Business Administration and Management, General
- Chemical Engineering
- Chemistry, General
- Clinical Laboratory Science/Medical Technology/Technologist
- Computer Science
- Construction Engineering Technology/Technician
- Dietetics/Dietitians
- Economics, General
- Electrical, Electronics and Communications Engineering
- Elementary Education and Teaching
- Engineering Technology, General
- English Language and Literature, General
- Environmental Studies
- Finance, General
- Foods, Nutrition, and Wellness Studies, General
- Food Science
- History, General
- Hospitality Administration/Management, General
- Hospitality and Recreation Marketing Operations
- Management Science, General
- Marketing/Marketing Management, General
- Mathematics, General
- Mechanical Engineering
- Natural Resources Management and Policy
- Nursing/Registered Nurse Training
- Occupational Therapy/Therapist
- Physics, General
- Plant Sciences, General
- Political Science and Government, General
- Poultry Science
- Psychology, General
- Sales, Distribution and Marketing Operations, General
- Social Work
- Sociology

Unity College

- Adventure Education Leadership
- Adventure Therapy
- Aquaculture and Fisheries
- Conservation Law Enforcement
- Ecology
- Environmental Analysis
- Environmental Biology
- Environmental Education
- Environmental Policy
- Environmental Science
- Forestry
- Landscape Horticulture
- Marine Biology
- Parks, Recreation and Ecotourism
- Wildlife
- Wildlife Biology
- Wildlife Care and Education
- Wildlife Conservation

University of Alaska Southeast

- Anthropology

- Biology/Marine Biology
- Economics
- English
- Environmental Science
- Government
- History
- Liberal Arts (Art, General Studies, Human Communication, and Language Arts and Communications)
- Mathematics
- Outdoor Skills and Leadership (certificate)
- Psychology
- Sociology

University of Mary Washington

- American/United States Studies/Civilization
- Art/Art Studies, General
- Art History, Criticism and Conservation
- Biology/Biological Sciences, General
- Business Administration and Management, General
- Chemistry, General
- Classics and Languages, Literatures and Linguistics, General
- Computer Science
- Drama and Dramatics/Theatre Arts, General
- Economics, General
- Elementary Education and Teaching
- English Language and Literature, General
- Environmental Studies
- Fine/Studio Arts, General
- French Language and Literature
- Geography
- Geology/Earth Science, General
- German Language and Literature
- Historic Preservation and Conservation
- History, General
- Interdisciplinary Studies
- International Relations and Affairs
- Latin Language and Literature
- Liberal Arts and Sciences/Liberal Studies
- Mathematics, General
- Modern Languages
- Music, General
- Music Teacher Education
- Philosophy
- Physics, General
- Political Science and Government, General
- Pre-Dentistry Studies
- Pre-Law Studies
- Pre-Medicine/Pre-Medical Studies
- Pre-Veterinary Studies
- Psychology, General
- Religion/Religious Studies
- Secondary Education and Teaching
- Sociology
- Spanish Language and Literature

University of Montevallo

- Accounting
- Art/Art Studies, General
- Art Teacher Education
- Audiology/Audiologist and Speech-Language Pathology/Pathologist
- Biology/Biological Sciences, General
- Broadcast Journalism
- Business Administration and Management, General
- Ceramic Arts and Ceramics
- Chemistry, General
- Commercial and Advertising Art
- Consumer Merchandising/Retailing Management
- Dietetics/Dietitians
- Drama and Dramatics/Theatre Arts, General
- Drawing
- Elementary Education and Teaching
- English Language and Literature, General
- Family and Consumer Economics and Related Services, Other
- Family and Consumer Sciences/Home Economics Teacher Education
- Family and Consumer Sciences/Human Sciences, General
- Fashion Merchandising
- Fine/Studio Arts, General
- French Language and Literature
- Health and Physical Education, General
- History, General
- Interior Design
- Kindergarten/Preschool Education and Teaching
- Management Information Systems, General
- Marketing/Marketing Management, General
- Mass Communication/Media Studies
- Mathematics, General
- Music, General
- Music Teacher Education
- Photography
- Piano and Organ
- Political Science and Government, General
- Pre-Dentistry Studies
- Pre-Law Studies
- Pre-Medicine/Pre-Medical Studies
- Pre-Veterinary Studies
- Printmaking
- Psychology, General
- Radio and Television
- Sculpture
- Social Sciences, General
- Social Work
- Sociology
- Spanish Language and Literature
- Speech and Rhetorical Studies
- Voice and Opera

University of Redlands

- Accounting
- Art & Art History
- Asian Studies
- Biochemistry & Molecular Biology
- Biology
- Business Administration
- Chemistry
- Communicative Disorders
- Computer Science
- Creative Writing
- Economics
- Education
- English
- Environmental Management
- Environmental Science
- Environmental Studies
- French
- German
- Global Business
- Government
- History
- International Relations
- Johnston Center for Integrative Studies
- Latin American Studies
- Liberal Studies
- Managerial Studies
- Mathematics
- Music
- Philosophy
- Physical Education & Athletics
- Physics
- Pre-law
- Pre-med
- Proudian Interdisciplinary Honors Studies

- Psychology
- Race & Ethnic Studies
- Religious Studies
- Social Science
- Sociology & Anthropology
- Spanish
- Speech
- Study Abroad
- Theatre
- Women's Studies

The University of Tampa

- Accounting
- Advertising and Public Relations
- Art
- Athletic Training/Sports Medicine
- Biochemistry
- Biology
- Biology-Secondary Education
- Business Economics
- Chemistry
- Communication
- Criminology
- Digital Arts
- Education (Elementary and Secondary)
- Electronic Media Art and Technology
- English
- English-Secondary Education
- Entrepreneurship
- Environmental Science
- Exercise Science and Sport Studies
- Film and Media Arts
- Finance
- Financial Services and Operations Systems
- Forensic Science
- Government and World Affairs
- Graphic Design
- History
- International Business
- International and Cultural Studies
- Liberal Studies
- Management
- Management Information Systems
- Marine Science (Biology or Chemistry)
- Marketing
- Mathematical Programming
- Mathematics
- Mathematics-Secondary Education
- Music
- Music Education (K-12)
- Music Performance
- Nursing
- Performing Arts
- Physical Education (K-12)
- Psychology
- Social Sciences
- Social Sciences-Secondary Education
- Sociology
- Spanish
- Sport Management
- Theatre
- Writing

The University of the South

- American/United States Studies/Civilization
- Anthropology
- Applied Art
- Art/Art Studies, General
- Art History, Criticism and Conservation
- Asian Studies/Civilization
- Biology/Biological Sciences, General
- Chemistry, General
- Classics and Languages, Literatures and Linguistics, General
- Comparative Literature
- Computer Science
- Drama and Dramatics/Theatre Arts, General
- Drawing
- Economics, General
- English Language and Literature, General
- Environmental Studies
- European Studies/Civilization
- Fine/Studio Arts, General
- Forestry, General
- French Language and Literature
- Geology/Earth Science, General
- German Language and Literature
- History, General
- International Relations and Affairs
- Latin Language and Literature
- Literature
- Mathematics, General
- Medieval and Renaissance Studies
- Modern Greek Language and Literature
- Music, General
- Music History, Literature, and Theory
- Natural Resources Management and Policy
- Philosophy
- Physics, General
- Political Science and Government, General
- Psychology, General
- Religion/Religious Studies
- Russian Language and Literature
- Russian Studies
- Social Sciences, General
- Spanish Language and Literature

University of Tulsa

- Accounting
- Anthropology
- Applied Mathematics
- Art History, Criticism and Conservation
- Arts Management
- Athletic Training/Trainer
- Audiology/Audiologist and Speech-Language Pathology/Pathologist
- Biochemistry
- Biology/Biological Sciences, General
- Business Administration and Management, General
- Chemical Engineering
- Chemistry, General
- Communication Studies/Speech Communication and Rhetoric
- Computer Science
- Drama and Dramatics/Theatre Arts, General
- Economics, General
- Education, General
- Electrical, Electronics and Communications Engineering
- Elementary Education and Teaching
- Engineering Physics
- English Language and Literature, General
- Environmental Studies
- Film/Cinema Studies
- Finance, General
- Fine/Studio Arts, General
- French Language and Literature
- Geology/Earth Science, General
- Geophysics and Seismology
- German Language and Literature
- History, General
- Information Science/Studies
- International Business/Trade/Commerce
- Kinesiology and Exercise Science
- Legal Professions and Studies, Other
- Liberal Arts and Sciences/Liberal Studies
- Management Information Systems, General
- Marketing/Marketing Management, General
- Mathematics, General

- Mechanical Engineering
- Music, General
- Music, Other
- Music Teacher Education
- Nursing/Registered Nurse Training
- Petroleum Engineering
- Philosophy
- Physics, General
- Piano and Organ
- Political Science and Government, General
- Psychology, General
- Religion/Religious Studies
- Sociology
- Spanish Language and Literature
- Sport and Fitness Administration/Management
- Voice and Opera

Warren Wilson College

- Art
- Biology
- Business & Economics
- Chemistry
- Creative Writing
- Education
- Engineering
- English
- Environmental Studies
- Global Studies
- History & Political Science
- Humanities
- Integrative Studies
- Mathematics
- Modern Languages
- Outdoor Leadership
- Philosophy
- Psychology
- Religious Studies
- Social Work
- Sociology/Anthropology
- Women's Studies

Washington College

- American/United States Studies/Civilization
- Anthropology
- Art/Art Studies, General
- Biology/Biological Sciences, General
- Business Administration and Management, General
- Chemistry, General
- Computer Science
- Drama and Dramatics/Theatre Arts, General
- Ecology
- Economics, General
- English Language and Literature, General
- Environmental Studies
- Foreign Languages and Literatures, General
- French Language and Literature
- German Language and Literature
- History, General
- Humanities/Humanistic Studies
- International Relations and Affairs
- Latin American Studies
- Liberal Arts and Sciences/Liberal Studies
- Mathematics, General
- Multi-/Interdisciplinary Studies, Other
- Music, General
- Philosophy
- Physics, General
- Physiological Psychology/Psychobiology
- Political Science and Government, General
- Pre-Dentistry Studies
- Pre-Law Studies
- Pre-Medicine/Pre-Medical Studies
- Pre-Veterinary Studies
- Psychology, General
- Sociology
- Spanish Language and Literature

Westminster College

- Accounting
- Airline/Commercial/Professional Pilot and Flight Crew
- Art/Art Studies, General
- Aviation/Airway Management and Operations
- Biology/Biological Sciences, General
- Biology Teacher Education
- Business/Commerce, General
- Business/Managerial Economics
- Business Administration and Management, General
- Chemistry, General
- Communication Studies/Speech Communication and Rhetoric
- Computer Science
- Elementary Education and Teaching
- English Language and Literature, General
- Finance, General
- History, General
- Human Resources Management/Personnel Administration, General
- International Business/Trade/Commerce
- Kindergarten/Preschool Education and Teaching
- Management Information Systems and Services, Other
- Marketing/Marketing Management, General
- Mathematics, General
- Nursing/Registered Nurse Training
- Philosophy
- Physics, General
- Political Science and Government, General
- Psychology, General
- Social Sciences, General
- Social Science Teacher Education
- Sociology
- Special Education and Teaching, General
- Willamette University
- Anthropology
- Art/Art Studies, General
- Art History, Criticism and Conservation
- Biology/Biological Sciences, General
- Chemistry, General
- Classics and Languages, Literatures and Linguistics, General
- Comparative Literature
- Computer Science
- Drama and Dramatics/Theatre Arts, General
- Economics, General
- English Language and Literature, General
- Environmental Science
- Fine/Studio Arts, General
- French Language and Literature
- German Language and Literature
- History, General
- Humanities/Humanistic Studies
- International/Global Studies
- Japanese Studies
- Kinesiology and Exercise Science
- Latin American Studies
- Mathematics, General
- Music, General
- Music Pedagogy
- Music Performance, General
- Music Theory and Composition
- Philosophy
- Physics, General
- Piano and Organ
- Political Science and Government, General

- Psychology, General
- Religion/Religious Studies
- Sociology
- Spanish Language and Literature
- Speech and Rhetorical Studies
- Violin, Viola, Guitar and Other Stringed Instruments
- Voice and Opera

Willamette University

- Anthropology
- Art/Art Studies, General
- Art History, Criticism and Conservation
- Biology/Biological Sciences, General
- Chemistry, General
- Classics and Languages, Literatures and Linguistics, General
- Comparative Literature
- Computer Science
- Drama and Dramatics/Theatre Arts, General
- Economics, General
- English Language and Literature, General
- Environmental Science
- Fine/Studio Arts, General
- French Language and Literature
- German Language and Literature
- History, General
- Humanities/Humanistic Studies
- International/Global Studies
- Japanese Studies
- Kinesiology and Exercise Science
- Latin American Studies
- Mathematics, General
- Music, General
- Music Pedagogy
- Music Performance, General
- Music Theory and Composition
- Philosophy
- Physics, General
- Piano and Organ
- Political Science and Government, General
- Psychology, General
- Religion/Religious Studies
- Sociology
- Spanish Language and Literature
- Speech and Rhetorical Studies
- Violin, Viola, Guitar and Other Stringed Instruments
- Voice and Opera

Acknowledgments

The author wishes to thank Jill Balkus, Laurie Barnett, Lynne Brett, Maria Dente, William Levith, Christina Renzi, Brandon Rogers, Andrew Sandley, Justin Scheckler, Leah Tracosas, Frank Webster, Lindsay Weiskittel, Daniel Williams, and Garrett Ziegler.